OCTAVIO PENNA PIERANTI

# PUBLIC SERVICE BROADCASTING RESISTS

## The search for independence in Brazil and Eastern Europe

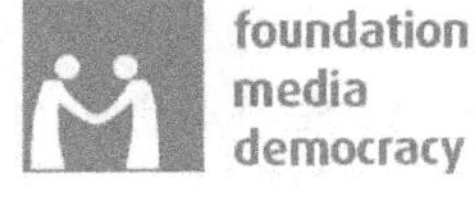



Sofia, 2020

To the (still) young Octavio,<br>
who will one day realize that communication<br>
goes beyond his favorite "episodes",<br>
heroes and villains

# Table of Contents

# Acknowledgements

This book is the result of research that began in Brasilia, but soon stretched out to include five countries overseas. I relied on the support and attentiveness of several researchers from each of these countries, both in person and remotely, including educational institutions and civil society entities. This work would not have been possible without the collaboration, dedication and support from the following interlocutors: Andrej Skolkay, David Smahel, Michał Głowacki, Nikoleta Daskalova, Pavel Sedláček and, particularly, Valentina Marinescu, who not only provided me with a number of contacts but also took it upon herself to contact them. She also became a friend, willing to talk for hours about my research and the situation in Eastern Europe. I would like to thank all my interviewees, whose names and profiles are presented in the following chapters, for their eagerness to share their stories and memories about communications in their respective countries.

On this side of the Atlantic Ocean, I would like to thank Murilo César Ramos, a friend and key reference for decades in communication politics research in Brazil, as well as my postdoctoral internship supervisor for the Faculty of Communication Postgraduate Program at the University of Brasilia (FAC/UnB), where this book was born. I would like to thank Fernando Paulino, Rafiza Varão and Vanessa Negrini and their partnership with FAC Livros, a dynamic publisher established in the FAC/UnB, which was responsible for the original publishing of this book in Portuguese and my previous one entitled, "Public Service Broadcasting Politics in Dilma's Government". Over the last ten years I have had the privilege of contributing towards a public communication project in Brazil in my time as head of office (and other positions I have held) at the

Brazil Communication Company (EBC). A part of this book is a reflection of my studies and experiences during this time. Special thanks goes to Tereza Cruvinel, the first manager of EBC, and all those who dedicated themselves to this project.

Last, but certainly not least, I thank my family for their understanding and support throughout this project, one that involved travelling, reading dozens of texts, and countless hours spent on editing. During this period, my wife, Miriam Wimmer, with the help of my parents and my mother-in-law, redoubled their efforts in raising our son Octavio, a lively, curious, intelligent boy. May those characteristics instilled in him help to build a better country in the future.

# The late construction of public communication: two cases

*Tereza Cruvinel*[1]

Public service broadcasting, in addition to being a poorly understood concept, is also a poorly documented experience, except for in a few countries where it has developed and achieved a high degree of consolidation, namely in Central Europe. The merits of this new book by Octavio Penna Pieranti are two-fold: it helps toward overcoming these two aforementioned shortcomings by providing conceptual elements while also rescuing important experiences for building public service broadcasting systems.

Pieranti draws a comparison of two experiences which, due to their later development (in relation to the emergence of the first public service broadcasters and the level of global broadcasting), did not have to start from the ground up; they were, instead, able to start by converting pre-existing state-governmental structures into public communication systems. These two experiences occurred in Brazil, represented by the creation of the Brazil Communication Company (EBC), and in Eastern European countries which, after the collapse of Real Socialism, were committed to transforming state ownership into public.

Pieranti makes his comparison based on a combination of personal experience and research. After working with digital

---

[1] Journalist and first director and president of the Brazil Communication Company – EBC (2007-2011).

content in the Ministry of Culture, and coordinating the First National Communication Conference (Confecom) in 2009, Pieranti helped establish the EBC. As head of office his work was crucial towards solving the obstacles and dilemmas the project faced. His postdoctoral research at FAC / UnB on Eastern Europe and its transition from state to public led him to visit some of the countries in the region, where he interviewed professionals, managers and researchers, and collected some striking data and statistics on the current reality of public service broadcasting in that part of the world.

As one might expect, he starts by establishing conceptual frameworks that in his view (a view which is also shared by many intellects) are needed to distinguish between public systems. Private broadcasting is a business activity aimed at financial gains, even if it does provide a public service, while state broadcasting is run by the State and designed for the institutional communication of public powers (not just governments, as Judicial and Legislative branches all over the world have created and maintained their own structures of communication). Public service broadcasting, however, finds itself in the space between the State and society, and must be managed with the direct participation of society. The State will always be its biggest investor, but not its only one, which, in turn, helps mitigate the dependency on the State. Programming should focus on information, culture, public debate and the strengthening of citizenship, and avoid political proselytism, including useless content created only to gain audiences. Although audiences are important in terms of legitimacy, they must be built through the relevance and originality of programming.

The part of this book which focuses on Eastern Europe is of particular interest as it provides us with an insight into a reality which we really know very little about, especially with regard to public service broadcasting. It begins with a rich descriptive review of that fast-moving point of time that resulted in the fall of the Berlin Wall, overthrew seemingly strong governments, and ended the former Soviet Union. After the collapse of socialism, state broadcasting systems started transitioning to capitalism in a variety of ways. For example, Germany, which already had a public system on the western side, opted to integrate its systems, while in Russia it was privatization that prevailed. Most countries tried to convert to public systems, but many years later, almost all of them take a backseat to private broadcasters, have internal dependencies, and a confused external perception about their real nature.

With regard to Brazil, Pieranti covers the erratic stance adopted by the Brazilian State on public service broadcasting which, over the years and passing of different governments, has resulted in the creation of multiple, overlapping, and poorly defined legal structures such as Radiobrás, TVE from Rio de Janeiro / Acerp, and the network of state educational broadcasters. The Federal Constitution of 1988 would establish complementarity between state, public and private systems, leading to former President Lula issuing Provisional Measure nº398 in 2007, which was then passed into Law 11.652,[2] the framework on which the EBC and principles of public communication were created. The EBC, however, would eventually be built based on the combination of those old structures, with all its benefits and drawbacks. Added to this is

---

[2] According to the Federal Constitution of Brazil, the President can publish "temporary laws" (named Provisional Measures) regarding some themes. These Provisional Measures must be approved by the Congress (which can also modify them) in 60 days (can be prorogated to 120 days) or they lose effect [Editor's note].

the fact that the law gives the EBC the dual role of providing services to the government (state communication) and managing public broadcasters; its framework favoring those who are in opposition to public communication, disqualifying the project and accusing it of continuing to serve the interests of the current government and ruling party.

What the EBC inherited from the old state systems was, essentially, assets. Despite the production and transmission structures for both Radiobrás and the ACERP being completely scrapped, the EBC still inherited valuable real estate property (mainly from Radiobrás), although to date the company has not been able to convert that property into more useful assets. On the other hand, it inherited only three television channels (in Brasilia, Rio de Janeiro and Maranhão) and was not given a national network, even for the rebroadcasting of TV channels. This provided to be an ostacle to building an audience and to society identifying with public channels which, in 2016, with the impeachment of President Dilma Rousseff, contributed greatly to the new government being able to quickly deconstruct the company without much resistance. This was different from what happened in Eastern Europe, where the former state systems almost always had networks with wide national coverage.

The comparison of experiences and the conceptual debate make this book from Octavio Penna Pieranti an important reference for those who are interested in public communication as an element of democracy. It provides us with reflection and elements to correct paths to a future where the political scene would allow for previously prohibited projects to be carried out, including the creation of a public service broadcasting system which would guarantee plurality and complementarity.

# Thoughts on public service broadcasting: the importance of comparative studies

*Valentina Marinescu*[3]

The main focus of this book *"Public Service Broadcasting resists: the search for independence in Brazil and Eastern Europe"* is to analyze the transition from the state broadcasting model to the Public Service Broadcasting (PSB) one in Central and Eastern Europe, and Brazil. This volume presents the reader with a solid piece of comparative research. The author – Octavio Penna Pieranti – has an extensive academic background. He holds a degree in Social Communication/Journalism from Rio de Janeiro Federal University (UFRJ), a Master's degree in Public Administration, and a PhD in Administration from the Brazilian School of Public Administration and Business at Fundação Getúlio Vargas (EBAPE / FGV), with a post-doctorate from the University of Brasília (UnB). Octavio Penna Pieranti is also a civil servant and has worked at the Brazilian Ministry of Communications (MC) and Ministry of Culture (MinC), at the National Tele-communications Agency (ANATEL), and at the Brazilian PSB, Empresa Brasil de Comunicação (EBC). To date, his academic research has been published in 7 books (by university and academic publishing houses) and more than 30 articles (published in academic journals), most of which are dedicated to public policies and regulations in the communications sector.

---

[3] Full Professor, Department of Sociology, Faculty of Sociology and Social Service, University of Bucharest.

This book is the result of Pieranti's post-doctorate studies and is written in a classical structure. It is divided into three main parts: first, the author debates the end of socialism and the transformation of the electronic media system in Europe; he then goes on to present the creation of the Brazilian PSB (EBC); and, lastly, he depicts the current scenario of the transition both in Central and Eastern Europe and Brazil. The author carried out his field work in five Central and Eastern European countries (Poland, Czech Republic, Slovakia, Romania and Bulgaria), where he interviewed audiovisual industry professionals, public service broadcasters, and researchers.

It is important to mention that Octavio Penna Pieranti uses the term "Europe" to describe a specific region of the continent, that is, Central and Eastern European countries. The main reason for this comparative research was based on the fact that the creation and development of the public service broadcasting model in Western Europe was linked to its historical consolidation of democracy, and broadcasting had already been established on said Public Service Broadcasting model either immediately following World War II (the United Kingdom, Germany or Holland) or, in the case of some countries, had transitioned to state-owned television after the end of dictatorships in the twentieth century (for example, in Portugal).

But, as Octavio Penna Pieranti rightly points out, this transition only began in Central and Eastern European countries in 1989, with the fall of the socialist regime (Mihelj, 2014, pp. 7-16)[4]. This occurred close to the point in time when the new

---

[4] MIHELJ, Sabina. Understanding Socialist Television: Concepts, Objects, Methods. **Journal of European Television History and Culture**, 3, n. 5, 2014, p. 7-16.

democratic federal Constitution in Brasil was passed in 1988. Pieranti also looks at the following similarities between Brazil and the aforementioned Central and Eastern European countries: both regions started their transition after the fall of authoritarian regimes; the new PSBs made use of the existing infrastructure, channels and employees from state broadcasting; and, most importantly, there was a significant lack of debate in civil society around the concept of PSB and its adoption into law, both in Brasil and in Central and Eastern Europe.

In the last part of the book, Octavio Penna Pieranti describes the current audiovisual market of Central-Eastern Europe and Brazil, and concludes that public TV has mostly lost its market share and is not a market leader in Europe anymore. He also noticed that public radio is more successful in European markets, with a few exceptions like Germany, Poland and the Czech Republic, where the market share of all public TV channels is higher than 30%. In other countries (such as Romania and Ukraine) the market share of PSB is lower than 5%. Regardless, the market share of PSBs for most of the countries analyzed here lies between 5% and 30%.

In addition, Pieranti presents those countries' legislation for the audiovisual domain and the conceptual framework of the term "public", referencing the history of this term in both regions of study. He notes that, although the PSB situation is not the same in all European countries under study, guaranteeing "independence" is still a daily challenge in those societies, despite the fact it is mentioned in most legislation. Octavio Penna Pieranti stresses the centrality of the concept of "independence" in relation to governments and to the market. He also analyzes how different aspects of this concept are viewed not only through legislation, but also in the daily lives of these PSBs. One extremely problematic aspect of legislation, as it pertains to so-called "independence", is the manner in which PSB directors from both Europe and Brazil are dismissed. According to the stipulation within the legal regulations, this is not a very complicated process. The dismissal of PSB directors has become quite a common occurrence over the last few decades in Europe and Brazil. Parliament in Poland and Brazil even changed the law in order to facilitate dismissals, while in Romania, the law did not protect these individuals and, as a result, it was much easier to dismiss them (Sükösd and Bajomi-Lázár, 2003, pp. 15-17)[5]. Thus, as Octavio Penna Pieranti questions, if the directors of PSBs can be dismissed at any time, how can they be independent? What guarantees the independence of management in the face of economic and political external pressures?

Pieranti mentions other challenges such as the fact that PSBs have huge financial problems (as is the case for Romania and Bosnia), that the market share for PSBs in this geographical region has dropped, and that their transition to new television (e.g., the so-called "Internet world") is not yet complete.

On a more current level, the book highlights some interesting aspects related to the history of democracy and audiovisual markets which are common both to Europe and Brazil. There are some interesting coincidences between the countries when it comes to historical events. Octavio Penna Pieranti notices that "Martial Law" was declared on the same day in Poland and Brazil (December 13th), although in different years:

---

[5] SÜKÖSD, Miklós, BAJOMI-LÁZÁR, Péter(ed). **Reinventing media: media policy reform in East-Central Europe**. Central European University Press, 2003.

1968 for Brazil[6] (Zaverucha, 1999, pp. 43-73) and 1981 for Poland[7] (Paczkowski, Byrne, Domber and Klotzbach, 2007, pp. 461-4730).

Furthermore, Pieranti explains the interdependence between the PSB's independence and the development of democracy in Europe. We can look at Romania as an example: after the collapse of the socialist regime, Romania (including other countries in the so-called "socialist block") went through a double transition: a political and ideological movement from a one-party system to a pluralist one, and an economic change from an almost total monopoly of state ownership to private ownership in all domains of social and political life. The first type of transition (political) occurred at the legal level and took around ten years to complete, starting with passing a new democratic Constitution and legal framework for political life, democratic elections for Parliament, and establishing institutions which guarantee that democratic principles function correctly in the country. The second transition (from a state-owned economy to a private one) is still ongoing. In relation to the PSB, this led to the development of a private audiovisual sector which was, and remains, mainly dependent on a foreign flux of capital and programs[8] (Mungiu-Pippidi, 2008, pp. 88-101). One example of this type of competition is the so-called "media wars", defined by K. Jakubowicz and M Sükösd (2008, p. 13) as "the continued struggle for media independence [...]. In media wars, journalists, editors, their

---

[6] ZAVERUCHA, Jorge. Military justice in the state of Pernambuco after the Brazilian military regime: an authoritarian legacy. **Latin American Research Review**, 1999, p. 43-73.

[7] PACZKOWSKI, Andrzejet al (ed). **From Solidarity to Martial Law: the Polish crisis of 1980-1981: a documentary history**. Central European University Press, 2007.

[8] MUNGIU-PIPPIDI, Alina. How Media and Politics Shape Each Other in the New Europe. **Romanian Journal of Political Science**, 8, n. 1, 2008, p. 88-101.

unions, media managers and civic groups fought in various coalitions with governments, oppositions, political and as well as business clans"[9].

But, as Gripsrud[10] (2007, p. 488) showed, Central and Eastern Europe has its own specific nature, levels, and forms of modernization which are even reflected in the audiovisual domain: e.g., PSBs in that region.

Nowadays, even though a number of scientific research centres and universities are working on explaining the transformations in the audiovisual field in Central and Eastern Europe or, separately, in Brazil, none of the researchers have made a comparative, transcontinental study. The innovative nature of Octavio Penna Pieranti's book results from the fact that, in my opinion, it is the first such book that deals with this comparative analysis. Using existing literature (over 70 volumes cited in general reference) and personal field work investigation, this book has proven to be a fundamental piece of research for both experienced researchers and students interested in international relatons, in media and communication studies, and in transnational comparison.

---

[9] JAKUBOWICZ, Karol, SÜKÖSD, Miklós (ed). **Finding the right place on the map: Central and Eastern European media change in a global perspective.** Intellect Books, 2008, p. 13.

[10] GRIPSRUD, Jostein. Television and the European public sphere. **European Journal of Communication,** 22, n. 4, 2007, p 479-492.

# QUESTIONS AND ANSWERS

# I

This book is about murder. It's about suppression, a lot of it. It's about accusations of espionage, about rights violations and underhanded politicians. It's about occupied buildings, about strikes, a lot of them, and numerous protests. It's about the end of dreams, realities and countries. But it's also about hope, solidarity, and generosity; and struggle and resistance.

What this book is really about is democracy, or rather, plural, real and possible democracies. It's about fragile democracies and stronger democracies. Democracy that goes beyond voting, beyond elections. Democracy not only as a political regime but as an environment for guaranteeing rights (some fundamental), representation, and political debate.

This book is about public service broadcasting in democratic contexts, more specifically, the transition from state-owned broadcasting to public systems in Brazil and in Central and

Eastern European countries. There is some observable degeneracy within the microcosm of public service broadcasting and its history in these countries, yet there are also important strengths. Before addressing these strengths, however, we need to answer a few questions.

*Why broadcasting?*

Over the last few centuries several authors have devoted themselves to examining the importance of mass communication in contemporary society. I do not intend to rehash all the dimensions and aspects of this debate; however, since this book starts off with the collapse of socialist regimes in Central and Eastern Europe, a brief review of Marxist writers on this subject is most appropriate.

Yet before we move forward, I shall briefly explain why I opted to use the term *socialist* rather than *communist*. These two terms have been used interchangeably. The official names of the Soviet Union and Romania, for example, referred to *socialist* republics, but the parties governing them called themselves *communists*. Other variations also existed: Albania opted to use the term *labor* to identify their ruling party. I will not address the theoretical justifications for why each individual country adopted their specific nomenclatures; I also do not want to confuse the reader or erroneously refer to all concepts as being synonymous. Thus, I decided to use the term socialist as it is originally defined by Marx, who identified socialism as the stage between capitalism and communism. In this political transition period, the state was seen as the revolutionary dictatorship of the proletariat:

> "What we have to deal with here is a communist society, not as it has developed on its own foundations, but, on the contrary, just as it emerges from capitalist society; which is thus in every respect, economically, morally, and intellectually, still stamped with the birthmarks of the old society from whose womb it comes" (MARX, 2005, p. 22).

The role of the press as a central element in the power struggle was present in the works of leading theoreticians on Marxism. Antonio Gramsci (2004) defined the press as a private apparatus of hegemony and Louis Althusser (1987) identified it as part of the ideological apparatuses of the state which, from the ideological point of view, are subordinate to the ruling class. But even before these theoreticians, the perception that the press needed to transform was already present in the work of Karl Marx (2006), who had defended the need for a "people's paper", in contrast to a bourgeois press associated with large media. What kind of press would that be? The major leaders of the Russian Revolution had an idea, and also implemented the concept. In Trotsky's words:

> "the right of ownership of printing presses and workshops is primarily the responsibility of peasants and workers, who represent the majority of the population. The bourgeois is in second place, because it is an insignificant minority" (REED, 2002, p. 329-330).

Lenin predicted that the state, in socialist countries, wanted to intervene in the sector, and stop the monopoly of publicity, an essential resource for the financing of mass communication. This intervention would be justified as a way of extending freedom of the press, removing it from the scope of journalistic companies and bringing it closer to a real concept of freedom of expression. If this is extended to all, its concept should also be reviewed in the new model:

> "It seems that this is a violation of freedom of the press. That is incorrect. It is about broadening and re-establishing the freedom of the press, because freedom of the press means that the opinions of all citizens may be freely published" (LENIN, 1976, p. 154).

A question posed by Gramsci is perhaps a good summary of everyone's understanding: "If the school is of the state, why not journalism, which is the school for adults?"

Even in the first decades of the twentieth century, radio and TV a few years later broadened the prospects for mass communication, enhancing what the first authors following Marx associated with the press. Whether for reasons pointed out by these authors or supposedly nobler (and not always sincere) reasons such as the search for national integration or the valorization of national culture, all countries have promoted development of their public service broadcasting networks. This process was implemented and managed directly by the state (at least in most European countries) or enjoyed the economic benefit and incentive of this actor (a situation experienced by most American countries).

In the 21st century, the Internet and the proliferation of new platforms that arise from it appear to have left the old mass media behind. All day in the major urban centers of the country we are constantly connected to the Internet which, according to some, indicates the progressive loss of relevance for radio and TV. Their end is near, say the most exalted ones.

I understand that this understanding, at least for the Brazilian reality, is false. On one hand, there is no doubt that the growth of the Internet produces new actors in public debate (and other not-so-new actors who have already been working with traditional mass communication) and poses a challenge to radio and TV broadcasters which, to a certain extent, try to reinvent themselves. On the other hand, a good portion of society does not have permanent access to the Internet, contrary to traditional media. Completely replacing one medium with another is not a rapid process – in fact, it is not even necessary.

Evidence shows us that public service broadcasting will still continue to be important in Brazil for the next few years. A diverse range of entities – public and private companies, foundations, and associations – still require new grants. These same entities make crises worse because revenue must be divided with the Internet, but also due to management problems, which has always been the case. The digitalization of TV continues. New audiovisual content is steadily produced in the hope of having a display window in traditional media. Criticism or praise of a program with a large audience can contribute to the success or failure of personalities, economic activities, or public policy.

And the old mediums, the ones that have not yet been left behind, are still being watched or listened to. More than that, they seem to be a part of citizens' lives in perhaps an unexpected way. Federally-funded research on media consumption in the country in recent years has contributed to this perception. The user rate for TV and radio has increased, while the number of people who had never previously used those mediums has decreased:

**Table 1: Weekly TV use in Brazil (%)**

|  | **2014** | **2015** | **2016** |
| --- | --- | --- | --- |
| 7 days per week | 65 | 73 | 77 |
| 6 days per week | 3 | 4 | 2 |
| NEVER | 3 | 4 | 3 |

**Source:** Prepared by author, based on Secom (2014; 2015; 2016).

**Table 2: Weekly radio use in Brazil (%)**

|  | **2014** | **2015** | **2016** |
| --- | --- | --- | --- |
| 7 days per week | 21 | 30 | 35 |
| 6 days per week | 2 | 3 | 1 |
| NEVER | 39 | 44 | 33 |

**Source:** Prepared by author, based on Secom (2014; 2015; 2016).

Here, we can see that from 2014 to 2016, the percentage of interviewees who watched TV and listened to the radio at least six days a week increased by 11 and 13 points (more than 16% and 56%). The percentage of respondents who never listen to the radio dropped 25% from 2015 to 2016.

There are other significant percentages apart from these. The survey for the 2016 edition showed that 34% of respondents said they watched TV for 3 hours or more daily, from Monday to Friday. This percentage rises to 37% on weekends. In addition, the percentage of respondents who reported listening to the radio for more than 3 hours during the week and at weekends was 19% and 29%, respectively. Unless one mistrusts the research methodology – and I see no reason to do so – we can conclude that society's dedication to public service broadcasting is considerable.

Good results continued in the sector in 2017. From January to August, an average of 47% of TV sets was turned on between 7am and 12am, which is a 17.5% increase from 2012. Also in 2017, Globo and Record registered their largest average audiences since 2011 (CASTRO, 2017).

This perception of success does not only pertain to Brazil. The European Broadcasting Union (EBU) monitors the performance of radio and TV in Europe every year. From 2013 to 2018 average television viewing time fell 2 minutes and average radio listening time fell 14 minutes in Europe. But the averages are still very high:  3h35m per day for TV and 2h22m for radio. In 2016, European citizens watched an average of 3 hours and 40 minutes of TV per day, four minutes more than what was registered in 2011. They also listened to an average of 2 hours and 24 minutes of radio per day, an eleven-minute decrease from five years earlier. In 2015, the top three Central and Eastern European countries for average TV viewing time were: Bosnia (each citizen watched an average of 5 hours and 40 minutes of TV a day), Romania (5 hours and 29 minutes) and Serbia (5 hours and 15 minutes). The countries registering the least amount of average viewing time were Iceland (1 hour and 50 minutes) and Switzerland (2 hours and 4 minutes, in the German cantons).

However, Central and Eastern Europe is the region where this medium's audience has grown the most. The Czech Republic and Slovenia are two countries whose populations watch the least amount of television, but the average is still high: 3 hours and 26 minutes a day. Things change slightly when it comes to radio consumption. Statistics show that Russia (4 hours and 12 minutes per day), Estonia (3 hours and 43 minutes) and Ireland (3 hours and 35 minutes) have the highest average radio listening times. The country registering the lowest listening time was Croatia at 1 hour and 16 minutes (EBU, 2019a, EBU, 2019b, EBU, 2017a, EBU, 2017b, EBU, 2016a, EBU, 2016b). We can see that public service broadcasting in Brazil and Central and Eastern Europe is still present in the daily lives of a large part of their populations.

*Why public service broadcasting?*

In order to answer this question we need to define "public service broadcasting". It will be defined in the pages of this book, but for now, it is important to note that it is different from state and private broadcasting – which are designated in the Brazilian Federal Constitution as different systems. In theory, private entities within the private broadcasting system operate for profit - even though service broadcasting is considered a public service. The state system, on the other hand, is maintained by the state, and is devoted to the institutional communication of government. The public system is the responsibility of public entities, but it is subject to mechanisms of government by actors outside the state. It relies on other sources of funding outside the public budget, and its programming is guided by values such as building citizenship and promoting public debate, and does not contain institutional content from government or any other content based solely on increasing audiences. In addition, public service broadcasting must be equidistant from editorial ideologies and the demands of governments and markets; their audiences are those who are naturally drawn to independent, critical, and less superficial programming. I emphasize that this summary is only a starting point to be looked at further in the following chapters.

Service broadcasting is still important in the 21st century, and so is public service broadcasting, but for different reasons. TV and radio stations are present in everyday life, even with all the increasing access to new media. However, this is not always the case for public service broadcasting which, depending on the country, has very low audience levels. The question then is: why is it important?

One argument is its complementary nature in relation to other broadcasters; it helps to offset the progressive deregulation of service broadcasting. The obligation to broadcast certain types of content, such as educational or independent productions, has been removed or reduced, however, that does not mean we can simply expect private broadcasters to transmit them. It is up to public service broadcasting to continue meeting this demand if such types of content are considered important on a national level (JAKUBOWICZ, 2010).

That argument is related to another: public broadcasters are needed to expand pluralism in mass communication. The perception of the importance of this extension is an old one; it is shared by authors cited in this book and gains new strength with the MacBride report, written by a committee appointed by UNESCO in the 1970s to address the new communications landscape. It was published in Portuguese under the expressive name "Many Voices One World" (UNESCO, 1983). In this case, pluralism is understood as diversity in the supply, use and distribution of media for: (1) ownership and control; (2) media genres and forms; (3) political views; (4) cultural expressions and; (5) local and regional interests. Public service broadcasting is linked to these aspects because it is not controlled by private groups and the type of programming it broadcasts. Thus, it is no coincidence that the Council of Europe's Committee of Ministers considered that the lack or under-representation of public media (i.e., media other than radio and TV) poses a risk to pluralism, with member states "ensuring public media has a safe and adequate financing model and organizational structure (...)" (LEUVEN, 2009, p. 53). The amount of funding and the number of new employees are considered to be a significant risk to the lack or under-representation of public media.

In turn, pluralism is related to the construction of democracy. From Alexis de Tocqueville (1973) to Robert Dahl (2001), many authors claim that the existence of different media controlled by different public and private entities is a key element of democracy and its conceptual variations. The role of the media varies according to each author, but it is commonly related to ensuring access to information, defending the right to communication, promoting public debate, strengthening national culture, and monitoring the legally constituted public authorities and large economic groups which led to the literary term "watchdog" being applied to media. One of the criticisms of this view, as stated earlier, was put forward by Marxist authors who drew attention to the media's connection to the ruling class.

This controversial issue is not central to the remainder of this book. It is important to draw from it, however, the consensus that pluralism is a key element for the construction of democracy. Since public service broadcasting is related to the affirmation of pluralism, it is also related, by extension, to the construction of democracy. On the other hand, Marxist authors and their defense of the transformation of the concepts of freedom of expression and the press and the creation of a "people's paper" led to the extinction or nationalization of existing media and the creation of new media under the umbrella of the state in socialist Central and Eastern European countries. As we shall see, public service broadcasting emerges from this scenario in the 1990s, in parallel with the collapse of the old regimes.

*Why Central and Eastern Europe?*

The first edition of the Joseph Stalin biography, written by Isaac Deutscher, a Polish writer, communist and anti-Stalinist, was published in 1949. The work was as much a classic as it was controversial. Deutscher was accused of being sympathetic toward Stalin, and he countered this criticism by stating that he was one of the first anti-Stalinist communists, but he could not fail to recognize Stalin's role in building socialism. Deutscher continued to write about this in further texts until the Khrushchev government's denunciation of Stalin's crimes made the topic too critical and tense. In his original text, Deutscher contextualized the advance of socialism (already in progress at the time) as a series of early and rapid conquests of nations marked by historical socioeconomic difficulties:

> "Between the two wars, nearly all those peoples had been stranded in an impasse; their life had been bogged down in savage poverty and darkness; their politics had been dominated by archaic cliques who had not minded the material and cultural retrogression of

their subjects as long as their own priveleges had been safe. That whole portion of Europe had emerged from the Second World War and from the hideous 'school' of Nazism even more destitute, savage and helpless. It may well be that for its peoples the only chance of breaking out of their impasse lay in a *coup de force* such as that to which Stalin goaded them. In Poland and Hungary the Communist-inspired land reform fulfilled, perhaps imperfectly, a dream of many generations of peasants and intellectuals. All over Eastern Europe the Communists, having nationalized the main industries, vigorously promoted plans for industrialization and full employment such as were beyond the material resources and the wit of native 'private enterprise', notoriously poor in capital, skill and enterprise. With fresh zeal and ambition they took to hard educational work, trying to undo the age-old negligence of previous rulers. They did much to calm nationalist vendettas and to promote co-operation between their peoples; in a word, they opened before Eastern Europe broad vistas of common reform and advancement" (DEUTSCHER, 2006, p. 557-8).

In this scenario of intense change the communication systems of socialist countries began to rise or grow. Comparisons between public service broadcasting in Brazil and the countries of Central and Eastern Europe may be surprising. More common examples of public service broadcasters, even in Brazilian literature, are usually the BBC from the UK, PBS from the U.S., and even ARD and ZDF from Germany. Articles and books, written by Brazilian researchers in Portuguese, examined these models and their history extensively (LEAL FILHO, 2008; WIMMER, 2014).

The early 21ˢᵗ century, following the approval of Argentina's "Ley de Medios" and changes made to legislation in other South American countries, saw Brazilian researchers beginning to examine the new directions of public service broadcasting on the continent – including Brazil (BECERRA *et al.*, 2012). Other publications dealt with the contexts of major European, North American, and South American references (INTERVOZES, 2009).

It is undeniable that, in terms of historical importance, the BBC, PBS, ARD and ZDF are major players in the service broadcasting landscape. It would not be an exaggeration to say that these broadcasters legitimize their concept by demonstrating, in practice, that another "type" of service broadcasting is possible. Perhaps this is why they are considered a kind of benchmark to be reached by those countries where public service broadcasting is still under development, like Brazil.

There is, however, a group of countries that have also adopted these same goals, but have faced, and are still facing, challenges and difficulties very similar to those of Brazil: countries in Eastern and Central Europe escaping the socialist regimes which ended in the late 1980s and the early 1990s. This observation may seem even stranger to those readers who imagine that the scenario of communication in those countries follows Lenin's principle of media having three main functions: propaganda, provocation, and organization (VARTANOVA, 2012).

An important part of this book is the demystification of this view – not Lenin's conception of what media in socialist countries *should* be (which is not the focus of this book, anyway), but rather the preconception of what it actually was. In the next chapter we will look into this idea further. For now, we are pointing out the fact that broadcasting in those countries should not be seen *solely* as a machine for propaganda. Audience was important and formats were used that are successful around the globe such as entertainment and popular programs. Some transmitted content was even used to criticize the politics of the regime (MIHELJ, 2014).

The first similarity in terms of the context and history of public service broadcasting in those countries and in Brazil is that although political propaganda was ingrained in their state broadcasters, adopting established radio and audiovisual formats was (and is) important for seeking an audience.

A second similarity is the origin of public service broadcasting models from the late 1980s. Unlike in Western Europe, public service broadcasting in Central and Eastern Europe and Brazil is run by broadcasters controlled directly by the government without any social control mechanisms and no compromise with any independent editorial line. Public service broadcasting inherited its legacy of good and evil from the creation of these broadcasters: it starts with a physical infrastructure and skilled technicians to operate it, and an on-air programming grid. Yet it inherits a state communication built on defending the government, including an organizational culture which is hard to change.

Mihelj and Downey (2012) argue that the analysis of media models should take into account other aspects that condition them. Although most countries have taken steps to consolidate democracy, there are some important behaviors that were established before 1989. This is due to a number of elements: the economies are not as strong as those of Western Europe so there are limited resources for intense change; cultural factors; previous behavioral patterns can weaken the independence of journalists and prevent them from acting as critical observers. Many of these aspects ring true with the reality in Brazil.

Brazil and Central and Eastern European countries adopted public service broadcasting at the same time. In Brazil, it first appeared in legal text in the 1988 Federal Constitution, even though it would only become regulated decades later. In Central and Eastern Europe, it started in 1989 with the first countries to break from socialism. However, this change in Central and Eastern Europe would happen much faster than in Brazil, as we shall see below.

In both national contexts, the concept of public service broadcasting rose through the emergence of democracy, which succeeded authoritarian regimes and even came before the first elections where the population was able to vote for candidates in multi-party elections. These governments had within them the foundations of the pre-existing state system which would serve as a starting point for the new system. In other words, in both realities, public service broadcasting is seen as one of the many new elements of the birth of democracy.

Even before these authoritarian regimes, these countries had no lasting experiences of public service broadcasting – at least not one guided by the principles of the contemporary model. There was no "public service broadcasting culture"; this culture would have to be developed by the actual broadcasting professionals themselves, adapting and changing how they worked with programming. It was developed by civil society, which needed to understand what it should expect from the new broadcasters and how to monitor them, and by the government, which needed to adapt to new broadcasters which mainly ran on public resources and were linked to the state, yet had autonomous editorial lines.

At the turn of the 1980s, the organization of civil society was still fragile, notably the portion that presented demands in communication. In Central and Eastern Europe, the rash of demonstrations that eventually led to overthrowing the socialist regimes did not usually have any structured demands for communication. Brazil already had entities concerned with this agenda, notably from professional segments or the academic environment. Even still, they did not have much of a voice and public service broadcasting was not a major issue in society at that time.

There were no public service broadcasters, no culture of this type of broadcasting, and no structured demands from much of civil society for them. And, therefore, there were no regulatory structures capable of defending the autonomy of public service broadcasters in relation to public power. In the best-case scenario, these structures would emerge and develop as a result of the transformations broadcasters were undergoing; in the worst-case scenario, they simply would not exist.

To date, the mechanisms for ensuring the autonomy of public service broadcasting in most of these countries do not always hold up to radical changes that can occur to the national power structure. This leads to operating rules being altered and a disregard for leader mandates and mechanisms of social control (DRAGOMIR, 2010).

There were also not enough resources, neither in Brazil nor Europe, for large experiments. In Central and Eastern European countries, the budget for public service broadcasting had to compete with all the other segments of society trying to adapt to democracy under disadvantageous macroeconomic scenarios. In Brazil, although the EBC was created during a prosperous economic phase, with the support of numerous resources in its early years, it was still necessary to modernize its previous infrastructure. When there were not enough resources for major innovations, the solution was to draw inspiration from Western models that have been in use for decades (MUNGIU-PIPPIDI, 2003).

All these similarities notwithstanding, there are several others that go well beyond the field of broadcasting which we shall go over in the next few pages. When a Brazilian walks through the streets of Bratislava, the capital of Slovakia, he or she notices some similarities between the Slovak language and Portuguese: their words for police (*polícia),* history (*história),* humor (*humor*), satire (*satira,* also written with no accent), and this (*este*) are the same in both languages. Also, martial law was introduced on December 13th in both Brazil and Poland, which seems like more than just a coincidence. Seeing Bulgarians celebrate when their national soccer team unexpectedly wins a match is something Brazilians can also relate to.

The aim here is to demonstrate that there is no prejudice against the models adopted in Central and Eastern Europe. The difficulties and challenges facing service broadcasting in Brazil, including the transition from an authoritarian government to a democratic one, share more in common with the history of these aforementioned European countries than the well-delineated scenario of Western Europe. Among these challenges is having a public system which works for the public, and the search for models defined at the national level:

> "(...) experience shows that the *Public Service Broadcasting (PSB)* model, most clearly represented by the BBC, is difficult to export to different cultural contexts. Even in Eastern Europe, the term PSB is usually

just a poor disguise for state broadcasting" (VOLTMER, 2010, p. 154-155).


*Who is speaking?*


An attentive reader will have already realized that I sometimes write my narratives in the first person singular. I do this because I believe the reader has the right to know my point of view, as well as to differentiate my personal observations from the analysis and conclusions obtained from other authors.

There are two specific moments in which I use the first person singular. The first is when I analyze the Brazilian case: I was director of EBC from May 2010 to January 2011. Before (at the Ministry of Culture) and after that period (at the Ministry of Communications), I worked with issues related to public service broadcasting. Thus, some of my observations are empirical and relate to these periods.

The second moment I use the first person singular is with regards to my thoughts about the transition in Central and Eastern European countries. This book is the result of research I did for my postdoctorate in Social Communication at the Faculty of Communication, University of Brasilia (FAC/UnB). I was in Poland, the Czech Republic, Slovakia, Romania and Bulgaria in March 2017 to conduct interviews, talk with researchers and industry professionals, give lectures, and participate in discussions. I felt it important to briefly mention the histories of the following people with whom I had had conversations with from my time in those countries. Most of these interviews are complements to the bibliographic and documentary references for this work. I interviewed the following professionals (in alphabetical order):

**Andrej Skolkay** is the research director at the School of Communication and Media in Bratislava, Slovakia. He has been involved in investigating the regulation of mass communication, the relationship between communication and politics, and journalistic coverage of corruption cases.

**Andrzej Krajewski** is a journalist. He was a correspondent for Polish public broadcasters in Washington from 1990 to 1994, and an adviser on matters of freedom of expression for the Polish broadcasting regulator (KRRiT). He has written articles and book chapters on media and democracy.

**Euclides Quandt de Oliveira** was Minister of Communications from 1974 to 1979 during the Ernesto Geisel government. Before that, he was chairman of the National Telecommunications Council (Contel) from 1965 to 1967 and Telebrás from 1972 to 1974. He was a retired Navy officer (electronics specialist) and a member of the Military Cabinet for the Castello Branco government. He passed away on July 19, 2013.

**Franklin Martins** was Chief Minister of the Secretariat of Social Communication, Presidency of the Republic (Secom-PR) from 2007 to 2010, during the second term of then president Luiz Inácio Lula da Silva. He is a journalist and has worked for Rede Globo, TV Bandeirantes, Portal IG and O Globo newspaper, among others.

**Irina Margareta Nistor** was a translator for *Romanian Television* (TVR) when, in the late 1980s, she began translating illegal copies of banned films. She was well known throughout Romania and her story was told in the movie *Chuck Norris vs. Communism*. She is currently a TV host and film critic.

**Nikoleta Daskalova** is coordinator for the Media Monitoring Lab at the Media Democracy Foundation in Sofia and is a member of the Bulgarian team for the European Union Media Pluralism Monitoring project. She was the rapporteur for the Balkan Media Barometer: Bulgaria 2014, as well as the author of other studies in this field.

**Pavel Sedláček** is a professor at the Department of Media Studies and Journalism, Masaryk University in Brno, Czech Republic. He conducts research and teaches in the areas of media education, ethics, and journalism history. He served as an associate researcher at the University of London and Webster University.

**Raina Konstantinova** began her career at *Bulgarian National Radio* (BNR) in 1973. Since then, she has held various positions at the station, eventually becoming Assistant Director. She was Radio Department Director for the *European Broadcasting Union* and a member on the BNR Public Council. She has presented with the *"Orphan Wanderer"* Award, awarded by the BNR.

**Romina Surugiu** is an associate professor of journalism and media studies at the University of Bucharest. She served on the board of the *Romanian Public Television Company* (TVR) from 2012 to 2015, and heads a research project on the history of television in Romania, Bulgaria and Belgium.

**Stanisław Jędrzejewski** is a professor at the Department of Social Sciences, Kozminski University, Warsaw, Poland. He was a member and deputy coordinator of the Radio Committee for the *European Broadcasting Union*, a board member for *Polish Radio* (PR), a member of the National Broadcasting Council, and coordinator of the PR Board of Directors.

**Tereza Cruvinel** was the first female CEO of Empresa Brasil de Comunicação (EBC), from 2007 to 2011. She is a journalist and has worked at O Globo (where she wrote one of the country's leading columns in political journalism for 21 years), Globonews, Rede TV!, TV Brasília, Jornal de Brasília, Correio Braziliense, Jornal do Brasil, and the website Brasil 247.

**Václav Mika** was Managing Director of Radio and Television of Slovakia (RTVS) from 2012 to 2017. Previously, he was Managing Director of *TV Markíza* and *Radia Express*, president of the Association of Independent Radio and Television Broadcasters, and has held a number of media positions and activities since 1986.

# THE END

**II**

On October 7, 1989, Erich Honecker should have been happy. *Should have been*. East Germany, the "socialist state of workers and peasants", celebrated its 40th anniversary, reaching a level of production and consumption which surpassed that of other European socialist countries.

At the social level, the indices measuring the quality of life were substantially higher in East Germany than in the other bloc countries, reflecting a culture of public policies typical of social welfare states (HERTLE, WOLLE, 2004). At the economic level, the country had broken away from its tradition of agriculture in favor of heavy industry and the production of consumer goods. East of the Berlin Wall there were companies that were or would be competitive or even recognized internationally such as Carl Zeiss, founded in the city of Jena, for optical technology. Although many products were still unavailable, consumption flourished on a national level.

*"Let us plough, let us build/Learn and create like never before/and, confident in existing strength/A free generation rises up"*. These lyrics from the national anthem of East Germany in 1949 (preceded and followed by other lyrics which talk of peace, equality, and labor for the country) announced the creation of the new German state, the Deutsche Demokratische Republik (DDR). At the end of World War II and up until 1949, Germany was divided into four occupation zones to be administered by the United States, Great Britain, France and the Soviet Union. The Soviet Union occupied eastern Germany and seemed to be content to maintain it as an occupation zone. However, this Soviet inaction did not sit well with political parties and other local political entities which pushed toward (and succeeded) in founding a new country. Despite Soviet opposition at the time (BANDEIRA, 2001; HUBER, 2008), a socialist state was born, one which was quite distinct from the others. It formally enforced multipartism: even though the Sozialistische Einheitspartei Deutschland (SED) has won all direct elections in the country's history by a wide margin, its parliamentarians were members of the Christlich-Demokratische Union Deutschlands (CDU), Liberal-Demokratische Partei Deutschlands (LDP), and other parties – which were not commonly known as opposition to the government (HUBER, 2008).

Plough, build, learn and create like never before. These verbs from the third stanza of the DDR national anthem also rang true for their neighbor, West Germany. Both were destroyed by the bombings from previous years. Being from the same national territory and the same world war, the two nations were separated by a fragile border throughout the 1940s and 1950s. Residents of one country often worked in the other, especially in Berlin, the capital city of the DDR. One only had to cross the street and come back at the end of the day, but they didn't all make it. The exodus to West Germany was massive. But as its population began to decline, the DDR made moves to limit the exodus of its citizens. Rumors of a wall separating the eastern and western portions of the city surfaced, yet were quickly denied by the government. On August 13th, 1961, East Germans woke up to find soldiers patrolling their streets, preventing them from crossing the border. Thus began the construction of the wall.

This, however, was in the past. On October 7th, 1989, Erich Honecker had reason to celebrate. Not only was he celebrating the anniversary of *his* People's Republic, he was celebrating his own trajectory: he had been a supporter of the Communist Party of Germany since adolescence, and was arrested by the Nazi German government; upon release, he continued his political activities in the Soviet occupation zone; he was a member of the SED, and held a number of positions within the party, ultimately being appointed First Secretary of the Central Committee at the age of 58 in 1971; he became chiefly responsible for the fate of East Germany after this year. He was also elected Chairman of the State Council in 1976.

In short, Honecker and his compatriots, in October 1989, were like characters whose images *could have been* printed on a set of stamps to commemorate the Republic's anniversary: they were smiling and looking confident while going about another day of work.

But the reality was harsher. Thousands of Germans had traveled to Czechoslovakia in the previous months. They tried to enter embassies of western countries, mainly West Germany, or traveled to Hungary to try to cross that country's border into

Austria. On October 2nd, sealed trains from Czechoslovakia carrying more than 10,000 refugees started crossing seeking asylum at the West German embassy, crossing through East Germany towards the other side of the wall. Honecker agreed to the crossing as long as no one left the train halfway through the journey and everyone accepted the confiscation of their documents.

Inside the train, refugees from Dresden tore their eastern documents and money apart and threw them out the train windows. Demonstrators gathered at the station in hopes of boarding the train, but were being driven back by police. The station was ruined and confusion spread as a result. On the same day in Leipzig, some 10,000 protesters took to the streets shouting "we'll stay here", announcing their willingness to resist. Within a few days, those same people in the same city with thousands of new protesters would shout "we are the people" (TAYLOR, 2009).

And on October 7th political leaders from many socialist countries were in attendance for the celebrations. Mikhail Gorbachev was in attendance to witness the demonstrations, some of which were bold. During the commemorative parade, youth group protestors began chanting "Gorbi" and "Gorbi, help us!" Over the next few hours, Gorbachev, theoretically the momentary representative of the humanization of socialism – an issue we shall return to – would have the opportunity to provoke Honecker, a symbol of the old guard (TAYLOR, 2009).

The events in East Germany did not represent the beginning of the end. At most, it was the middle of the end. In the West, a striking image of the time was the number of queues and how much they grew. In Brno, Czechoslovakia, people queued up to buy toilet paper (SEDLÁČEK, 2017); in Romania there was a monthly food ration, which included one kilo of sugar and six eggs (NISTOR, 2017), but buying meat, milk and other foods was very difficult. Up until the 1970s, goods could be bought anywhere in the country, but in the second half of the 1980s, people who resided outside of Bucharest, for example, could not buy inside the capital. On Christmas Eve, 1989, people had to wait in the cold to get eggs, an essential ingredient in holiday recipes – yet there was not always enough for everyone (SURUGIU, 2017). Interestingly, Bulgarians associate queues with the period immediately following the end of the socialist regime, when economic reforms resulted in many products being unavailable; there were empty shelves across the country, and hyperinflation reached an alarming 2,000% in 1996.

Other indications of major problems also existed. In Romania, the bloc country which probably suffered the most from the economic conditions of the 1980s, power outages were common and indoor heating was reduced or cut during the day. In the months of November and December 1989, when the average temperature in Bucharest dropped to about -5°C, buildings like the University of Bucharest Law School, partially lined with marble, students and teachers had to have class in freezing classrooms. In Warsaw, the capital of Poland, neon signs, once symbols of prosperity in the 1970s, were being turned off because they consumed too much energy. Many were even thrown away (and recovered decades later) as they were considered to be a thing of the past. A dependence on Western brands grew in East Germany, some of which were obtained as payment from West Germany for the release of political dissidents. In Czechoslovakia, whose economy was supported by heavy industry and war, the Gross Domestic Product (GDP) continued to grow until 1988, but less so than in previous decades. In the meantime, the government's lack of credibility spread throughout the country and the outcry for the freedom to travel abroad increased.

At the time, a part of the population held official jobs and other parts held clandestine ones. In Poland, Andrzej Krajewski was editor of Firma, a magazine aimed at small businesses. He also held a semi-legal job as a guide and interpreter for correspondents for Japanese newspaper Yomiuri Shimbun and American newspaper Washington Post, and an *illegal* job as editor of the clandestine weekly CDN; the Polish acronym for "It Continues". Irina Nistor was a translator for the state-run television station in Romania and, after 3 p.m., she provided the dubbing for all the characters in prohibited American films. The tapes were sold illegally to the few Romanians who could afford a VCR and set up home movie clubs to watch them with their neighbors. Movie smuggling and underground trade grew, and Irina's voice became famous, as in the movie "Chuck Norris versus Communism".

Sounds of change echoed in the early 1980s in the People's Republic of Poland. In 1981 the government tried to repress dissatisfaction through the introduction of a new Martial Law, claiming it was necessary in order to prevent Soviet tanks from invading the country and repeating what had happened in Czechoslovakia and Hungary in previous decades:

> "When Martial Law was introduced on December 13th, 1981, studios and transmitters were secretly relocated to a hidden location, possibly the Military Academy, about 2 km from the original site. (...) At midnight they began arresting people, TV programming was interrupted, and the next morning all the Polish children woke up their parents asking: 'Where

is Teleranek?' *[A Sunday-morning children's TV program in Poland – 'ranek' in Polish means 'morning'].* In its place was General Jaruzelski saying, 'The time has come...' This transmission was not broadcast from its usual location, but from the hidden one. People would arrive at work and the police would say: 'there is no work, go home. We'll let you know when you can come back'. It was a dramatic experience. The people on TV were in uniform. Some of them were not high-ranking military personnel; their uniforms were plain, with no badge. One of them I had met in New York, in 1986, where he was working for a local Polish channel" (KRAJEWSKI, 2017).

This incident is sadly coincidental with Brazilian history: exactly twelve years before December 13th, the date when Polish Martial Law was introduced, Brazil had issued Institutional Act Number Five and experienced some of its most traumatic years under military dictatorship.

Opposition to the Polish government gained strength in the following years. In the first half of 1988, striking workers demanded the legalization of the Solidarity union which had previously been forced underground after having supported the government throughout the decade. Lech Walesa, one of the union's main leaders, had become a popular figure even outside the continent. The government agreed to hold dialogues and began the process that would be known as the "Round Table". In April, 1989, the union was legalized and parliamentary elections were scheduled for June of that same year. Solidarity's victory was far greater than expected: its candidates won every possible seat in the Sejm, the lower house of parliament, and 99 of 100 in the Senate. In August, two parties from the socialist coalition broke the alliance with the Polska Zjednoczona Partia Robotnicza (PZPR) and announced their support for Solidarity. There was no solution left for Parliament other than to appoint a new Prime Minister after the resignation of the former. On August 24th, Tadeusz Mazowiecki was sworn in as the first non-communist head of government since the early postwar years – without any backlash from the Soviet Union.

Since the mid-80s, the Hungarian government had taken small steps towards liberalizing the government. The January 1989 package already provided for union pluralism, freedom of association and the press, a new electoral law, and a revision of the Constitution. In May, still before the new Polish reality, Hungary began removing barbed wire to open up its border with Austria. Thousands of citizens would pass through this border in the following months. In June, Imre Nagy, the country's leader who was executed after Soviet troops invaded in 1956, was rehonored and re-buried and given head of state honors, along with four other colleagues. The ceremony was broadcast live and hundreds of thousands of Hungarians turned up to show their support. The first half of that year also saw the beginning of rounds of negotiations between local political forces, leading in the following months to adopt a set of measures for the political system, including the decision to hold multiparty elections for Parliament. By year's end, the Hungarian Communist Party had advocated democratic socialism, committed itself to free elections and to multipartism, and the country was renamed by removing the term "Popular". The elections took place in March 1990.

With such open changes in Poland and Hungary, things were set to get worse in East Germany. On October 16th, 1989, an estimated 120,000 people were already taking to the streets in Leipzig in demonstration. The next day, a meeting of the Politburo planned for the removal of Erich Honecker: his removal was requested by each member. Honecker, in a bid to maintain longstanding party practice, voted for his own removal. Egon Krenz, his successor, was in the wrong place at the wrong time. The economy was worse than expected, the demonstrations were just starting to grow, and measures of distension only led to outcries for more freedom rather than ease tensions.

What happened on November 9th, 1989, was unexpected. Things were starting to look quite desperate: over the previous 24 hours more than 20,000 Germans had left neighboring countries and were heading toward Austria. Nevertheless, Günter Schabowski, spokesman for the Central Committee, held what one might call an unusual press conference. He read a note about the imminent adoption of new travel regulations, noting that some transitional rules would be adopted before said regulations would come into effect. Among such rules was the permission for permanent emigration between all border crossings, including those between East and West Berlin. Journalists were intrigued and asked if the note was correct. And when would it be possible to leave the country freely through the border crossings? Schabowski looked at the note again, hesitated a little, and replied, "immediately, without delay".

The situation would be hard to believe if the images were not available today. In the hours that followed, thousands of East Germans proceeded toward the Berlin Wall. The border guards had not received any specific orders and shortly opened the gates. It was another chapter in the collapse of socialism in Europe, but the images of the wall being destroyed, of people sitting on top of it or crossing through the border were very impactful. For many of the people from my generation, these are the major images representing the end of that regime, of that time, of that part of history. By the end of the following year, both East and West Germany would begin an intense and frantic transition back into a unified country (on a political level), but the fall of the wall meant this was all but a certainty.

November of 1989 was also a defining month for Czechoslovakia. Demonstrations continued to grow, constituting what would come to be known as the "Velvet Revolution". By the end of that month, all Communist Party leadership resigned, announcing the end of the one-party rule. In December, President Gustáv Husak appointed the country's first largely non-communist government since 1948, and then resigned. On December 29th, Václav Havel was appointed President of Czechoslovakia. Alexander Dubček, the legendary reformist Prime Minister, one of the hallmarks of "socialism with a human face", toppled in 1968 during the Prague Spring, was elected President of the federal parliament. In June 1990, the first elections were held under the new format, and on January 1st, 1993, the country was split into two countries – the Czech Republic and Slovakia.

The exodus marked Bulgaria in the mid-1980s and, to this day, brings shame to some of its inhabitants. Initially, the Bulgarian government encouraged citizens of Turkish origin to change their names and, due to political differences, authorized for their departure from Bulgaria. About 200,000 people ran to the border with whatever they could carry. To this day, an election day in Bulgaria is marked by the arrival of numerous buses crowded with voters from Turkey.

In the 1980s, the regime was regarded as one of, if not *the*, most loyal to the Soviet Union. The ironic sense of humor so characteristic of Eastern Europe was still on display: "In Bulgaria, we opened the umbrella before it started raining in Moscow";

"What is the Bulgarian-Soviet friendship? It is a cow fed in Bulgaria and milked in the Soviet Union".

Laughter, however, was not the most common reaction at the end of the decade. Demonstrations also began to take place in the country in October and November 1989. The starting point was in Ruse, a northern port city in Danube, on the border with Romania. The pollution caused by the chemical industry led people to stage demonstrations which eventually began to spread. On November 10th – one day after the fall of the Berlin Wall had begun – Bulgarian TV aired a live broadcast of the Communist Party meeting which culminated in the removal of Todor Zhivkov, the party's Secretary-General since 1954. His more liberal successor, Petar Mladenov, began to lift the restrictions on the freedom of expression and assembly, which led to new demonstrations and the formation of anti-communist movements. The first multiparty elections since 1931 were scheduled for December in the following year. In the interim, political forces agreed on rules for the transition to democracy. The Communist Party announced its break from Marxism-Leninism and adopted a new name – the Bulgarian Socialist Party. In June, that party won the elections.

Nicolae Ceaușescu is a separate – and dubious – character in this story. Just over three years after succeeding leadership of the Romanian Communist Party as Secretary-General he did not allow the country's troops to participate in the invasion of Czechoslovakia, and publicly advocated further liberalization of its regime. The following year, the government-run TV station was the only one in the socialist bloc to air a live broadcast of US astronaut Neil Armstrong landing on the moon (SURUGIU, 2017b). Because of these demonstrations (and others) the Soviet Union became suspicious of the Romanian leader, and their relationship became more and more distant, with capitalist countries keeping a hopeful eye on the country. In 1960s Romania there was a reasonable supply of consumer goods, and foreign films used to arrive in local theaters only about a year after their initial release. An anti-abortion law was enacted at the end of the decade, leading to an increased number of illegal abortions being performed in clandestine clinics without proper health care, which included the birth of unwanted children. This problem would be portrayed in the 2007 film "4 months, 3 weeks and 2 days", which won awards and honors in many film festivals (NISTOR, 2017). In 1971, Ceauşescu visited China, North Korea, and Mongolia, and was impressed with Kim Il-Sung's government. This led him to establish a cult of personality inspired by the one surrounding the North Korean leader.

By the end of the 1980s, the crisis in Romania had grown, in part due to Ceauşescu's strange decisions. He decided to pay off all foreign debt the country had, a decision supposedly influenced by his wife, Elena. He also ordered the "pharaonic" construction of the new Romanian Parliament, currently the world's second-largest civilian building. Covered in marble, with gigantic, spacious corridors and rooms, the palace underwent several design changes initiated by Ceauşescu during its construction.

Even so, in November 1989, Ceauşescu was re-elected leader of the Romanian Communist Party for a five-year term. On December 21st, he delivered a speech in which he called for a demonstration of support for the government, which was met with a chorus of boos. The images of a stunned Ceauşescu trying to silence the crowd have swept the globe and, to this day, are still striking. It is strange to think that the ruler of a country could have been so alienated for so long that he was unaware of the mood of a society subjected to deprivation. Short anecdotes can help to better understand that moment:

> "Every school had a picture of Ceauşescu, and in each one of those pictures only one of his ears was visible. In Romania, the expression 'having one ear' means 'being crazy'. One day, someone noticed this and all the photos were replaced in every school in the country. On TV, only one anchor was allowed to wear glasses so as not to remind Ceauşescu that he was old, as he associated wearing glasses with old age. Films about the elderly were also not allowed to be shown. His speeches were typed on a special typewriter with very large letters so he didn't have to wear glasses" (NISTOR, 2017).

While diligent advisors were concerned with redefining the image of Ceauşescu, resistance occurred, including inside Romanian TV which, at the time, was run by Constantin Petra:

> "Constantin was a pensive person. For example, he did not stop the elevators. You might find that that is not such a big deal, but the TV building had 13 floors. Believe me when I say: not stopping the elevators at that time, although Ceauşescu wanted to reduce energy consumption, was an act of courage. He let the teams continue to film Ceauşescu's speech while he was trying to silence the crowd's booing. We would not have these images if the team had not continued to shoot. Once again, it was an act of courage; he could have stopped the filming" (NISTOR, 2017).

Resistance grew, the defense minister appeared to be dead, and the army turned against Ceauşescu, who continued to try (unsuccessfully) and calm protesters outside the Party Central Committee. He and his wife were arrested while trying to escape, tried by a makeshift court, and were executed. In his defense, Ceauşescu allegedly refused to acknowledge the court's authority and sang "The International" before being shot. An interim council announced elections for 1990 which were to be held in May. In the confusing end of the decade in Romania, more than 1,000 people were shot which, to this day, is still a mystery as to where or why it happened. A cemetery was built in the middle of the capital for the victims.

In the span of about one year, between 1989 and 1990, socialism had collapsed, from the northern port of Gdansk in Poland to the southern village of Podkova in Bulgaria. It was not just a transformation of political systems in Poland, East Germany, Czechoslovakia, Hungary, Romania, and Bulgaria. At that time, the Soviet Union was also losing support throughout the European continent, from the north to the south. The following years saw the fall of two other socialist countries on the continent; these countries, however, were not entirely in accordance with the Soviet Union.

Yugoslavia differed greatly from other socialist countries: it was a federation in which a number of social rights prevailed. The federation, made up of six republics and two autonomous provinces (later recognized as republics which are culturally and ethnically distinct from one another) remained largely united thanks to Marshal Josip Broz Tito. After his death in 1980, ethnic tensions and liberal pressures increased. In 1990, representatives from Slovenian and Croatian communist parties broke from national structure and negotiated, with the opposition movements of these republics, multiparty elections. In December of that same year, Slovenian citizens voted to separate from the federation. The army announced that it would not accept the separation of the country, which led to several civil wars that only delayed the changes. Conflicts spread throughout the republics until the federation came to an end in the 1990s.

Albania was once considered the most closed-off country in Europe. Perhaps this is due to the fact that, as early as 1990 when the socialist countries began their transformations to democracy, some people believed this transformation would never happen in Albania (JOFFILY, 1990). The death of Enver Hoxha in 1985, after 40 years serving as head of state, led Ramiz Alia to come to power. The new First Secretary of the Albanian Party of Labor began slow, liberalizing changes, and loosened restrictions on travelling abroad in 1990. The 1991 elections saw the communists emerge as the victors, with Alia serving as president, but demonstrations led to the inclusion of non-communists in the government. The demonstrations did not stop. New elections held in 1992 saw Sali Berisha become the first official non-communist head of government in the last 53 years (although he had been a member of the Albanian Party of Labor in previous decades).

In the meantime, the Soviet Union itself had collapsed. Since 1989, Gorbachev's reforms had been facing more resistance, a reflection of the changes occurring in the allied countries and the country's growing domestic economic problems. The first elections with real opposition from the 15 USSR member republics were held in 1990, and the Communist Party was defeated in six of them. Declarations of independence began in the following months. In August 1991, hardliner party members attempted an uprising, placing Gorbachev, who was then on vacation, under house arrest. The coup failed, with significant opposition from the population and the President of the Republic of Russia, Boris Yeltsin, but events started to gain momentum. From the months of August to December, ten republics declared independence. Leaders from three of the most important republics – Russia, Ukraine and Belarus (later to be renamed Belarussia) – announced the creation of the Commonwealth of Independent States. Gorbachev announced his resignation on Christmas Day, the Soviet flag was lowered in the Kremlin, and the Russian flag was raised. By the end of that year, the USSR would formally cease to exist.

# III

The ensuing transformations obviously transcended the political system and spread throughout the lives of the public and all economic areas of these countries, including the broadcasting sector, the subject of this book. Some aspects from previous years and the transition appear to be crucial toward understanding the media sector in Central and Eastern European countries.

The first aspect concerns the effect Western capitalist countries had on socialist life, on a number of levels. These countries were seen as antagonists, as references in terms of consumption patterns; as sources of public pressure for political transparency; as broadcasters of anti-socialist propaganda; and as funders of opposition movements toward the government. They were, for different reasons, threats to socialism – and they studied and were familiar with the Central and Eastern European countries. Western governments and businesses were ready to act, both before and after the local European governments were removed.

Moreover, one cannot overlook the relationship between the Soviet Union and its main ally states. The former would not only be a major reference for military alliances – such as the Warsaw Pact, which allowed for the temporary occupation of ally nations in order to suppress uprisings and riots – but it was also a strategic maneuver. In the context of public service broadcasting, this alliance materialized in the form of the International Radio and Television Organization (OIRT). Founded in 1946, the entity united country members, including western capitalist countries. In 1950, with the exception of Finland, some members left the OIRT to found the European Broadcasting Union (EBU). In addition to European socialist countries, the OIRT aligned with other bloc allies from around the world, including Afghanistan, Algeria, China, North Korea, Cuba, Yemen, Nicaragua, Syria, and Vietnam. The purpose of the organization was to strengthen technical cooperation and the exchange of content among member countries; they even created a television network called Intervision. In 1993, the OIRT merged with the EBU. Additionally, the satellite communications service organization Intersputnik was also active (BEUTELSCHMIDT, OEHMIG, 2014).

The alliance included the Soviet Union providing economic support to its allies. The amount of financial support depended on each nation's reality and the problems they faced, which generated controversy and internal disputes. East Germany is a good example of this. It cost more to finance that nation as it combined repression with a pattern of consumption and technological advancement unrivalled by its allies. This price was paid, to some extent, by the USSR. The German satellite was viewed as a drain on Soviet resources, more so than the rest of the bloc, drawing scathing criticism from some of its leaders. Lavrentiy Beria, chief of the Soviet secret police (NKVD) under Joseph Stalin, was one of the most vocal in this regard, claiming that East Germany made no sense and would not exist without Soviet leadership. He was correct there as the country did not actually exist until the USSR took it over in the post-war years. And one could say he was correct again, this time about the future, as the country was incorporated by West Germany once Soviet funding became scarce. However, the present did not agree with him: Beria, aspiring to succeed Stalin, was executed.

When Mikhail Gorbachev repeatedly stated publicly, in June 1989, that the Soviet Union would no longer interfere with its allies' construction of socialism, he was not merely adhering to the people's right to self-determination. This political move was followed by a reduction to the economic subsidies associated to the allied countries. In the previous four decades, these allies had largely depended on the Soviet economy and were not prepared for such a disruption as they had long been ruled by leaders deep-rooted in power. These same allies continued to depend on external resources and favorable economic relations, so the most logical path was to adopt the Western capitalist model. And so, with heads hanging low, the former Soviet allies began to copy the solutions adopted by their new Western partners, including opening up the public service broadcasting market to private enterprises, and turning former government-controlled broadcasters into public ones, in accordance with Public Service Broadcasting (PSB), which some countries in Europe had ascribed to since before World War II. As we shall see, this might have been the goal, but it would have to be adapted to current possible contingencies.

Of course, there was the issue of social dissatisfaction with state-imposed surveillance in previous decades and the lack of protection for individual and collective rights, from a liberal perspective, even if they eventually appeared in legal texts. The secret service agencies were dedicated to monitoring the activities of each country's citizens, in addition to international activities, and there were many of them. Once again, the East German apparatus was a reference: its political police, the Ministerium für Staatssicherheit (or Stasi), is regarded as the most extensive security service of all the Soviet-aligned countries, and might possibly hold that same reputation if compared to other eras and national contexts. One out of every 180 East Germans is estimated to be a Stasi official. In the USSR, the ratio was 1 person out of every 595, in Czechoslovakia 1 out of 867, and in Poland 1 out of 1,574. In terms of permanent professionals and permanent or occasional collaborators, some authors estimate that one out of four residents in the country was linked to Stasi (FUNDER, 2008; HOFFMANN, 2012).

The desire for less vigilance and more freedom was a component towards dismantling the old socialist model and was also reflected in public service broadcasting. More than changing from state to public with the inclusion of more social participation, old programs and professionals identified with the old regime were being replaced. Programs were substituted in stages, as it was not possible to overwrite the entire schedule overnight. The "Der schwarze Kanal", a political propaganda program, was briefly eliminated from the East German broadcasting just before the fall of the Berlin Wall and after the freedom of the press was granted; one of the rights secured in the days following Honecker's deposition. The children's television program "Sandmännchen" survived reunification and is still broadcast. Derived from a Scandinavian tale, the character was a man who physically resembled Santa Claus, and put children to sleep. Although West Germany created its own version, it was the eastern version that was popular on local television. The "Sandmännchen" would often meet with his Mongolian and Vietnamese friends (who came from aligned countries), as well as visit space (or the cosmos, in Soviet bloc jargon) to commemorate the achievement of Sigmund Jähn, the first German (and easterner) to fly in space. It was, in fact, a reciprocal tribute, since Sigmund had carried a miniature Sandmännchen on his flight as part of the Soviet Union's Interkosmos program.

On the other hand, the situation for those professionals who politically identified with the old regime during the transition period did not receive the same affection as Sandmännchen did. A lustration policy had begun in the countries of the old bloc or, in other words, a purification of the new model was being performed by punishing the servants of the old regime. Of course, it was not possible to simply get rid of all public servants with ties to the old government as doing so would result in a severe lack of experts needed to carry out even basic public administration activities. Yet, purification was what they wanted, and victims were to be a natural consequence of this process.

Depending on each country's law, the repercussions included the investigation of one's life history, dismissal from public office, inability to be appointed to new positions, public exposure, and imprisonment. In reunited Germany, citizens were given the right to access their files in the secret police, and the government assigned teams to organize the paperwork. Files were shredded prior to the Stasi offices being overrun by the population, but only some of them were shredded. The work of organizing the files therefore consisted largely of trying to piece together bits of torn paper which had been thrown into large bags.

In the Czech Republic, more than 210,000 people had their life history investigated up until 1993. In 1994, before the parliamentary elections, 12,000 Hungarian authorities were legally investigated for their possible collaboration with the secret police. From 1992 to 1994, the Albanian government fined seventy authorities from the Communist period, a total which amounted to $60,000. Ten were arrested. In Lithuania, a parliamentary committee investigated the Komitet Gosudarstvennoi Bezopasnosti (KGB) files. The first shipment of documents alone contained 2,400 boxes with more than 31,000 citizen verification files and more than 11,000 investigation files (ELLIS, 1996).

Rudolf Zukal refused to accept the Soviet invasion of Prague in 1968. He voted against it in an assembly, lost his teaching job at the Prague University of Economic Sciences, and would spend the next two decades working with an excavator, cleaning lakes in Bohemia. He participated in the opposition to the Czechoslovakian government, was rehabilitated, and in 1990 regained his job at the university and was elected deputy after being appointed to head the Ministry of Education. Life seemed to be moving forward again, but in 1991, his cooperation with the secret police had been discovered. Thirty years earlier, he had won a scholarship to study in Vienna. There, he met with a former friend from college who knew he was working for the Ministry of the Interior, to which the secret police were linked. She used to talk to him and answer his questions about university life, a situation that got worse when he was blackmailed for having an extramarital affair with her. He eventually received money to attend parties and hang out with fellow college students. In 1991, after living at length as a dissident, Zukal was given two alternatives: he could resign as a deputy, or have his name publicly disclosed and try to explain himself to his colleagues. Six lawmakers had resigned for similar reasons, but he opted for the second alternative. He had his name read, as well as information about his collaboration, alongside ten other parliamentarians in the crowded lobby of the Federal Assembly. Zukal explained the situation but was avoided in Parliament. He received letters calling him an agent. He did not want to apply for a new term (ROSENBERG, 1999).

Jenny Gröllmann was a popular actress in East Germany and continued her career after the reunification. In 2006, she received a surprise: her ex-husband, Ulrich Mühe, father of her daughter, and also an actor (he played the remorseful Stasi agent in "The Lives of Others", which won the Oscar for Best Foreign Language Film in 2006), gave an interview for a book about the movie in which he accused his ex-wife of being a Stasi informant. Gröllmann denied the accusations and the case was publicly debated, with alleged evidence and interpretations used as an argument for both sides. In 2008, the Berlin Supreme Court ruled that the charge was unfounded and prohibited the press from referring to the actress as a Stasi informant. None of the protagonists in this story survived to see the outcome of the legal dispute: Gröllmann died in August 2006; Mühe in July 2007; and, in 2008, Helmut Menge, the secret police officer who mentioned her in his reports. They were all victims of cancer (SCHNEIDER, 2015).

These two stories became famous and were even retold in books translated into Portuguese. Many others did not become so famous, but even so, the events that occurred years or decades before still ended up disrupting the career of many professionals back then, including public service broadcasters.

The two examples cited above also show that punishments were not restricted to authorities who were undeniably linked to the previous government or who directly committed violations of individual rights. That is to say, while searching for more freedom, the punishment (not always resolved in the courts) did not guarantee the right to a full defense, nor did it guarantee that alleged offenses committed decades earlier would be tried.

Was the goal, in fact, to guarantee full rights, or was the transition a process of building the possible, of regulating freedom and providing limited advances with openness to capital, redistribution of wealth (for the few) and diminished state authoritarianism? The search for an answer to this would end up diverting the focus of this work; however, it is interesting to see that, even after the overthrow of socialism, how some politicians and parties that once ruled Romania, Bulgaria, Albania, and other countries, remained in power and have now abandoned the classic Marxism-Leninism ideology.

The contradictions extended to Gorbachev's self-confidence. There is no doubt as to the central role he played in transforming the world between the late 1980s and early 1990s, which would have an impact in the decades to follow, including the need for leftist political forces to search for other models. But to what extent did adhering to the principle of self-determination actually defend the increase of rights so inherent in a democracy? Gorbachev's Perestroika defended the restructuring of the state and the role it played; and no less important was Glasnost, associated to the idea of state transparency and dialogue with the public, cultural openness, and freedom of expression. Gorbachev wrote about freedom of the press:

> "One of the signs of general revitalization is that our press increasingly prefers dialogue to monologue (...). It is much more beneficial to diversify authorship so that all citizens have the opportunity to speak up, so

that socialist pluralism, as it were, is represented in each publication in its entirety (...). Not everyone likes our style, however. This is especially true of those who are not used to living and working under the conditions of glasnost and explicit criticism, who are unable or unwilling to do so. They express dissatisfaction with our mass media and sometimes even demand that glasnost be restrained, suppressed" (GORBACHEV, 1987, p. 85-86).

The role of the press, however, is not restricted to promoting debate and defending transparency and cultural openness:

"The press must become increasingly effective. It should not leave the lazy, profiteers, opportunists, repressors of criticism and demagogues alone; but rather actively help those who work altruistically for perestroika (...). It is important to emphasize that the press should unite and mobilize people rather than disassemble them and create dissatisfaction and lack of confidence (...). The interests of deepening socialist democracy and intensifying people's political maturity require a fuller use of the mass media to discuss public and state issues, to broaden public control, to actively engage in greater accountability, for stricter discipline at work, for the observance of socialist law and order, and against violations of social principles and ethical standards of the Soviet way" (GORBACHEV, 1987, p. 87-88).

Thus, the press should foster public debate, and at the same time, cooperate with the selfless workers who advocate

perestroika (i.e., the government itself) without creating dissatisfaction and distrust. It should collaborate with discipline at
work, observance of law and order and oppose violations of
ethical standards.

This was the scene of contradictions in which the public
service broadcasters of old European socialist countries began
their restructuring.

# IV

The public service broadcasting policies of the socialist countries had two fronts. The first concerned their relationship with foreign broadcasters, whose signals were directed to their territories. This was a controversial issue. Even though, in the 1920s and 1930s, each country had the right to control radiowaves within its own territory, there was no consensus on the limits of transmission from one country to another. This problem increased due to ideological polarization, to an increase in the number of short and medium wave radio broadcasters, and to the increasing popularity of receivers for picking up these radio band signals.

During World War I, Germany used radio for propaganda purposes, and did not respect its territorial limits. In the 1920s, the USSR also used radio for propaganda purposes. By 1939, 25 countries were broadcasting internationally. The United States created The Voice of America broadcaster in 1942. All major countries participating in World War II operated similar services.

The problem increased over the following decades, and by 1983 governments in at least 80 countries were broadcasting in more than 30 languages. Private broadcasters did the same (KRASNER, 1991).

Television offered even greater potential as a tool for propaganda, but it came with more technical complexities. The first of these complications had to do with the range of the signal, which was lower than the aforementioned radio bands, and thereby led (and leads) to lower coverage. Moreover, unlike radio, the technical standards of television differed between Western countries and Central and Eastern European countries. There were two ways to circumvent this obstacle: adapt the emission or the reception.

The standards for black and white television were the same in East and West Germany. When East Germany adopted a new standard for color TV that was incompatible with Western Germany, the latter began broadcasting on both standards so that its programming would continue to be available in East Germany. In Hungary and Czechoslovakia, it was common for the public to adapt the receivers so that they could watch Western programming (KRASNER, 1991).

The popularization of TV and its subsequent technologies led to other forms of propaganda, one of which was reported in the Romanian documentary "Chuck Norris versus Communism". Bootleg videos of American films dubbed in Romanian became commonplace. People watched these films in makeshift movie clubs or in the homes of those who had expensive display equipment, and who would charge their neighbors to come over and watch them. This bootleg business grew into a vast network of piracy, and the films, acting as tools of propaganda, revealed the consumer goods and standard of living that were available in the West. The domestic distribution and screening of American films was prohibited.

The way to combat unwanted foreign broadcasts was to create structures to deliberately scramble or block signals, thus preventing people from being able to listen to them, a practice known as radio jamming. Many countries with different political systems have adopted and would adopt this practice over time. The Soviet Union has practiced it since the 1930s; Austria, Germany, and Italy during World War II, with Francoist Spain following suit shortly after. The same is true even today in North and South Korea, including other regions of the world. These attempts at jamming radio signals are not always successful, because the restrictions can be circumvented by broadcasting – programming from the Soviet Union was broadcast across more than 60 separate frequencies.

The other aspect of public service broadcasting policies in socialist countries concerns domestic broadcasting, i.e., the content that is made available to the local population. This was a growing concern as the number of households with television sets was growing at a similar rate as Western countries.

**Table 3: Number of residents per television set**

| Country | 1965 | 1975 | 1980 |
|---|---|---|---|
| United States | 3.6 | 3.1 | 2.8 |
| United Kingdom | 4 | 3 | 2.9 |
| France | 7.4 | 3.5 | unavailable |

| Country | 1965 | 1975 | 1980 |
| --- | --- | --- | --- |
| Italy | 8.6 | 4.6 | 4.2 |
| Portugal | 48.8 | 12.8 | 7.1 |
| East Germany | 5.1 | 3.4 | 2.6 |
| West Germany | 5.3 | 3.2 | 2.9 |
| Czechoslovakia | 6.6 | 4 | 3.6 |
| Hungary | 12.2 | 4.4 | 3.9 |
| Soviet Union | 14.4 | 4.6 | 3.5 |
| Yugoslavia | 34.3 | 7.7 | 5.9 |
| Bulgaria | 44.5 | 5.8 | 5.3 |

**Source:** MIHELJ, 2012.

In 1980, the number of residents per television set in East Germany was similar to that of the United States and the United Kingdom; the number of residents per television set in Czechoslovakia, Hungary, and the Soviet Union was lower than in Italy; and the number in all the socialist countries listed above was lower than in Portugal.

The role that propaganda plays in radio and TV has been well documented and is quite evident: it followed the lives of each country's top leader; there was an emphasis on international demonstrations in partner countries (which showed how important the country in question was to the rest of the nations); and political party speeches and events amounted to long hours of programming. There was, however, another kind of TV and radio, one that went unnoticed by those who only watched political content.

In the mid-1960s, programming in Eastern and Central Europe was under pressure to adapt to a style of mass communication, in order to reach an increasing number of households. The launch of the first *Sputnik* satellite in 1957, and others that came after, changed how content would be exchanged and transmitted throughout the world. For the public, this meant greater access to different content, even more so in regions that picked up Western broadcasting signals. Even in places that did not pick up these transmissions, like in parts of Romania, it was still possible to watch broadcasting programs from more liberal countries or countries which had access to more diverse content such as Hungary, Yugoslavia and Bulgaria.

Thus, in the 1960s, the European socialist countries began to slowly license foreign content, including more national and local content on popular culture, in addition to maintaining the sports, drama and educational content they had been broadcasting since their inception (IMRE, 2012). This trend continued in the following years. Honecker, while attending a party convention, even described East German television as boring and demanded that the programming include more entertainment. In the Soviet Union, Leonid Brezhnev reportedly talked about the need for entertainment, noting that "Soviets have the right to relax in front of the television after a day's work" (MIHELJ, 2012, p. 18).

The inclusion of more entertainment content not only drew citizens in socialist countries away from Western broadcasting, it also helped to preserve television as an important means of communication between the state and society. Conversely, if a broadcaster only transmitted propaganda, it would tend to lose credibility as an information medium.

There was also a pragmatic reason for transmitting licensed content. The decision to import programming was not only about having access to quality content, but transmitting that content for as long as possible since not enough of it was produced locally. Thus, foreign content would fill the gaps in programming schedules and eventually become the main attraction for each channel.

And that is exactly what happened. In the early 1970s, 32% of Hungarian television content was imported from the United Kingdom, France and West Germany. Eighty percent of the foreign content on Yugoslavia's Belgrade TV was produced in countries outside the socialist bloc, 40% of which came from the United States. In the early 1980s, 43% of imported content in Central and Eastern Europe had originally aired on Western television stations, while another 45% came from other socialist countries. The imported content consisted mainly of variety shows, cartoons, TV series and movies. "Lassie" became popular in Yugoslavia; "Flipper", "Joe Mannix" and "Chicago" in 1960s and 70s Romania; "Forsythe Saga" and "David Copperfield" in the Soviet Union, and "Zorro, Mickey Mouse Club", and "Disneyland" were well received in Poland between 1959 and 1962 (MIHELJ, 2012).

By 1989, when the socialist bloc was beginning to crumble, local television networks were already covering most of the countries. The major radio and television stations were available in the 1990 edition of the "World Radio TV Handbook", a directory started in 1947 of almost every major radio and TV station on Earth, which includes their basic technical data. I prepared the following maps in order to better show the reader how public broadcasting stations were distributed throughout each country. In addition, I briefly summarized these broadcasters' transition to the PSB model, after the overthrow of the socialist regime.

The following pages contain examples of three different models of transition: (a) incorporation, where one public broadcaster in the socialist bloc is consolidated into another broadcaster previously from a different country (as was the case with East Germany); (b) fragmented, where one public broadcaster split up into several different ones, just as the country to which it once belonged did (for example, Yugoslavia, Czechoslovakia and the Soviet Union); and (c) continuity, where transition over to the PSB model occurred within the same structure that existed before the overthrow of the socialist regime (the other countries in the list).


*Albania*


In 1989, Radiotelevisione Shqiptar broadcasted a single TV program from 5 p.m. to 9 p.m. daily, and again on Sundays from 9 a.m. to 2:30 p.m. As we can see on the map, the main stations were located in the cities of Berat (channel 9), Elbasan (channel 6), Gjirokaster (channel 7), Kükes (channels 12 and 39), Peshkopl (channel 8), Pogradec (channel 11), including the capital, Tirana (channel 10).

According to some authors, Albania overlooked public administration reforms when it transitioned to democracy. This led to a weak government system and the spread of corruption which, by the way, was not exclusive to the new Albanian government. Reforms attempted to meet international guidelines,

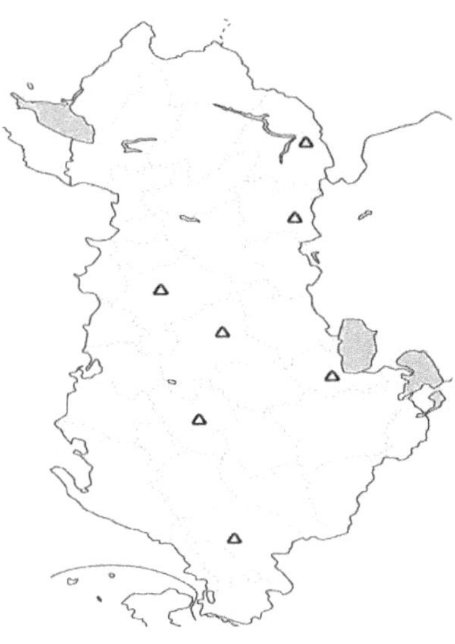

**Source:** Provided by author, based on WRTH (1990).

but public administration continued to be characterized by strict hierarchical structures (CEPIKU, MITITELU, 2010).

In 2006, the public broadcaster RTSH ran both the public TV station, TVSH, which was broadcast on one national and three local channels, and Radio Tirana, which broadcasted on two national and four local channels; this contained one program for Albanians residing outside the country and another in a foreign language. RTSH coverage reached around 80% of the country (LONDO, 2006). A few years later, the company created a second TV channel, in addition to launching a number of digital TV channels featuring sports, arts and culture programming.

*East Germany*

The transition to public broadcasting in East Germany was quite different from that of other European bloc countries. First of all, local broadcasters had infrastructure and daily broadcast times that were compatible with stations in many western countries.

An important part of the public broadcasting infrastructure remained in East Germany with the division of the country after World War II. East Germany inherited the 1939 Inselsberg tower (another aerial tower was built in the early 1970s, in the same transmission facility) and mountains that were good sites for installing other transmission towers, such as the Brocken and the Helpterberg.

**Figure 2: TV Stations in East Germany**

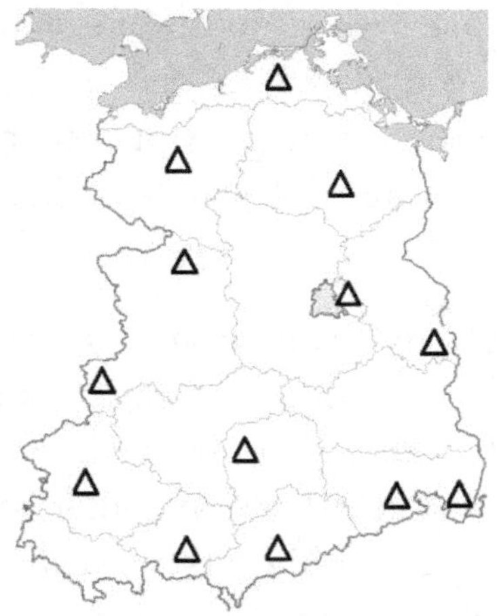

**Source:** Provided by author, based on WRTH (1990).

Radio and TV stations were run by different entities. Rundfunk der DDR was the organization for the radio stations and, in the late 1990s, two national programs were created, one focusing on Berlin, and the other on youth programming, temporary and regional broadcasts, and other international stations.

In 1989, the main TV stations in East Germany were located in the capital city of Berlin (channel 5), and in the cities of Brocken (channel 6), Cottbus (channels 4 and 53), Dequede (channel 12), Dresden (channel 10), Helpterberg (channel 37), Inselsberg (channel 5) Karl-Marx-Stadt (channel 8, now called Chemnitz), Leipzig (channel 9), Löbau (channel 27), Marlow (channel 8), Schwerin (channel 11), and Sonneberg (channel 12), covering virtually the entire country. That same year, *Deutscher Fernsehfunk* (or DFF), previously called *Fernsehen der DDR* from 1972 to 1990, had two regular national schedules. In the late 1980s, the main channel broadcasted 105 hours per week, the only channel to do so. At the same time, public broadcasters from Italy (RAI), Portugal (RTP) and Greece (ET-1) broadcast 86, 85 and 56 hours per week, respectively (WRTH, 1990).

However, these other public broadcasters were not in direct competition with the DFF; that competition would come from West German public broadcasters, but it was an uphill battle competing against one of the major public systems in Europe, and the world. In fact, East Germany is considered as one of the birthplaces of public TV, with regular programming (even back in 1935) and one of the first to manufacture and sell television receivers.

Nevertheless, the DFF did not shy away from conflict. Television was born in East Germany at a time when its main allied countries were more in tune with radio and how to massify it. The GDR began construction on a state television center in Adlershof, Berlin, in June 1950 (shortly before the first Brazilian broadcast). A regular television service, with two hours a day of programs, began on December 21, 1952; the same day as Joseph Stalin's birthday. That same year, West Germany resumed its experimental test broadcasts. In January 1956 East Germany's "test" period of expanding transmissions ended which, by this time, was already broadcasting in several other cities, including Berlin. The DFF was thus officially created.

From 1956 to 1989 the total number of hours transmitted steadily increased, in large part due to the creation of the country's second channel (DFF2) in 1969, the same year that color transmissions were introduced (three years before the first color broadcast in Brazil). In January 1957 West Germany's main public service broadcaster, ARD, broadcast 6,930 minutes over the course of 31 days, while DFF broadcast 2,735 minutes over 27 days (HEIMANN, 2006). Since the ARD did not broadcast programs on

Mondays, the average broadcast time per day was very close between the two broadcasters: 233.5 minutes for ARD and 197.6 minutes for DFF. The following years saw an increase in numbers, especially with creation of the second channel in 1969: DFF broadcast 3,007 hours of programming in 1960, 6,028 hours in 1970, and 8,900 hours in 1989. Foreign programs made up 35% of programming hours in 1964, compared with 45% in 1972, this increase being the result of a policy for expanding international partnerships. By the mid-1970s, DFF had commercial agreements with broadcasters from more than 70 countries. The largest partner in the socialist bloc was the Soviet Union, and in the capitalist bloc it was the great adversary, West Germany. Most of the programming was sports, political news and entertainment (BEUTELSCHMIDT, OHEMIG, 2014).

Competition between West and East German broadcasters was quite one-sided in the 1960s. By 1966, Western public broadcasters had 20 studios and 10,775 employees, compared to 1 studio and 2,354 employees in DFF. The annual budget for the DFF was 1.11 billion West German marks, and for ADR it was 127 million East German marks. Officially, the currencies had the same value, but in practice they operated at a 1:4 ratio – which represented a difference of 1 to 38 in the budget (DITTMAR, 2005). When it came to international radio, distance was even more important. The international broadcaster *Deutsche Welle* from West Germany has been broadcasting in 29 different languages to various countries around the world since 1953. In 1992, it became a TV station when it inherited the team and structure of the RIAS-TV broadcast facilities, which was connected to the USIA, used to broadcast propaganda to Central and Eastern Europe. RIAS-TV no longer made sense in the post-Cold War world, and instead focused on efforts to broadcast antisocialist programming (CHALABY, 2010).

In the late 1960s, a major change began to occur to East German television. In neighboring Czechoslovakia, local television had supported the more open form of socialism experienced during the Prague Spring, representing the desire of a significant part of the population. The SED, the ruling party in East Germany, appeared to take more notice of the potential of television as a mass medium. In September 1968, it unified all the individual organs which were working in tandem with the DFF, and producers had to continually prove that they were 'in tune' ideologically with the government. When Erich Honecker replaced Walter Ulbricht as the country's top leader in 1971, programming began to adopt a more liberal bias, open to new international and entertainment formats. A state commission in the East German Council of Ministers was held on broadcasting, and the Deutscher Fernsehfunk was renamed Fernsehen der DDR. Up until the mid-1960s, the DFF had struggled to attract West German viewers, and by the end of the decade, it started to switch its focus more toward its own domestic audience, which it pursued even further in 1972 (DITTMAR, 2005; KOCHANOWSKY, TRÜLTZSCH, VIEHOFF, 2012).

Nevertheless, competition between broadcasters from both countries was fierce. Images of protests in East Germany in the late 1980s (notably those that began in Leipzig and spread across the country) were being transmitted into East German homes, thanks to Western programming. This programming also gave a voice to dissidents and critics of the socialist regime. In an authoritarian state marked by its social surveillance, pluralism was surprisingly present in the lives of most citizens: by the end of the 1980s, it was estimated that between 11% and 13% of DDR residents only watched the DFF; about 20% watched only western broadcasts; and the remaining population watched both. These numbers are a little surprising considering that popular imagination seemed to suggest that the DFF was fairly unimportant, even among its own countrymen. However, studies like this one show that it was more important than previously thought (BRÜCHER, 2000; DITTMAR, 2005).

The structuring of the programming schedule itself somewhat contributed to this phenomenon: as of 1957, the 7:30 p.m. daily broadcast of "Aktuelle Kamera", the main television newscast of DFF, was sandwiched between the "Heute" newscasts (on the West German channel ZDF, which aired at 7 p.m.) and the "Tagesschau" newscasts (on another West German channel ARD, which aired at 8 p.m.). Thus, German viewers could effectively watch three news programs from three different broadcasters in two different countries, one after the other. Over time, amid the country's growing economic and political problems, ratings for the DFF and DFF2 declined, partly due to the lack of credibility attributed to their newscasts. In 1982, the average programming audience was 33%, the lowest percentage up until that time. In 1989, on the eve of the fall of the regime, "Aktuelles Kamera" had an average audience of 4%. Audience ratings for variety shows and programs continued to be considerably higher (BRÜCHER, 2000; BEUTELSCHMIDT, 2001).

Weeks before the Berlin Wall and the other borders of East Germany were pulled down on November 9th, 1989, the DFF began to change...once again, but this time it went in another direction. The SED's Central Committee lifted the restrictions on rights as a way to appease protesters, which led to the control over the press being abolished on October 19th. That brought an immediate change to programming: debates on issues such as freedom to travel and the situation in Leipzig (the birthplace of the protests) began to air on radio and TV; authorities were subjected to criticism and had difficult questions to answer;

reports even contained images showing the inside of Stasi barracks; and political propaganda programs, such as *Der Schwarze Kanal*, ceased broadcasting (OBERST-HUNDT, 2000).

On October 3rd, 1990, Germany officially completed its reunification process. The DFF's lifespan was coming to an end. By December 31st, 1991, DFF had changed its name, overhauled its programming, had to compete with satellite TV (which was a new trend in the east), and prepared to be integrated into the West German public service broadcasting system, as we shall explain further on in this text. On January 1st, 1992, television sets would no longer receive any transmissions from DFF.

Shortly before that, in December 1989, the new, transitional East German government had its plans outlined for the future. Hoffman-Riem (1991) listed the stages of development for these plans as follows: (a) reunification had not yet officially been confirmed at that time, and the government set up a commission to debate the country's new communication law. This law was promulgated in February 1990, and recognized the freedom of opinion, information and communication. It also provided for a new regulatory body for monitoring, and not controlling, the mass media. Even the SED newspaper declared it had broken ties with the party. This legal transition was conducted by the same people who ran the SED, which led to many concerns; (b) the new East German market then started receiving West German print media; (c) what happened next was a forced co-operation between west and east, one which was affected by a crisis of credibility, a curiosity about western products, and economic conditions of competitors (in public broadcasting, West German media did not want to cooperate with East German media, which was struggling to restructure itself and survive); (d) and lastly, there were gaps in the legal and regulatory frameworks which, as reunification was approaching, were replaced by West German rules, practices, and even technical assistance, yet all the while, the increasingly weak neighboring country of East Germany had to be respected.

In the mid-1990s, the Treuhandanstalt (THA), the East German agency responsible for preparing former state-owned enterprises for privatization, began its operations. It was the largest holding company in the world at the time. The East German public broadcasting market was redefined and adapted to the Western model, and did not offer many opportunities for large reforms. Thus, the public broadcasting model and commercial broadcasters were also assured in the eastern part of the new country (HOFFMAN-RIEM, 1991).

The public service broadcasting structure in the east, however, was technologically outdated and its labor force was viewed as being bloated as it reached up to nearly 13,000 employees, a large number of whom were politically committed to the old regime. Layoffs at DFF began quickly. In 1990, there were 7,500 professionals working at DFF, by the end of March 1991 that number dropped to 4,700, and in September there were only 3,500. Up until the mid-1990s, most of the layoffs hit Stasi, especially administration and technical staff. In July 1990, the state stopped funding the DFF, and the company was left to obtain its own funding. There were not many layoff announcements for the 5,400 radio employees at the time. When Rüdolf Mühlfenzl from West Germany took over the public broadcasters in January 1991, he presented a plan to lay off more than half of the 12,900 employees in the following months. Half of the remaining 6,300 employees were to be fired by September. These numbers were never reached. Earlier that same year, a total of 9,600 questionnaires were distributed among employees, inquiring about their connection to Stasi. The questionnaires were then analyzed and any responses that warranted further investigation were separated. Two representatives from the Church were responsible for this analysis. They determined that: 162 employees were to be interviewed further due to questionable answers in their questionnaires; 202 employees (93 from TV stations) had relations with *Stasi*; 197 (106 from TV stations) were fired; 627 (375 from TV stations) were no longer fit to occupy leadership positions; 45 left the company during this investigation period; and 646 (375 from TV stations) were allowed to keep their jobs. The consequences were small. There were still some unresolved situations by the time the station ceased operations in December 1991: the 659 orchestra and choir members, as well as the 40 dancers, were given temporary contracts until the end of June 1992; between 3 and 4 thousand of the 13,000 employees held other positions in state broadcasters like technicians, journalists and singers. A new choir and orchestra were put together with many of those aforementioned musicians. In all, about half of the employees were relocated. Some 5,300 East German public broadcasting employees were dismissed and rewarded a compensation of DM 2,000 to 29,000. The NFL, a liquidation company, paid out about DM 9 million in compensations in 1991 and another DM 14 million in 1992 (HICKETHIER, 1998; DOHLUS, 2014b).

In addition to the staff, there was the legacy of equipment and infrastructure. The equipment was divided among the new state public broadcasters. Their technical directors selected what they needed from the inventory. During the first few months of 1992, 70% of the equipment had already been redistributed. Much of the outdated equipment and "generic" assets were sold to broadcasters from other countries or to professionals in Germany. The sales of assets amounted to about DEM 25 million. In terms of constructed facilities, there were a total of 48 sites with 231 buildings, ranging from 173,000m² to 451m², a total of around

760,000m²; two thirds of which was in Berlin. Most of the properties were sold, and those that were not, were incorporated into the equity of public broadcasters. There were a number of buildings, in Berlin alone there were installations both in Adlershof (with an area of 173,000m²) and Johannisthal (110,000m²), a filming area in Köpenick, a parking lot in Alt-Glienicke, a storage room for machines in Schönefeld, a complex in Grünau, and dozens of offices, warehouses, workshops, studios, editing stations, among many other structures. In addition to these were complexes in Rostock, Dresden, Halle, Gera, Leipzig, and Karl-Marx-Stadt (later renamed Chemnitz). And then there were the East German radio and TV archives: about 390,000 music tapes, 134,000 videotapes and 120,000 film reels of programs or production, six million press clippings, 5,400 meters of written material, more than 250,000 photos, 2.3 million negatives, and more. The West German broadcasting archive Deutsches Rundfunkarchiv was responsible for the DFF archives, which were kept for a period of two years, free of charge, and were the responsibility of each individual state (DOHLUS, 2014a; DOHLUS, 2014b).

At the time of reunification the new states in East Germany could choose whether they wanted to maintain their public broadcasters or whether they wanted to merge them with existing public broadcasters, on the premise that DFF would cease broadcasting on January 1, 1992. The DFF decided it would fully integrate into the West German public broadcasting system. In the first half of 1991, it was clear that it would not be realistic, financially-speaking, to include more than two new broadcasters in the five states. By February 1991, the Mitteldeutsche Rundfunk (MDR) was established for the states of Thüringen, Saxony-Anhalt and Saxony, three states that were governed by CDU at the time. The highest positions in the company were given to employees from ARD; the lowest positions were held by professionals from the east. The other states, Mecklenburg-Vorpommern and Brandenburg, as well as the capital Berlin, were considering joining the SFB, which operated out of West Berlin. What they actually did, however, was something different: the Mecklenburg-Vorpommern station joined the NDR, which transmitted for other western states; the state of Brandenburg created its own public broadcaster, Ostdeutschen Rundfunk Brandenburg (ORB), and Berlin joined SFB. In 2003, the SFB and ORB merged to become the Rundfunk Berlin-Brandenburg (RBB). All public broadcasters were members of the ARD, and the new states all switched to the West German model. The national public broadcasting channel, ARD, included programming from regional public partners linked to local governments in its national schedule. The ARD benefited from the incorporation of the new states into its structure and was able to use the old DFF1 channels to broadcast national programming. The frequencies used for DFF2 broadcasts were made available to the newly-formed regional stations. ZDF, the second national public channel in West Germany, operating as a centralized structure, began broadcasting to the new states across previously unused channels. Other operations that did not clearly adhere to the media structure of West Germany were either canceled or completely overhauled. One example was the radio station Jugendsenders DT64, a youth-oriented East German broadcaster which lost its frequency to the RIAS (American radio station in Berlin). The station's employees were not consulted about this change, but they were already in the process of looking for partnerships in the private sector in order to continue broadcasting (HICKETHIER, 1998).

As one might imagine, the process of shutting down the East German broadcasters was neither simple nor consensual. In some cases, some of the transitions during the reunification process led to feelings of discontent against Westerners, as it seemed they considered themselves superior and wanted to reduce or simply eliminate the eastern legacy. This position of West German superiority led to feelings of inferiority or outrage among East Germans (HOFFMAN-RIEM, 1991).

In this sense, reunification could be seen as a takeover and replacement of previously existing living conditions. This sentiment is broadly explored in the movie "Good Bye, Lenin!", which was also successful outside Germany. In addition to the sense of guilt and abnegation the son feels toward his mother, the film includes signs of "Ostalgie" (a German play on words for the nostalgia for East Germany) which many East Germans felt at the time. The film was praised for its discussion on this topic yet received criticism for allegedly romanticizing a society which was marked by its submission to an authoritarian regime and its widespread mass surveillance.

Critiques of the new model coming from the field of public service broadcasting, for example, those formulated by Hoffman-Riem (1991) and Hickethier (1998), focus on the fact that there were a number of directions that could have been taken, ones that could have involved restructuring the public broadcasting model for all of Germany. Discussions were held in this regard, but in public service broadcasting (and in other sectors), the final decision was restricted to a small group of people largely from West Germany, some of whom had been temporarily transferred to East German structures.

In the months following the end of Perestroika, Bulgarian radio employees were given lists with the names of people who could not be interviewed. Before that time, managers counted on their employees to censor themselves. The lists angered the employees who, contrary to the rule, continued to conduct interviews, even knowing that they would never be broadcast (KONSTANTINOVA, 2017).

One of the first noticeable changes to television programming (once Zhivkov had resigned and socialism began to crumble in Bulgaria) was the greeting message anchorpeople used to address their viewers: "good evening, comrades" was replaced with "good evening, ladies and gentlemen", which at one time was considered a bourgeois expression (DASKALOVA, 2017).

At the time, Balgarska Televizija broadcast two national programs, the main one aired nine hours a week (except Mondays) and 17 hours on Saturdays and Sundays. On Friday nights, it broadcast programs from the Soviet channel, Ostankino. The main television stations were located in the capital Sofia (channel 10) and in the cities of Belogradcik (channel 12), Botev Vrah (channel 11), Burgas (channel 7), Kjustendil (channel 10), Sliven (channel 12), Strumni Rid (channel 9), Shumen (channel 5), Tolbukhin (channel 12, renamed Dobrich) and Varna (channel 9). Similar to other countries in the socialist bloc, radio stations in Bulgaria were also run by separate agencies. Both these agencies are referenced in international literature under their English abbreviations: BNT (Bulgarian National Television) and BNR (Bulgarian National Radio).

The first radio station in the country dates back to the 1930s, which was later run by the state. The BNT, however, was founded in 1959. The two national television programs continued to broadcast, gradually adding regional content to their schedules. In 2002, BNT's regional channels were broadcasting between 4 and 5 hours per day, only one or two hours of which are programs originally produced by these stations (RAYCHEVA, 2004).

**Figure 3: TV Stations in Bulgaria**

**Source:** Prepared by author, based on WRTH (1990).

*Czechoslovakia*

By the end of 1989, Czechoslovakia's main TV stations were located in the capital Prague (channels 1 and 7), in Banska Stiavinica (channel 40), Bardejov (channel 4), B. Bystrica (channel 7), Borský Mikulás (channel 42), Bratislava (channels 2 and 31), Brno (channels 9 and 49), Ceské Budejovice (channels 2 and 36), Cheb (channel 26), Domazlice (channel 24), Gottwaldov (channel

41), Hradec Králové (channel 6), Jáchymov (channel 7), Jeseník (channel 4), Jihlava (channel 11), Klatovy (channel 6), Kosice (channel 6), Liberec (channel 8), Modrý Kamen (channel 12), Námestovo (channel 4), Nové Mesto (channel 12), Ostrava (channels 1 and 42), Plzen (channel 10), Poprad (channel 5), Ruzomberok (channel 9), Sturovo (channel 9), Susice (channel 9), Trencín (channel 10), Trutnov (channel 11), Uherský Brod (channel 21), Ustí n. Labem (channel 12), and Ziline (channel 11). These channels included more than a thousand re-broadcasts. At the time, two schedules were broadcast, the main one being for 97 hours a week.

**Figure 4: TV Stations in Czechoslovakia**

**Source:** Prepared by author, based on WRTH (1990).

There was an air of prosperity among the broadcasters. The new building for the radio station in Bratislava, the future capital of Slovakia, began broadcasting in 1985 after sixteen years of construction. To this day, the inverted pyramid-shaped building, referred to as a special ship, is an architectural reference in the city. It was an imposing building that housed the TV station and was the tallest in the city from 1974 to 2002, but is currently closed. In 1987, the network achieved some of its best results to date: 140 national television programs were produced, as well as many children's programs (MIKA, 2017).

The transition was a quick one: journalists from the radio station decided to cover the demonstrations in late 1989 and the station's management team joined suit (SKOLKAY, 2017). In the period of one week, the journalism departments for both the radio and TV stations were restructured and, within a matter of days, the departments for public relations and the programs' visual identity for were also restructured.

In January 1990, the CST (Czechoslovakian Television) was separated into two units, one operating in the future Czech Republic and the other in Slovakia. This was the beginning of the separation between the two broadcasters, which would further separate with the breaking off between TV and radio. At the same time procedures were starting to take place to distribute the patrimonial rights of construction between the new units of the future countries. Since most of the artists were identified as supporters of the Velvet Revolution, station employees kept their jobs, for the most part (MIKA, 2017).

In 1991, the new Broadcasting Act was published and Czechoslovakia was the first country in the socialist bloc with a new law in this sector. The Slovak Television and Slovak Radio Act (SMATLAK, 2000) was announced earlier that same year, before the country split. The separation of the broadcasters was peaceful, as was the regime change and the division of Czechoslovakia. The history of public broadcasting in the country, however, would still go on to experience moments of tension, as we shall look at later.

Hungarian television was born early, in 1936, when its first trial transmissions were being broadcast. On May 1, 1957, Magyar Televizió aired its first regular broadcast, covering its Labor Day festivities. Also in that same year, Hungary established the first content exchange program between other socialist bloc countries (Czechoslovakia, Poland, and East Germany), called Intervision. The amount of foreign content increased over time, and in the early 1970s, 32% of its television content was imported from the United Kingdom, France, and West Germany (IMRE, 2012; MIHELJ, 2014).

In the first half of the 1960s, the total number of broadcasting hours per week jumped from 22 to 40. In 1989, two separate programs were transmitted, the main one broadcasting approximately 74 hours per week. The major stations were located in Budapest (channel 1), Csávoly (channel 28), Györ (channel 8), Kab-hegy (channel 12), Kékes (channel 8), Komádi (channel 7), Miskolc (channel 9), Nagykanizsa (channel 1), Pécs (channel 2), Sopron (channel 9), Szentes (channel 10) and Tokaj (channel 4). There are currently four national broadcasts, including one which is aimed towards expatriates overseas residents and radio programs.

# Figure 5: TV Stations in Hungary

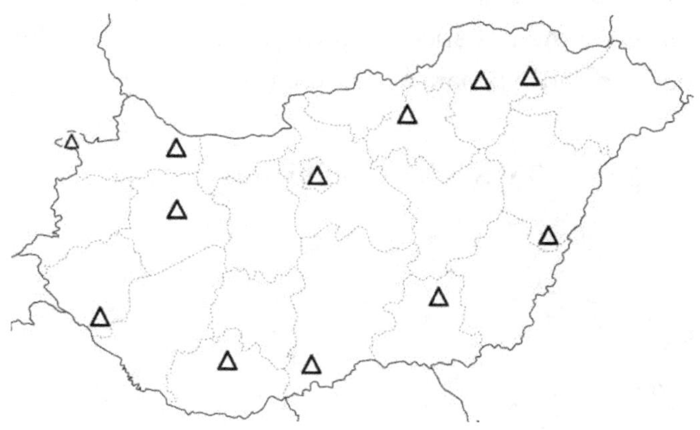

**Source:** Prepared by author, based on WRTH (1990).

*Poland*

By the end of 1989, Telewizja Polska was broadcasting two national programs; the main one broadcast 81 hours per week. The main stations were located in the capital Warsaw (channels 2 and 27) and in the municipalities of Bialystok (channel 8), Bydgoszcz (channel 1), Gdansk (channel 10), Jelenia Góra (channel 30), Kielce (channel 3), Katowice (channel 8), Klodzko (channel 38), Kraków (channel 10), Koszalin (channel 8), Lódz (channel 7), Lublin (channel 9), Olsztyn (channel 9), Opole (channel 43), Dick (channel 2), Plock (channel 29), Poznan (channel 9), Przemysl (channel 24), Rabka (channel 36), Rzeszów (channel 12), Sledice (channel 52), Suwalki (channel 5), Szczecin (channel 12), Wroclaw (channel 12), Zamosc (channel 10), and Zielona Góra (channel 3). The radio stations were operated by Polskie Radio. Public service broadcasting in Poland would become more complex in the following years, especially after digitalization: in 2017, there were twelve national TV channels on the air, two of which were generic and the others aimed at specific audiences, not to mention dozens of regional and radio broadcasting channels.

**Figure 6: TV Stations in Poland**

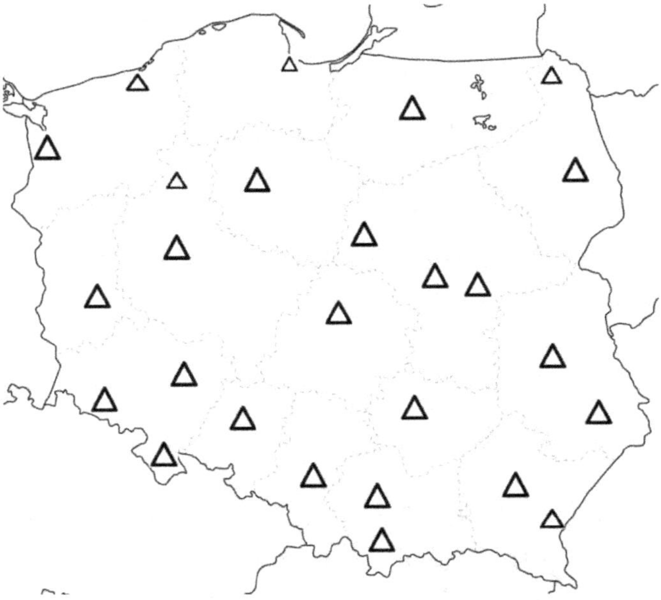

**Source:** Prepared by author, based on WRTH (1990).

The communication agenda, different from other countries in the socialist bloc, was already being discussed even before the regime had ended. Since the beginning of this period there has always been organized opposition in Poland, sometimes resulting in public demonstrations, even though they never reached the level of those in Hungary in 1956. These organizations were articulated in specific environments, which contributed toward strengthening the Solidarity labor union.

Opposition also manifested through media. Since 1956, the Catholic Church has had the right to publish newspapers. As of the mid-1970s, the number of illegal publications increased. In December 1981, with the introduction of martial law, about 1,200 journalists were expelled from the official media and an estimated 2,000 publications were edited.

In 1988, a group composed of Stanisław Jędrzejewski (who was interviewed for this book), Karol Jakubowicz (whose story will be described below), and others, was devoted to elaborating a draft for public service broadcasting which would provide for the creation of a regulatory model similar to the French one. In 1989, the opposition, which until then had requested a space to broadcast its own programming, defended the "socialization" of Polish mass communication in meetings with the government (SPARKS, 2008; STĘPKA, 2010; JĘDRZEJEWSKI, 2017). For a while, after the end of the regime, old practices would return – as they did at the end of the first half of 1990:

> "I started as an international correspondent in the United States in August 1990. The previous station was effectively communist. The station didn't use it, but it took nine months to change. When I went to sign my contract, I realized that the salary was very low. I had lived in the United States for three years and was aware of the local reality. I complained, and the clerk responded, 'But, Mr. Andrzej, this is not your whole salary'. 'What about the rest of it?' 'This is normal', she replied. The correspondents received part of their salary from the Ministry of Foreign Affairs – they were spies, they were agents! No one actually said that, but it was

obvious. Luckily, my wife is a journalist and I didn't have to become a spy (KRAJEWSKI, 2017)".

*Romania*

Televiziunea Română's first transmission was broadcast on the last day of 1956. In 1968, a second local channel began broadcasting. The radio stations were members of another entity: Radio Română.

Up until the late 1960s, as described in Mustata (2012), Romanian television went through what came to be known as the "age of scarcity", marked by a lack of aesthetic, institutional and professional identity. Even still, some of its programs won international awards. Its main content was adapted from radio, as was the case in several other countries. From that time forward, while Gheorghiu-Dej was serving as first secretary of the Romanian Communist Party and as the country's prime minister, television was thought of as a means to simultaneously "educate" and entertain. Once appointed director of the newly established state television network in the early 1960s, Silviu Brucan was given autonomy to change programming. In 1964, TVR and the BBC signed a technical cooperation agreement and English formats would be broadcast on local programming. Political satire and programming from the BBC began to be transmitted at that time.

With the death of Gheorghiu-Dej in 1965, Nicolae Ceauşescu took over as General Secretary and leader of the country. Sworn into office in 1967 with the approval of the IX Congress of the Communist Party, Ceauşescu, seeking political affirmation, started to criticize the country's previous period more frequently and thus proposed changes. The 1970s became known as the great phase of Romanian TV. Children's programming, such as "Aventurile lui Val Vartej", and weekly magazines such as "Telecinemateca" and "Teleenciclopedia" became popular. Critical and popular investigative journalism programs such as "Reflector" also emerged. It was only in 1977 that the program would fall under government rule, with its format revised directly by the party's Director of Propaganda. The total number of broadcast hours increased substantially in the 1970s. In 1957, television broadcasts reached a total of 571 hours; 1,369 hours in 1961; 3,161 hours in 1971; 4,642 hours in 1975, and 5,377 hours in 1980. The "age of availability" had arrived (MUSTATA, 2012).

The good times, however, would soon come to an end. The country's economic situation worsened in the early 1980s amid the new massive construction projects implemented by the regime and the determination to pay off the foreign debt. Heavy demands were made in all areas of the country in order to achieve this goal, including severe power cuts to save energy.

Out of the 100 or so newspapers in circulation in the country, 40 are left. As of 1985, Romanian radio, having transmitted since 1928, cut its broadcast time in half; it had reached 230 hours per week between the two national channels. The second TV channel was shut down. Transmission times for the main channel (programming was only 2 hours a day, at night, during weekdays) were drastically reduced. The length of broadcasts was extended on Saturdays and Sundays, but the channel never broadcast more than 22 hours a week.

Political control over the station has increased since the beginning of the decade. Up to half of the broadcasting time on weekdays was spent on advertising programs. A committee made up of, but not restricted to, the station's president and vice-president decided on what kind of foreign content would be broadcast. They avoided movies containing church scenes, sex, or kissing on the lips – kisses lasting up to 3 seconds long were permitted, but were edited if lasted longer. On the other hand, films with very large families were welcome as they were seen as helping to stimulate population growth. There is a strange contradiction here: If sex was unwelcome and kisses on the mouth could only be shown ever so briefly, how was it that procreation was encouraged? (NISTOR, 2017)

The only mass media available to the entire population were foreign broadcasts which transmitted in Romanian, such as Free Europe radio, Voice of America and the BBC, among others. Some of these broadcasts actively spread anti-socialist propaganda (MARINESCU, 1995). Some stations from neighboring socialist countries were also transmitted in some cities: Western Romanian received Hungarian and Yugoslav programming, particularly from the Serbian station; and in the capital Bucharest the alternative was Bulgarian TV, which broadcast subtitled movies on Friday nights. In both cases, the cult of personality of rulers was not nearly as intense as the one practiced by the Romanian station. "Leka nosht, detsa!" ("Good night, children!") is a Bulgarian expression that Romanians who were born in the late 1970s or early 1980s still use today (NISTOR, 2017; SURUGIU, 2017).

Figure 7: TV Stations in Romania

**Source:** Prepared by author, based on WRTH (1990).

In the winter of 1989, Romania's main TV stations were located in the capital city of Bucharest (channel 4) and the cities of Arad (channel 12), Bacau (channel 10), Baia Mare (channel 10), Birlad (channel 5), Bistrita (channel 3), Brasov (channel 10), Bucegi (channel 6), Cimpulung (channel 8), Cluj (channel 11), Comanesti (channel 12), Constanta (channels 8 and 10), Cozia (channel 12), Craiova (channel 8), Delta (channel 6), Deva (channel 12), Dobrogea (channel 3), Galati (channel 7), Gheorghieni (channel 5), Iasi (channel 9), Magura (channel 9), Mangalia (channel 11), Oradea (channel 3), Petrosani (channel 10), Piatra (channel 6), Semenic (channel 3), Sibiu (channel 7), Suceava (channel 4), Tirgu Mures (channel 12), Timisoara (channel 9), Tulcea (channel 12), Turnu Magurele (channel 2), Varatec (channel 7), Vascau (channel 8), and Zalau (channel 6).

Days after the overthrow of Ceauşescu, radio and TV broadcasters began to call themselves "free". TV broadcasts were accompanied by the letters FRT ("Free Romanian Television") for quite some time. The second TV channel started operating again. This did not mean, however, the immediate adoption of programming independent from the government. Irina Nistor (2017) recalls dubbing for the movie "The Animal Farm", based on George Orwell's eponymous book on authoritarianism, which was released in January 1990. Her audacity led to complaints from one of the station's directors who stated that opposition to Ceauşescu did not mean criticism of socialism as a whole – it was important to see the "more human face" of the system. Another event with deeper repercussions would follow: protests began against those who took power (former Ceauşescu supporters and socialists, albeit a bit more liberal), but television did not broadcast them, arguing that they were unable to get good images because the weather was cloudy and there was not enough light. It was clear that the term "Free Romanian Television" should have been relativized at that time (NISTOR, 2017).

Initially, public broadcasters were still regulated by a 1990 decree which kept them under the control of the Presidency of the Republic. Its director was appointed by the Romanian president and the two director-generals (one from TV, one from radio) were appointed by the Prime Minister. A new law for these broadcasters was not approved until 1994 (MARINESCU, 1995).

Total transmission times began to rise rapidly. Public radio stations broadcast 30,148 hours in 1989; 52,309 hours in 1990; and 118,619 hours in 2002. There were 5 channels: a news channel, two music channels, one youth channel and one rural programming channel, plus an international station with 6 studios located in different cities, totalling 2,301 employees. Broadcasts from public

TV stations jumped from 1,795 hours in 1989 to 8,541 hours in 1990; 9,997 hours in 1993; 13,095 hours in 1996; 14,197 hours in 1999; 25,111 hours in 2002; and 35,040 hours in 2005, comprised of three national channels, one international channel and about 2,700 employees (COMAN, 2009).

This movement was accompanied by an expanded infrastructure for the production and transmission of broadcasters. The main public channel in the mid-1990s already covered 98% of the country and transmitted 144 hours per week, while the second channel was re-opened and covered 60% of the country with 93 hours of content transmitted per week. Televiziunea Română had 49 production stations and 12 production studios. Seventy percent of the transmissions were original programs and the reamining 30% consisted of foreign content (MARINESCU, 1995).

In fact, foreign productions played an important role in the restructuring of Romanian TV. As soon as the regime had been overthrown, Romanian TV had plans to stop broadcasting only 2 hours per day on one channel and start all-day broadcasts on two channels. Since there was not enough local production to meet this demand, the immediate solution was to re-broadcast more and more Western programs. The second channel transmitted television newscasts from Spanish, French, German and English broadcasters for three years, during which time local productions were increasing to meet said demands. Attempts were also made to revive old Romanian programs, but the ones from the final phase of socialism were unsuccessful. The opposite occurred with formats such as *talk shows* and Q&A programs. Religious programs were also broadcast on Sunday mornings (MUSTATA, 2012).

This renewal of old programs took place during a time of severe crisis, one which worsened soon after the collapse of socialism and reduced the Romanian economy to a level well below that of the 1980s. Economic reforms decreased for almost twenty years. Between 1993 and 1996, the Romanian Gross Domestic Product plummeted by 30%. The following year, in 1997, a stabilization plan was implemented, but that failed, and the GDP fell by another 12% (CEPIKU; MITITELU, 2010). In the first decade of the new century, the economic situation started to see improvements and the country began to steadily grow.


*Soviet Union*


Up until 1991, all Soviet radio and television broadcasters were funded and controlled by the state's governing body of broadcasting, the USSR State Committee for Broadcasting (Gosteleradio). There were five national TV channels, two with almost universal coverage. The First Channel, which was transmitted to 99.8% of Soviet households, contained more general programming with an emphasis on news. The second channel, transmitted to 95 percent of households, broadcast documentaries, cultural and children's programs, drama, and content from other regions in the country.

The third and fifth channels focused mainly on events in Moscow and St. Petersburg, respectively. The fourth channel broadcast educational programming for children and adults. The 14 national radio stations were broadcast across the entire country (VARTANOVA, ZASSOURSKY, 2003).

There was much less foreign content on Soviet television than in the other socialist bloc countries: in the 1970s, 5% of Soviet

Union broadcasting was foreign, while in Poland that figure was 17%, and in Bulgaria, 45%. In the 1980s, that number reached 8% in the USSR, and ranged from 24% in Czechoslovakia to 30% in East Germany (MIHELJ, 2012). Some authors argue that, over time, Soviet broadcasters developed a certain level of independence (BECKER, 2004). Added to this was a robust print media system: it was estimated that in 1974 an impressive 18 billion copies of newspapers and other periodicals were published in the capital Moscow alone – an average of more than 49 million copies per day (BALANENKO, BEREZIN, 1974).

The main TV stations featured on the map were located in the capital of each republic: Yerevan (Armenia), Baku (Azerbaijan), Minsk (Belarus), Tallinn (Estonia), Tblisi (Georgia), Alma Ata (Kazakhstan), Riga (Latvia), Vilnius (Lithuania), Kishinev (Moldova), Moscow (Russia), Kiev (Ukraine) and Tashkent (Uzbekistan). There were also broadcast relay stations located in the interior. The main Soviet channel broadcast 60 hours of programming per week.

The transmission system was by far the most complex in the socialist bloc due to the geographical expanse of the country. It had eleven time zones so scheduled content had to be organized well. There were about 900 major stations in the country and 4,000 relay stations, as well as 3,000 cable distribution systems and 90 Orbita stations, a Soviet system that broadcast satellite TV signals.

The Soviet Union also had an international TV service which broadcast main local programming throughout the Allied countries (the Russian language was taught in these other countries at different levels). Soviet programming was available on channels in Bulgaria, Czechoslovakia, East Germany, Hungary, and Poland.

**Figure 8: TV stations in the Soviet Union**

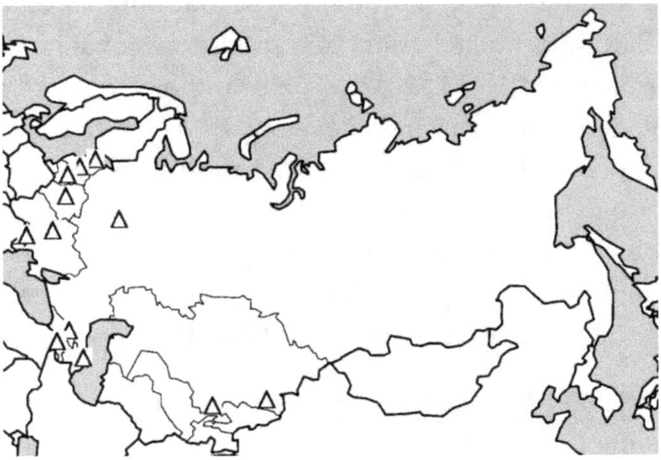

**Source:** Prepared by author, based on WRTH (1990).

The broadcasters in the former Soviet republics experienced very different transitions from one another. There were some simpler transitions, such as in Latvia, which has four public radio stations and two TV stations. And there were far more complex transitions, such as in Russia, the expanse of which covers nine time zones.

The history of Russian public service broadcasting is based on private investors. Russian Public TV in the 1990s was operated by a publicly traded company whose shares were still majority owned by state entities.

A new state-owned media holding company was created in 1999 (VGTRK) which operated the television channels Rossia (also called Channel 1 or ORT), Sport, Vesti-24, Bibigon and Kultura, and operated the radio stations Mayak, Kultura and Rossii, including 89 regional TV broadcasters (some of these were created in subsequent years). In 2002, regional broadcasters, previously controlled by local authorities, lost their financial independence and became dependent on the VGTRK. In 1999, the entire technical transmission infrastructure for these channels came under the responsibility of the VGTRK; however, two years later, they were passed on to another state-owned company, RTRS. This company had 10,500 relay stations but the state budget only covered about 10% of RTRS spending (KIRIYA, DEGTEVERA, 2010).

Public broadcasting experienced a turnaround in 2001 when the ORT was transformed into a commercial broadcaster (still called Channel 1 or Pervyi kanal at the time), even though the state retained 51% of the shares. In 2012, the then-president Dmitri Medvedev, after declaring his support for the creation of a Public TV, signed a decree to establish a new station: the Obshchestvennoye Televideniye Rossii (OTR – not to be confused with ORT), which started operations in 2013 (VARTANOVA, 2015).

The role of the Russian government in mass communication goes further. The state and its related bodies became the chief owners of most media companies, a situation which only got worse in the 2000s. The same was true of the printing and distribution sectors, where municipalities also played an important role. Public broadcasting was also carried out by the state. The holding company VGTRK was established, as well as news agencies ITAR-TASS and RIA Novosti. Between 2010 and 2012, it was estimated that the Russian state had spent 174 billion rubles in support of the media (VARTANOVA, 2015).

One of the former Soviet republics possesses a striking resemblance to the situation in Brazil. Located on the border between eastern Europe and southwest Asia, with a population of just under 10 million, Azerbaijan chose a different path in the broadcasting transition process: it established a public broadcaster but continued to be owned by the state – upholding the idea of operating two systems simultaneously, the state and the public, the same idea that is upheld in the Brazilian Federal Constitution. During the privatization process the Azerbaijan government bought 51% of the shares of AzTV. The public broadcaster was then created, receiving resources and equipment from the state's second channel. A specific body was created to operate the public broadcaster which has been operating under the name Ictimai TV or iTV since 2005 – transitioning from a state broadcasting model to a PSB one. However, there was one difference: the state broadcaster AzTV expanded to include two other programs and continued to play the role of institutional government communication (ABASHINA, 2016). The existence of two broadcasters was a problem for the EBU as they both wanted to join the international body in 2007. The EBU decided to include ITV based on AzTV's denial of having connections with the government.

By the late 1980s access to programs from foreign public broadcasters was scarce. Those who did have access to foreign content either lived near the borders and were able to pick up signals from neighboring countries or received satellite channels or signed with pay-per-view providers. Both of these options were generally unavailable in socialist countries.

*Ostankino*, the name given to the Soviet state broadcasting tower, expanded. The government began to set up terrestrial relay networks in the bloc countries which received the station's signals. Thus, *Ostankino* programs could be watched in Sofia (channel 31), Prague (channel 41), Bratislava (channel 50), Brno (channel 52), Dresden (channel 32), Karl-Marx-Stadt (channel 27), Cottbus (channel 8), Budapest (channel 11), Győr (channel 5), Warsaw (channel 51), including 29 other cities in five countries (WRTH, 1990). Only the socialist countries which were more critical of the Soviet Union – particularly Albania, Yugoslavia and Romania – were denied Russian broadcasts.

That doesn't mean reception was good – far from it. Reliable data on Ostankino audiences in socialist countries is lacking, but it is interesting to note that even industry experts, like the ones interviewed for this study, could not even remember the broadcasts. The Russian language was taught in these countries' schools, but even so, it was probably Soviet soldiers stationed in Allied countries or Russian expatriots who mainly watched Ostankino programming outside of the Soviet Union (MIKA, 2017; SKOLKAY, 2017).

Even more interesting is how this story ended – after all, the network was being put together in the final moments of socialist regimes. Again, there is not much information available on this, although it seems reasonable to suppose that the early years of transmission were the result of political agreements between partner regimes. This relationship would be marked by the exchange of transmissions from foreign channels in the Soviet Union, something which appears to not have materialized. In any case, the political changes forced a re-negotiation. The regulatory agency in Poland decided that its public broadcaster would assume the costs of Ostankino transmissions. The president of the Polish regulator, Marek Markiewicz, even declared the broadcasts as being "in the interest of the state". TVP leaders protested this repeatedly until, in 1996 or 1997, transmissions were interrupted. The national public broadcasting company of Italy, RAI, was also transmitted in Poland through a similar agreement.

This story is shrouded in mystery – probably not due to any attempts to conceal the past, but maybe it was just the language barrier, and that people probably just forgot about it. How long transmissions were broadcast for is not clear, nor is it clear if other countries continued broadcasting the Ostankino signal. Even this brief account of the Polish case was only possible thanks to one the respondents, Andrzej Krajewski who, at my request, managed to get hold of the exchange of messages between the regulator and a user named "Adam" from a Polish public archive on the Internet.

Ostankino formally stopped broadcasting in Poland about seven years after the collapse of socialism. The search for a new broadcasting model was already underway.


*Yugoslavia*


In 1989, the national public broadcasting system Jugoslovenska Radiotelevizija was present in all socialist republics of Yugoslavia. The main stations in Bosnia-Herzegovina were Bjelasnica (channel 5), Hum (channel 8), Kozara (channel 6), Majevica (channel 5), Pljesevica (channel 10, on the Croatia-Bosnia border), Trovrh (channel 9), Velez (channel 7), and Vlasic (channel 11). The main stations in Croatia were Beli Manastir (channel 8), Biokovo (channel 9), Cerovac (channel 8), Kalnik (channel 5), Labistica (channel 4), Mirkovica (channel 7), Pljesevica (channel 5), Psunj (channel 4), Sljeme (channel 9), Srdj (channel 6), and Ucka (channel 11). In Macedonia the stations were located in Crn Vrv (channel 6, on the Maja and Zezë mountain in Kosovo and Macedonia), Mali Vlaj (channel 9) and Pelister (channel 4). In Montenegro, the stations were located in Bjelasica (channel 12), Durmitor (channel 10), Lovcen (channel 8), Mozura (channel 33), and Sudjina Glava (channel 6). In Serbia the stations were located in Avala (channel 6), Besna Kobila (channel 8), Crni Vrh (channel 11), Delhi Jovan (channel 43), Jastrebac (channel 5), Kopaonik (channel 3), Ovcar (channel 8), and Tupiznica (channel 10). Lastly, in Slovenia, there were stations in Krvavec (channel 5), Kum (channel 3), Nanos (channel 6), Plesivec (channel 6) and Pohorje (channel 11). Yugoslavia's broadcasting system also covered the country's two autonomous provinces – Kosovo, with major stations located in Cviljan (channels 9 and 21) and Goles (channels 7 and 44), while Vojvodina had stations located in Crveni Cot (channels 10 and 24), Subotica (channels 5 and 43), Venac (channel 41) and Vrsac (channel 56). The length of broadcasting times varied depending on the republic or province.

Yugoslavia was different from other European socialist nations. For example, it was not a member country of the Warsaw Pact, and instead became a founding member of a parallel movement called the Non-Aligned Movement in 1961. The country's conception of rights was also distinct, and was reflected in mass communication.

Article 167 of the 1963 Yugoslav Constitution provisioned the right for citizens to express and publish their opinions in public media; however, there was no regulation to enforce this right. An important precedent occurred in 1985 when the Slovenian Supreme Court, still under socialist rule, ordered the main Slovenian newspaper Delo to publish an article written by a citizen criticizing a senior party official. That article was rejected by the editor. In 1991, after the breakup from the old system, a Slovenian minister proposed amendments to suppress the right to publish opinions; he believed that the pressure of competition in a capitalist system already guarantees the publication of opinions that are important to everyone (SPLICHAL, 1995).

# Figure 9: TV stations in Yugoslavia

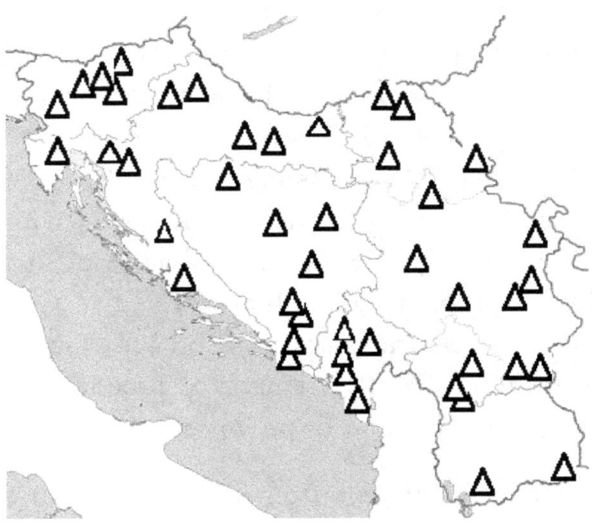

**Source:** Prepared by author, based on WRTH (1990).

The Yugoslav media were more numerous and plural than in any other socialist country. In 1989, its 23.72 million citizens watched nine different TV programs (one for each federal republic and three for minorities), listened to a total of 202 radio stations (28% of that content was news), and read 27 individual daily national newspapers and 17 different magazines. Tanjug, one of the ten largest news agencies in the world, had 12 offices located in a number of countries, and ranked 14th on the list of countries with the most book titles published per year (KREŠIC, 2012).

When Slovenia's state broadcaster began operations in 1958, there were about 700-800 televisions in the republic and a total of 4,000 in all of Yugoslavia; in comparison, 90% of US households were already using televisions. In 1989, there were over 4 million TV sets across the country. The funding for public broadcasting also differed from the model adopted in several of the socialist countries. TV advertising revenue in Yugoslavia increased from 6.8% of the total budget to 23.1%, between 1966 and 1971. In addition, important content was being included in its programming; for example, a television series broadcast in the 1960s which dealt with social problems such as unemployment (IMRE, 2012; MIHELJ, 2014).

A decentralized management with powers concentrated outside the state was traditional for Yugoslavia. The *partizan* resistance movement against the German invasion in World War II was itself decentralized, with each group acting on their own behalf in the separate federal states (by this time, each state had become its own country). In addition to expelling the remaining Germans, they also defeated right-wing groups that supported the monarchy – and supposedly did so without any support from the Red Army, leading to its eventual departure from the Soviet Union (AGUIAR, 2010).

Self-management was the prevailing form of organizational management, for the media as well, and delighted scholars in this field throughout the 1970s and 1980s. This practice was introduced in 1950 and, by 1955, attempted to introduce elements of market practices and a decentralized system for regional equality. Centralized planning had lost momentum, and was replaced by indicative and decentralized planning, based on the social welfare state model. Planning was to express all forms of political, social and economic relations, and its obligations were to be established by workers through self-management and social pacts. The means of production were owned by society, and not the state, whose intervention was meant only to ensure self-management. The governance of this model involved different organizations operating in different areas but, for each unit, the main body of power was the general assembly, which elected the Workers' Council. The council oversaw business activities, and decided that elected directors and executives would serve four-year terms, with the possibility to be re-elected. The cost of products and services were set by the market and wages varied from month to month depending on revenues (MOTTA, 1980).

In line with this system, the social control bodies in Yugoslavian print media had a duty to safeguard social interests in mass communication. These bodies were composed of two groups of delegates, one representing the media employees and the other representing the community which that particular media served. Among the duties were the appointment and dismissal of the company's communications director and its editors, but the chief editor and the executive editor were directly appointed by the party (SPLICHAL, 1995).

The situation changed after the overthrow of socialism and the breakup of the country, which occurred as a result of civil wars that spread throughout several of the republics. In accordance with the 1991 law, the newly independent Croatian government determined which companies previously controlled by society would now be controlled by the state (in a process known as "nationalization"), and which ones would be privatized. The Agency for Restructuring and Development (ARD) was created. Its leaders were appointed by the government and its role was to oversee this delegation process and elect the boards of directors for each individual company. Each board of directors would then define the direction their company would take (which did not always get the support of workers and former managers). As a result, most of the media became state-owned or co-owned by HDZ, the main local party (KREŠIC, 2012).

The situation for broadcasters in the former socialist republics varied in regards to their transition to the Western model. One of the most dramatic situations in all of Europe was that of Bosnia and Herzegovina, a country divided into two fairly autonomous entities, the Republika Srpska and the Federation of Bosnia and Herzegovina. Even after conferring with international consulting agencies, there was still no fully operational public broadcaster in Bosnia in 2008. A plan developed in 2000 by a BBC expert provided for two entities responsible for TV and radio transmissions, one for Republika Srpska and the other for the Federation. That same plan also provided for a national public broadcasting company and a national company that would act as a technical coordinator and distribute content among the other three entities. Radio Television Republika Srpska remained on the air and Federal TV was created out of the ashes of BHTV, a pre-war successor to RTV Sarajevo, which was a symbol of unity and resistance against Serbian aggression. The new national broadcaster, BHRT, had strict rules for linguistic parity (Bosnia, Croatian and Serbian) and alphabet (Cyrillic and Latin). It started operating in 2001 and, in 2004, started broadcasting nationally. The fourth corporation was not been created until 2008. In 2016, BHRT, in the midst of an economic crisis, announced it would suspend its transmissions, which led to strong concern from the EBU. If this were to happen, it would be the first time a public service broadcaster in Europe would have to interrupt its broadcasting due to financial difficulties (HOZIC, 2008).

# THE MIDDLE

V

Public broadcasting was not born in Brazil with the creation of the Brazil Communications Company (EBC) in 2007. Nor was it interconnected with the state, public and private systems laid out in the 1988 Federal Constitution. Even though these two events have changed the perspective of public broadcasting in Brazil, they are part of the history of radio in the country.

The Radio Society of Rio de Janeiro was founded in 1922, the same year that Brazil celebrated the 100th anniversary of its independence. Regular transmissions started one year later, sponsored by the Brazilian Academy of Sciences. Almost a decade later, the federal government signed decrees No. 20,047 in 1931 and No. 21,111 in 1932 in order to regulate the service and define public broadcasting (which up until that time consisted only of radio) as a national service for educational purposes; the Union would be its national network. Receivers could be used for non-commercial purposes by registering and paying an annual fee; in other words, a licensing fee. Public radio was then born: it was not linked to government or to private companies. Since it was a public medium, and it was the 1930s, it was regulated through a source of financing similar to that of public broadcasters in other countries – a fee had to be paid by those operating receivers (although the decree did not determine which entities this fee was to be paid to).

At the center of this birth of public radio was a group of scientists led by Edgar Roquette-Pinto. He had many occupations (coroner, anthropologist, teacher, writer, member of the Rondon Mission and the Brazilian Academy of Letters) but what he is most remembered for is his work as an educator. He argued that the new medium (radio) would be fundamental towards "educating" the population of a country with such a high rate of illiteracy. In 1936, he donated the station to the Ministry of Education and Health, and the Radio Society became known thereafter as Radio Ministry of Education, and then Radio MEC. Between 1936 and September of 1955, the station transmitted 66,197 hours of programming (an average of 3,484 hours per year). In the beginning of this period it was transmitting 849 hours per year (an average of 2.32 hours per day), and by the end it was transmitting 6,000 hours per day (16.4 hours per day), a trend that continued to grow in following years (MILANEZ, 2007a). The station is still currrently operating, under a totally different editorial line linked to the EBC.

However, the decades following the first radio broadcast in Brazil would demonstrate how quickly reality can differ from legislation. The first private broadcasters emerged during this period, and commercial advertising was their main source of funding. Television began operating in 1950, launched by the country's largest economic media group at the time, the Associated Dailies. The Brazilian Telecommunications Code (CBT) was enacted in 1962 with the aim of making the public broadcasting sector an eminently private one. The Brazilian Association of Radio and Television Broadcasters (ABERT) was founded as the main national entity for defending the interests of public broadcasting, and was strongly supported by the country's main commercial broadcasters. The President of the Republic at the time, João Goulart, exercised a veto against the CBT, but the National Congress voted against the veto (PIERANTI, MARTINS, 2007). With the veto now overriden, initiatives to regulate the sector more effectively could not be taken.

Meanwhile, this system was complemented by a group of federal government broadcasters. There were no significant initiatives from public broadcasters in the 1960s, either programmed or sponsored by civil society entities, which were at one time the hallmark of radio in Brazil. There were almost 40 non-private broadcasters operating in the country, scattered throughout various ministries such as Labor, Agriculture, Finance, Communications, Education and Culture. They generally transmitted content that did not hold much interest to private enterprises (such as providing public services) to areas lacking in economic potential.

One station stood out in this group: Rádio Nacional (National Radio). Since the 1940s, it was the crown jewel of radio. At the time, the federal government had decided to nationalize the railroad sponsoring companies which were in debt to the Union, including their subsidiaries and any other entity which they may have been connected to. This movement resulted in the creation of the Incorporated Companies of the Union Assets (EIPU), a diversified group of operations that, in addition to railroads, included refrigerated warehouses, paper manufacturers, newspapers and radio stations. Once the São Paulo-Rio Grande Railroad Company went through this process, Rádio Nacional was incorporated into the Union under Decree-Law No. 2,073 of 1940.

The Joseph Gire Building was inaugurated in 1929, at a time when the rest of the world was living through the Great Depression, and was the tallest skyscraper in Latin America. Located in the harbor area of Praça Mauá, this 22-floor building was easily visible from all of Rio de Janeiro, a city marked by its low buildings. The building would soon change its name to Edifício A Noite (the Evening Building), adopting the name of the evening newspaper that was headquartered there at the time (also incorporated into Union assets). But its most famous occupant over the following decades would be Rádio Nacional, having one of the nation's largest radio audiences. Its studios welcomed some of the country's leading artists and technicians, named icons of Brazilian popular communication, covered top teams and athletes in the country, started transmitting short wave broadcasts in 1942 to other countries like the United States, Europe and Asia in four languages, and brought on the so-called "Golden Age of Radio".

As the world began to experiment with a new medium that combined image with audio, Rádio Nacional was conducted its first experiments of implementing television in the country, in the late 1940s. The station received two grants to pursue this new form of media – one for Rio de Janeiro, which was eventually revoked and later granted to the company that owns the O Globo newspaper, and the other for Brasilia, which founded TV Nacional in 1960, ten years after Chateaubriand launched the first Brazilian broadcaster (JAMBEIRO, 2002; SAROLDI, MOREIRA, 2005). Thus, TV Globo was born, which soon became the leading broadcaster in Brazil, a position it would not relinquish until the federal government decided to get involved in television.

There was another educational broadcasting initiative, in Rio de Janeiro, but this one would have a happier ending. In 1952, city hall received a precarious grant for a second TV station, headed by Roquette-Pinto and Fernando Tude de Souza. After designing the project and ordering equipment from US suppliers, a new leader came to power and the plans were disrupted. Since the station had not yet been built, the grant was revoked by President Juscelino Kubitschek, who then assigned it to Mayrink Veiga Radio. Once again, the station was not installed and, in 1963, the grant was moved over to TV Excelsior. This new station was short-lived; broadcasting was stopped in 1970 under intense pressure from the military regime. Its next occupant, in 1973, was the Brazilian Center for Educational Television Foundation (FCBTVE), which founded TV Educativa, linked to the federal government. The FCBTVE had been created about six years prior and, until that time, produced educational content that was used by a number of broadcasters (including commercial ones) throughout the country as a way to meet the quota for educational programming on TV.

How did these broadcasting initiatives from federal government work? What united them was the term "educative": it was a group of broadcasters whose role was to educate and teach remotely. In some cases, like with Rádio Nacional, the programming went beyond education by also offering entertainment. In other cases, the main objective was to provide public services. This was all defined under the term "educational broadcasting" once the service had been regulated (initially on TV) through Decree-Law No. 236 of 1967.

The "television education" initiatives were established before the military dictatorship began which, once in power, would take over said initiatives, yet in the decades to come others would emerge: There was the National Educational Broadcasting Campaign (CNRE) from the Ministry of Education and Culture, created by Decree No. 49,259 in 1960; the National Telecommunications Council (Contel) policy guaranteeing educational channels; a working group created under Decree No. 63.592 in 1968 for refining the legal situation of educational broadcasters and another group created under Decree No. 65.239 in 1969 to set up an "advanced system of educational technologies" which included public broadcasting; the implementation of the National Teleducation Plan (Prontel); investments in a domestic satellite aimed at developing 'tele-education'; and the "Minerva Project", a subsidiary course created in 1970 which was suspended twenty years later (OLIVEIRA, 1992; 2006; BUCCI, 2008):

> "During my time at Contel, we worked closely with the Ministry of Education, which was interested in expanding the number of broadcasters working with education – not just in television, but radio as well. If I am not mistaken, in 1967, a Brazilian representative of UNESCO informed us that an educational satellite television system was already being designed in Canada. This gave us something new to think about (...). The Ministry of Education worked very closely with both Contel and the Ministry of Communications on the idea of how to bring education to the more remote areas of the country. It is interesting to know that the idea of a Brazilian satellite originally came from the Ministry of

> Education and Contel. Another interesting point was Prontel, but I don't know if it exists anymore. It was a Television Education Program, something along those lines. It was an organ within the Ministry of Education focused on educating through television. But then there was another problem, one that also arose in other countries and other areas: television signals from other countries would also be received, what to do about that? The Ministry of Education began to be opposed to the satellite system" (OLIVEIRA, 2006b).

The major driving force behind the advance of educational broadcasting, however, was Decree-Law No. 236 in 1967. It gave the Union, states, municipalities, universities and foundations the legal right to have grants and operate broadcasters without the need for a selection process. Programming included the transmission of classes, conferences, lectures and debates – a vision of distance education that, with the exception of a few restricted spaces in the programming schedule, would not survive for long. This theoretical construction was a response to pressures from international organizations with high hopes for the new medium, such as UNESCO and, at the same time, it was a desperate attempt to prepare the workforce for the growing industrialization of the country (JAMBEIRO, 2002). This same decree law also registered one of the hallmarks in the history of public broadcasting in the country: the ban on commercial advertising. From 1967 to 1975, nine educational broadcasters were created; six were linked to state departments of Education or Culture, such as TV Cultura from São Paulo, and the other three were run by the Ministry of Education and Culture, including Educational TV in Rio de Janeiro, operated by FCBTVE, and the pioneer station, linked to the Federal University of Pernambuco (PIERANTI, 2007).

Federal government broadcasters went beyond their programming schedule. The Radio MEC studios were used for recording albums; a total of 8,000 albums were recorded by 1955, an average of 400 per year. In addition, there was technical assistance and training activities. The FCBTVE trained professionals for educational television before operating a station. In 1969 there were more than 150 stations (MILANEZ, 2007a; MILANEZ, 2007b).

By the mid-1970s, Brazil already had dozens of educational broadcasters linked to the Union, states, municipalities and universities, all with their own plans for how to use "tele-education", a predecessor of distance education. The plans for mass training in this medium were not realized; however, the broadcasters existed. Many of these broadcasters were spread throughout a number of ministries with no coordination and little representation. In 1971, they were the object of analysis in the 1971 Motives Exhibition No. 118, a visionary document on the imminent future of the communications sector in Brazil, signed by then Minister of Communications, Hygino Corsetti. The text advocated for the creation, in the near future, of one entity capable of coordinating the radio and television services operated by the Union. That moment arrived in 1975 under the management of Euclides Quandt de Oliveira:

> "I don't know exactly where it started, but at some point the idea started to be tossed around: why don't all the radios come together in one group, in one administration, managed by the government? At the

beginning of the Medici government, when Corsetti entered, he did a preliminary study on the need for all broadcasting agencies to be run by one management group. This idea was presented by Medici in his first address to Congress. What's even more interesting is that Rádio Nacional was not happy with the creation of Radiobrás. This was an ongoing idea, but it never came to fruition. When the Geisel administration took over, the unification project was raised but the ministry was completely focused on the telecommunications network problem ... so they said 'get organized and go' and the ministry was given an obligation to organize. The basic idea had already been reduced ... the Rádio Nacional station was supposed to have international coverage. Why would we do a program for other countries? Very few people would listen to our programs, so let's cover our country ... Radiobrás' basic mission was to manage those companies and cover the Amazon area" (OLIVEIRA, 2006c).

However, the story of educational broadcasting was not limited to expectations about the new phase. While the Ministry of Communications was planning to expand the infrastructure in the country, oppression, violence and torture were imposed on the construction of Brasil Grande. Many professionals who were identified as being opposed to the military government were dismissed or removed from their jobs at Rádio Nacional. But there is another station which would suffer an even bigger setback.

Vlado was born in 1937 in the Kingdom of Yugoslavia. With the rise of Nazism and being of Jewish descent, his family decided to leave the country. They immigrated to Italy, where they lived in hiding before immigrating to Brazil, where Vlado graduated in philosophy and became the journalist Vladimir Herzog. He worked for the Estado de S. Paulo newspaper and the British BBC, in addition to teaching at the University of São Paulo's School of Communication and Arts. During this time he secretly participated in the Brazilian Communist Party. In 1975, he became director of journalism for TV Cultura (a station affiliated with the government of São Paulo) and faced fierce opposition in the Legislative Assembly from members of the ruling Arena party, such as the former president of Corinthians, Wadih Helu, and future president of the Brazilian Football Confederation (CBF), José Maria Marin. The Brazilian Army summoned him to testify about his connections with the communist party. He decided to go voluntarily the next morning. He never came back. The official news was that he had committed suicide, accompanied by a photo that circulated around the world in which it appeared Vlado had hung himself by his belt tied to his prison cell bars with his knees notably bent. Since he was actually taller than the cell bars which he allegedly hung himself from, he could not have committed suicide in that position. He had been murdered, and his death generated a number of acts of resistance: from investigative charges to religious groups honoring him, journalists had begun to mobilize. Within a few years, the military regime would collapse, and the slow and restricted process of punishing those responsible for such crimes had begun.

Torture and violence, however, were not methods practiced by the Ministry of Communications. The ministry dealt with infrastructure in the sector and had no hand in regulating content. Censorship was attributed to other organs. At the time of

Vlado's assassination, the ministry had implemented the newly created Radiobrás. In fact, the goal of providing more coverage for the Amazon (mentioned earlier) replaced the overseas shortwave broadcasting project. Even changing the focus of the nation's most powerful broadcasters, the Brazilian Broadcasting Company (Radiobrás), created through Law No. 6.301 of 1975 and linked to the Ministry of Communications, offered a rare opportunity to plan and enhance the performance of the stations linked to the Union. However, this expectation was short-lived due to the failing 'tele-education' policies and the Brazilian economy itself, which was taking its first steps into an era of hyperinflation. In practice, Radiobrás became a hub for the smaller, less profitable broadcasters which had no major programming projects and were much less important than the imposing, yet fragile, Rádio Nacional which would also feel the effects of the economic crisis, after many staff were dismissed due to their alleged support of the military dictatorship (SAROLDI, MOREIRA, 2005).

By the 1980s, Radiobrás had already become an unwanted company in the allied parties' frantic dispute over positions. Not even the publication of the new Federal Constitution, which advocated the complementarity of public, state and private broadcasting, could reverse the downward spiral. Some broadcasters simply shut down, while others, especially at the beginning of the New Republic, were donated or auctioned by the federal government. For example, Decree No. 95,955 of 1988 authorized the sale of fourteen radio stations (twelve on FM frequency and two on OM frequency) and one TV station in Porto Velho to the private sector and state and municipal governments. Company assets were simply handed over which led to a backlog of bureaucratic issues (BUCCI, 2008). The number of stations linked to the Union then began to fall (Graph 1).

The situation worsened in the following decades. Radiobrás had licenses for new stations in Porto Velho and Manaus, but they were never installed. From 1990 to 1992, 439 employees were laid off, another 32 quit, and the company was about to be closed by the Fernando Henrique Cardoso government. It was operated by different structures of public administration, from the Ministry of Communications to the Secretariat of Social Communication, even to the Chief of Staff Office:

**Graph 1: Variation in the Number of Federal Broadcasters in Brazil (1982-1988)**

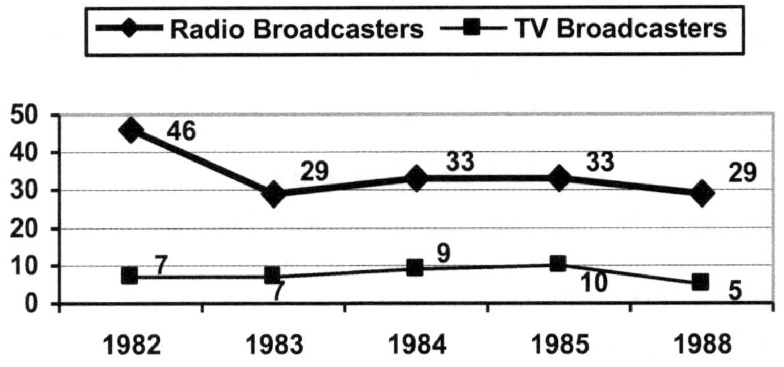


**Source:** PIERANTI (2011).

At the same time, educational public broadcasting had expanded in three very distinct ways. Public universities obtained their grants and no longer reported to Radiobrás, reverting back to the time when broadcasters were all spread out, something that the creation of Radiobrás was supposed to prevent. Some states and a few municipalities also obtained grants and adopted TVE

Rio de Janeiro or TV Cultura from São Paulo as their network heads. Lastly, foundations under private law, ones which were not necessarily linked to educational institutions, established broadcasters but did not follow the expected form for running a public education broadcasting service. As these grants were issued at the discretion of the federal government, they became instruments for providing favors and solving political problems. Several of these foundations operated like private broadcasters, but did not always have commercial advertising.

Even though it was run by the federal government, Radiobrás was not unanimous. It had no ties with TVE Rio de Janeiro or TVE Maranhão, nor with Radio MEC, which, at this time, was mainly broadcasting classical music programs. They were owned by a number of entities over the decades and, in 2002, came under the administration of the Roquette Pinto Association of Educational Communication (ACERP), a social organization linked to the federal government. In this same year, Radiobrás had 1,147 employees, four radio stations, two television stations, and an Internet news agency. ACERP had 1,302 employees working at the educational television stations in Rio de Janeiro and Maranhão, including two other radio stations (BUCCI, 2008).

Educational TV in Maranhão was a totally different project from the others. In 1969, the state government began operating it with the aim of expanding secondary education. The program was supposed to be received in educational institutions where students could watch and be monitored, according to the strict methodology of "tele-education". In 1986, the station was federalized but continued to operate in partnership with the state Department of Education. In 1996, there was an estimated 46,944 students enrolled; ten years later, that number dropped to only 492 students, all of whom were enrolled in a school in São Luís and another in Peri-Mirim. That same year the "tele-education" project was abandoned and the broadcaster began to relay TVE programming in Rio de Janeiro with local journalistic content (MILANEZ, 2007b).

In addition to educational broadcasters, there were other initiatives broadening the field of public communication in the country. Law 8,977 of 1995, known as the Cable Law, provided for the free and obligatory distribution of community and university channels. Furthermore, Law No. 9,612 of 1998 created the community broadcasting service, and with it, thousands of community radio stations were born.

As an intern at TVE Rio de Janeiro in 2002, I remember how we were looking forward to changes that were supposed to happen to the station under the Luiz Inácio Lula da Silva's government. At the end of that year we all thought that Lula's government was going to invest in TVE, recognizing its historical importance and its potential in the field of communication. We didn't know that the changes would take a few more years to be implemented – and we didn't realize how much it would be changed.

# VI

Lula's first term as President of the Republic was a complicated one. While it is true that the country saw public policies being put in place that definitely changed the living conditions of millions of Brazilians, the country also saw the first political crises of the term. And with those crises came the realization that the government was not communicating well: the President of the Republic did not speak to the most important mediums of communication; the important measures promised in his campaign went largely unreported; and the form in which official advertising was distributed harkened back to the previous model where a huge part of the resources were put into traditional media. It seemed to be a plot to transform the state system and government communication.

Or so it seemed. At the beginning of Lula's second term, Franklin Martins took over as Secretariat of Social Communication and took his executive secretary, Otoni Fernandes Jr., with him, both of whom were successful journalists. Together they revolutionized government communication as well as generated a feeling of antipathy from opposition media. While in government they created rules for the distribution of official advertising which included defining technical criteria for contributions and incorporating thousands of new media into one previously private club. They were protagonists of major communication processes such as the First National Conference on Communication (Confecom), the working group that proposed a new regulatory framework for the sector, and they championed the creation of the Brazil Communication Company (EBC).

Another important actor in public administration was the Ministry of Culture. Broadcasting was not just limited to the Ministry of Communications; it became important to the Ministry of Culture when Gilberto Gil took over as minister of culture (to be succeeded afterward by his executive secretary Juca Ferreira). Initially, the Ministry of Culture focused more on promoting audiovisual content, and then it focused on its own broadcasting as many commercial broadcasters were not interested, and after that it focused on alternative sources for distributing this material. Thus, policies and programs such as Culture Points, DocTV, AnimaTV, FicTV, We on the Screen and many others began to work with communication as they were created in an environment of intense social participation.

Never had the public communications sector been so organized and united. The combined performance of Abepec, Astral, ABTU and ABCCom (which were the educational, legislative, university, and community channels, respectively) which were available on cable TV made the "public field" important. The biggest exponent of this movement was the 1st National Forum on Public TVs held between 2006–2007 (being the last year of Lula's first term and the first year of his second). At the end of the event, the President himself criticized Brazilian TV, stating that a new station would be created to show what television was not showing. Technically-speaking, the message was unclear; politically-speaking, it was unmistakable and clear:

> "I would not say that Lula had a very clear conception of Public TV. He said: 'I don't want a blank TV, I don't want a government TV, I want a TV that helps people think, helps people understand the country, one that has serious journalism'. The Ministry of Culture, with Gilberto Gil at the helm, shared a very similar view to ours, to Secom's and to the president's about Public TV. So the vision that led to the creation of EBC and TV Brasil was built within the government quite quickly and easily" (MARTINS, 2013).

Added to this list is Tereza Cruvinel. She is a journalist who has been writing one of the country's most reputable political columns for the O Globo newspaper for decades. She was invited to take over the EBC as its first CEO. Her relationship with parliamentarians from different parties would be a decisive factor in getting the provisional measure for creating the company approved and converted into law, as well as generating opposition from traditional media.

In previous years, Radiobrás was dedicated to trying to implement a public broadcasting project under the management of Eugênio Bucci. The company changed its focus from institutional communication to the right to information – that is, the right of society to receive objective and truthful information in place of information from a governmental point of view. For

Bucci, "the state should be understood as a subcategory of the public; in other words, although not everything which is public should be state, everything that is state should be public" and broadcasters who act as stakeholders end up "guaranteeing patrimonialism" (BUCCI, 2008, p. 260-1).

Although the initiative was important, its success was relative: Radiobrás had a solid tradition of government communication, had no legal provision with which to change its operations, did not manage nationally relevant media, did not have institutionalized mechanisms for social participation, and was administratively weak. ACERP did not go through any similar process during Lula's first term.

Provisional Measure No. 398 of 2007 defined the Brasil Communication Company (EBC) as a public company linked to the Secretariat of Social Communication with integrated shared capital and assets constituted by the Union. It incorporated Radiobrás and, consequently, the former state broadcasters and their employees. Since it is a social organization, ACERP could not be legally incorporated so the EBC became responsible for operating ACERP's sister stations. The EBC was responsible for providing public broadcasting services and communication services (institutional) to the federal government. Basically, public service broadcasting like TV Brasil (the public television which replaced the old TVE and National TV of Brasilia), a number of radio stations (Radio Nacional), contracted government communication channels (NBr TV, initially a satellite-based subscription service) and the radio programs "Voice of Brazil", with news regarding the government, the Legislative and the Judiciary in the federal level, and "Coffee with the President", an interview with President of the Republic, all lived under the roof of the EBC. The EBC went far beyond traditional educational broadcasting; it provided mechanisms for public debate, developped critical awareness, fostered citizenship building, and supported measures for social inclusion and the socialization of producing knowledge and stimulating interactivity. The company's revenue came from multiple sources such as public budget, sponsorships, service provision – but not commercial advertising.

The company's CEO had a fixed term of office and could not be dismissed by the President of the Republic, a common practice up until that time. In addition, the management structure included a 22-member Board of Trustees, all with fixed terms, 15 of whom were from civil society, represting cultural diversity and a wide range of professions. This board was responsible for monitoring public channels, making sure that their programming was in accordance with legislation. It was also responsible for the removal of any director from office who received more than two motions of repudiation against them. There were also quotas that scheduled programming needed to meet: at least 10% of its weekly schedule must contain regional content and 5% must contain independent content. The EBC also established partnerships with other entities for the purpose of forming a National Public Communication Network.

National Congress incorporated some important additions in the text. The major addition was the creation of the Contribution for the Support of Public Service Broadcasting, which all telecommunication service providers and broadcasters paid to support the EBC. The provisional measure was approved on the last day at dawn. It was a boisterous session, culminating with the removal of some of the opposition parliamentarians from the plenary. Thus, Law No. 11,652 of 2008 was born, one of the most innovative laws in the history of public broadcasting in Brazil.

# VII

The first major challenge facing the EBC was its characterization as an authentic representative of public service broadcasting and not as a representative of "Lula's TV", a term coined by its critics. When I arrived at the EBC as chief of staff in the second half of Tereza Cruvinel's term, this dispute was still on the agenda.

There were at least two reasons behind the strong attempts at trying to label the EBC as just a group of state broadcasters with a new look: The first being tradition; the second being the structure of the company itself. Brazil had never had an entity that referred to itself (and was legally recognized as) a promoter of public service broadcasting. Previous instances in the field of public service broadcasting differed from this concept. The Federal Constitution of 1988 provided for three (different) broadcasting systems: public, state, and private. Mechanisms for daily social participation were provided by law through community radio stations, university and community channels were available on cable TV (after the approval of a new law in 2011, they became available on all pay-TV providers), and Radiobrás briefly tried to distance itself from government communication. However, the image of Union broadcasters and state educational broadcasters (who partnered with the EBC to create a National Public Communication Network) was historically associated with government communication. This government communication was often referred to as state communication, thus creating a clear confusion between the concepts of "state" and "government" which, of course, received a fair amount of criticism (RAMOS, 2013). These broadcasters reflected the views of federal or state governments, and had trusted their normal operations to appointed leaders who did not monitor social participation. In general, their journalism lacked credibility and was recognized for their children's, sporting, debate and educational programming. The situation was not much better in neighboring countries, and as a result, there was a lack of clear references to public service broadcasting. There was a legacy of government communication embedded in these broadcasters – and the EBC, like its Central and Eastern European sisters, had to take on that legacy.

The very structure of the company contributed to this confusion. The EBC was created to manage public service broadcasters but it was under legal obligation to provide institutional communication services to the federal government and was remunerated for this service. As such, it was and is responsible for federal government products such as "Voice of Brazil" and NBr which, by the way, up until 2016, had never been confused with public broadcasting products. The focus, the formats, and the narrative structures were almost all entirely different – and when they weren't, they should have been.

There was a consensus that this mixture was not ideal, which led to further criticism (RAMOS, 2013). In a perfect country, recognizing public broadcasting as a fundamental element for building a democracy would be natural, and government communication could be done through a different entity.

Although I do agree with this consensus, I side with the minority here and believe that, for pragmatic reasons, it is completely reasonable and possible for public broadcasting and institutional government communication to exist under the same framework. First, they have similar international references: as we shall see later in this book, some Central and Eastern European public broadcasting entities run legislative channels and are paid by their respective governments to produce specific products such as diaspora programs (country nationals who reside abroad). Moreover, in a country known for its challenges in public administration, it would have been unreasonable to abandon the structure the EBC was established under for the purpose of setting up an entirely new organization dedicated to public service broadcasting. This would have required a number of public procurements for the hiring of labor and a doubling of investments, which would run a high risk of failure as the transition to Digital TV, in progress at the time, used up all the frequencies available in major cities. Lastly, even if the federal government had had a significant parliamentary base at that time, it would not have been politically feasible to approve a totally new structure for public service broadcasting. In fact, the provisional measure for the creation of the EBC was about to expire, and was only extended when its contract period for that measure had ended. This leads me to believe that Brazil was correct in adopting the Central and Eastern Europe model, which made a similar transition. That was the possible model. Facing criticism was a routine occurrence at this early stage:

"Public TV began to face media criticism even before the provisional measure was issued. I think me being EBC president has somehow made it worse. I wrote a reputable column for Globo, I was a commentator at Globonews; I was part of the journalism elite. Seeing as how Public TV, from the outset, was viewed as the government's revenge for the unfriendly treatment it received from the political press, me being appointed as president also sparked reactions. They saw it as a kind of 'corporate betrayal', something that would not be forgiven during or even after my administration. There was also, and still is, a great deal of ignorance in terms of the difference between public and government communication and the role of Public TV. When we cited the BBC as an example, some were surprised to learn that it is public. Of course, there was an air of political radicalization between opposition and government in Congress. There was almost a promise held that the provisional measure would not be approved even though the support group for Lula's second term grew with the inclusion of the PMDB. The situation was even more complicated in the Senate. The government lost the vote to extend the CPMF, which was being negotiated at the same time as the EBC provisionary measure" (CRUVINEL, 2013).

The EBC was frequently criticized by a wide range of sources, including much of the traditional media. The company's management, with Tereza Cruvinel as president, and the federal government, particularly then-minister Franklin Martins and the President of Brazil himself, defended the EBC. They explained that public service broadcasting (not to be confused with government communication) was necessary for democracy and countries such as the United States, Europe, Japan and others recognized this.

The first principle for measuring the importance of public broadcasting is defending it as an alternative way of communicating, one not to be confused with state or private broadcasting, or the government or the market. This kind of broadcasting is different because its whole purpose is to be independent and equidistant from both state or private. Of course, there are some elements needed to ensure its independence, as we shall discuss further on. The EBC's first management group repeatedly defended its politics, thereby reinforcing its importance. This kind of defensive discourse became gradually less frequent, and after a few years had stopped completely. In 2017, contrary to the basic principles of public broadcasting, rumors were circling that there might have been a possible merger between public channels and government institutional communication products. This was not the only problem the EBC experienced; there were others regarding the structure of the company:

> "When I was invited to head the company, the other directors had already been chosen. It was a mistake to accept the position under these circumstances, I paid a huge price for it, but I don't regret it. It was a good fight and the legacy was good. A few days after I took office, I realized the extent of the difficulties I was going to face setting up and running the company with a board of directors where decisions I had not made were voted on. So, the directors did not choose and appointment me, which would have implications in terms of hierarchy. The top three (Director General, Director of Prog-ramming and Content, and Director of Relationship and

Networking) had been nominated by the Minister of Culture, Gilberto Gil, and they seemed to view me as an intruder among their midst. After all, I came from the Globo Organizations and, although it meant I had experience and gave me some professional value, it aroused prejudice and distrust. Of course, conflicts did not take long to manifest. But everyone knew that because of my time in Congress I would play a key role in approving the provisional measure. Soon after it was approved, and even before the sanction, I began to be openly challenged" (CRUVINEL, 2013).

The two main leaders of the entity were appointed by the President of the Republic. Symbolically, they were at similar levels, and the managing director was not the CEO's trusted choice. There was no mediation with National Congress, as is the case in other countries, and those who are nominated by parliamentarians are not presented as they are in regulatory agencies in Brazil (RAMOS, 2013). Apart from Tereza Cruvinel, only two directors remained in office until the end of the first term: José Roberto Garcez, who came from the former Radiobrás and was Director of Services at EBC, the area responsible for government communication, and Support Director Roberto Gontijo. Some of the first directors had previously held positions in the Ministry of Culture, a key political organ in support of the creation of the EBC. Everyone had left the company before that management came to an end:

"I don't think it should be linked to the Ministry of Communications because this ministry deals more with technology, the physical basis, and not with content. It could well have been the Ministry of Culture. In fact, it was a collective construction; it wasn't just

Secom that built it. I worked together with Juca (Ferreira), who was the executive secretary of MinC. At first, several people came from the Ministry of Culture to the EBC, including the Director General. It was a mixture and it was a mistake because the one to appoint the CEO should be the president of the company. It is the same as an Executive Secretary of a ministry not being appointed by the Minister. It doesn't work, because loyalty and a positive relationship don't work that way. The EBC could have been linked to MinC and I even think that, in the medium term, it should go to the Ministry of Culture. Remember that MinC played a key role in the Public TV Forum, which subsidized the creation of TV Brasil. But maybe President Lula thought that Secom, in a new light, would be in a good position to move the project along, so much so that he included that in the invitation he sent me" (MARTINS, 2013).

The problem of division was not just with the board. In its early years, the EBC took on graduates from Radiobrás and ACERP, two entities with very different internal cultures. Radiobrás was based in Brasilia and ACERP in Rio de Janeiro. The former was recognized for its role in government communication, but in the years immediately before its demise, it tried to devote itself to public broadcasting. Since ACERP was incorporated into the EBC and Radiobrás was not, a double chain of command was established for a few years: the heads of the EBC were not able to properly take control of teams made up mostly of ACERP professionals. This situation occurred in most of the units in Rio de Janeiro, such as the areas of journalism and production. So it came down to the goodwill of the ACERP coordinator. That double chain of command also occurred at the upper levels of management in both entities as ACERP was not a subsidiary of the EBC – it was actually contracted by the EBC to provide certain services.

From a legal point of view, the provisional measure that led to the creation of the EBC was developed by a working group over a two or three-month time period. There was no time to actually present the proposal as it still needed the approval and and mobilization of the 1st National Public TV Forum. The conversion of the text into law showed that this political deadline was correct. However, legal solutions were not drawn up during this process; they would be drawn up years later.

One of these solutions was the nature of the grants: the EBC was never able to unite all the federal government broadcasters, including those from federal universities and research foundations (which was, at one time, Radiobrás's dream). These federal broadcasters continued to operate autonomously; their connection with the National Public Communication Network was a fragile one and subject to the harsh political environment. Even the inclusion of new broadcasters to the EBC was not regulated until 2014, when the Ministry of Communications regulated new consigments to the Union. The EBC was then recognized as an entity which was able to secure these consignments quicker than it could traditional grants. There were also other background issues: It then recognized the EBC as an entity that could have these assignments, faster than traditional grants. There were other issues in the background:

> "The GT has a level of excellence and has been able to formulate some important institutional solutions, but I think it has made many mistakes regarding future operational issues, for example, opting for a public company format. Were other models studied, like a foundation or an institute? I don't know. The GT thought of a non-dependent public company with full financial autonomy to manage the public system. Editorial autonomy was ensured by subordinating the prog-

ramming guidelines to the Board of Trustees, but how can we guarantee financial autonomy to a company which lacks the revenues to maintain itself and is not able to explore commercial advertising? That was a problem that I later had to face. We had to change the nature of the company, from independent to state-owned. Of course, I would like to chair an independent company that could best apply its budget appropriations and reallocate resources without relying on Congress, one that could set its own wage policy, among other advantages. But in order to do that, it would need to generate its own revenue. Without exploring commercial advertising (what is correct), where would the revenues come from to modernize outdated structures and labor liabilities? As a dependent company, however, the EBC was subordinate to Union Budget rules, although my management always produced the resources we promised. When the economic area was at its worst, Franklin came in, went to the president and got things resolved" (CRUVINEL, 2013).

After Tereza Cruvinel left the EBC at the end of her mandate, Nelson Breve, former Secom Press Secretary during the Lula administration, took over as Chief Executive Officer. Breve was concerned with the company's structure and the definition and its strategic planning. A few months before the end of his term, Breve went back to his prior position at the Press Office and Américo Martins took his place, only to resign a little less than six months later. Several media outlets at the time (LIMA, 2016; MELO, 2016) reported that his exit could have been the result of political interference from the government. Martins denied these allegations in an official communication stating that he had left for personal reasons (AGÊNCIA BRASIL, 2016). From February to May 2016, a time when the political crisis in Brazil was worsening, the EBC operated with no CEO having been appointed. That month, a few days before being removed from office, Dilma Rousseff appointed Ricardo Melo, former Director of Journalism, as the new CEO of the company. Melo would be dismissed a few days after the new interim government was put in place, returned to office by injunction, and was removed once again due to a larger number of changes to the EBC.

Provisional Measure No. 744 of 2016 was forwarded to National Congress at the beginning of the Temer administration, and was later converted into Law No. 13,417 of 2017. It made important amendments to the law in support of the EBC's operations, one of which being that the CEO would no longer have a fixed mandate, which left the position open for Laerte Rímoli to assume. The EBC's Board of Trustees was also dismantled and replaced by a neutral Editorial and Programming Committee whose main duties were vetoed when the law was approved. This committee was not implemented, at least until the end of 2017. Thus, two institutes very closely linked to the independence of public broadcasting ceased to exist: the fixed mandate of key leaders and the guarantee of social participation bodies, which we shall discuss below. Very few manifestations followed these harsh measures.

The almost complete silence can be attributed to the weakening of the EBC. For years some of the company's staff had questioned the arrival of managers who were linked with the federal government. The term "revolving door" was even used to describe the entry of former Secom employees into the EBC. This may help to explain the affinity some of the company's professsionnals felt towards the new CEO, who promptly announced that some of the management positions would be held by permanent employees.

In addition, the EBC was looking to assert its leadership in the public broadcasting sector. Attempts to adapt the old state educational broadcasters to public broadcasting never happened. There were attempts to create social participation bodies, for example, in Bahia and Sergipe, but the states did not adopt the logic of fixed mandates for CEOs. In addition, TV Brasil continued its dispute with TV Cultura and Rede Minas to be the leading integrated network for educational broadcasters:

## Table 4 – Education broadcaster programming

| Program | Nº of broadcasts | % of all broadcasters |
|---|---|---|
| TV Brasil | 27 | 19.1 |
| TV Cultura | 26 | 18.4 |
| Rede Minas | 26 | 18.4 |
| Religious Programs | 22 | 15.6 |
| Own Programming | 18 | 12.8 |
| Futura Channel | 9 | 6.4 |
| Record News | 5 | 3.6 |
| NGT Network | 4 | 2.8 |
| Others | 4 | 2.8 |
| **Total** | **141** | |

**Source:** PIERANTI, FERNANDES, 2017.

TV Brasil was the preferred network for educational broadcasters operating in the country in 2017 by a narrow margin. This was largely because public educational broadcasters preferred TV Brasil. If you only look at the grants from private entities, then religious programming is in the lead, with TV Brasil in fourth place (PIERANTI, FERNANDES, 2017).

The Brazilian model for structuring public networks is quite unusual: the EBC is responsible for educating autonomous broadcasters, many of which are linked to private foundations or governments run by parties in opposition to the federal government. This hinders TV Brasil from expanding because the affiliation of state broadcasters in certain strategic municipalities is erratic. The federal government also failed to implement any effective alternatives, like a new consignment policy in all the country's capitals for the EBC. This inability to branch out is one reason for the lack of interest and relevance in public broadcasting.

Thus, the structure of the EBC's stations is not similar to those in Central and Eastern European countries, nor is it the result of a governing system in which it has precedence over other partners, as is the case with the German ARD. The problem of a model dependent on convincing autonomous broadcasters increases in a scenario where audiences are continually low, as shall be discussed further on.

Another aspect which appears to be unequal is funding for the EBC. The creation of the Contribution to the Promotion of Public Broadcasting – which could in theory take the place of a licensing fee – was an important innovation, but the telecommunications service providers (which are the major debtors) have been contesting it in court ever since its inception. The contributions are paid to the court and are not used. The *a priori* rejection of commercial advertising as a source of financing for non-private broadcasting in Brazil eventually led the EBC into the arms of the public budget. In this sense, it is worth analyzing the budget numbers over the last few years:

## Table 5: EBC's Budget (BRL) (2007-2019)

| | 2007 | 2008 | 2009 | 2010 | 2011 | 2012 | 2013 | 2014 | 2015 | 2016 | 2017 | 2018 | 2019 |
|---|---|---|---|---|---|---|---|---|---|---|---|---|---|
| 1) Appropriation Bill | 156040170 | 323720716 | 290422280 | 453911395 | 471116957 | 416332681 | 533510760 | 538362975 | 627526080 | 657433054 | 708409651 | 723382895 | 617088498 |
| 1.1) Previous year's variation % | | 107,46 | -10,29 | 56,29 | 3,79 | -11,63 | 28,15 | 0,91 | 16,56 | 4,77 | 7,75 | 2,11 | -14,69 |
| 2) Enforced budget | | 259378380 | 383005483 | 471566261 | 424495347 | 455560734 | 482937855 | 535646005 | 557246263 | 595616167 | 605909791 | | |
| 2.1) % of budget implemented | | 80,12 | 131,88 | 103,89 | 90,10 | 109,42 | 90,52 | 99,50 | 88,80 | 90,60 | 85,53 | | |
| 2.2) Previous year's variation % | | | 47,66 | 23,12 | -9,98 | 7,32 | 6,01 | 10,91 | 4,03 | 6,89 | 1,73 | | |
| 3) Personal and social contributions | 91954680 | 69917719 | 100543070 | 140138748 | 158331780 | 220449902 | 238283994 | 268663242 | 283669165 | 350114832 | 384808757 | 408102217 | 399576061 |
| 4) Investment | 10000000 | 104382941 | 111847704 | 109435587 | 93696953 | 29342328 | 58000000 | 18213000 | 26000000 | 31429128 | 15000000 | 11212270 | 11592800 |
| 4.1) Previous year's variation % | | 943,83 | 7,15 | -2,16 | -14,38 | -68,68 | 97,67 | -68,60 | 42,76 | 20,88 | -52,27 | -25,25 | 3,39 |
| 4.2) Investment implemented | | 121970139 | 95216110 | 94534180 | 44457831 | 44215635 | 30387301 | 32713000 | 7234526 | 8376968 | 27360984 | | |
| 4.3) Previous year's variation % | | | -21,93 | -0,72 | -52,97 | -0,54 | -31,27 | 7,65 | -77,88 | 15,79 | 226,62 | | |
| 4.4) % Predicted implementation | | 116,85 | 85,13 | 86,38 | 47,45 | 150,69 | 52,39 | 179,61 | 27,83 | 26,65 | 182,41 | | |
| 5) % Predicted budget investment | | 32,24 | 38,51 | 24,11 | 19,89 | 7,05 | 10,87 | 3,38 | 4,14 | 4,78 | 2,12 | 1,55 | 1,88 |
| 6) % Implemented budget investment | | 47,02 | 24,86 | 20,05 | 10,47 | 9,71 | 6,29 | 6,11 | 1,30 | 1,41 | 4,52 | | |

Source: PIERANTI, 2017.

The EBC's budget has increased over the last few years. For example, it had an increase of 16.56% in 2015 and 4.77% in 2016. However, most of these amounts are used to fund the company. It is better to examine item 4.2, which shows how much of the budget is spent on investments. There was a decrease in investments in every year from 2009 to 2013, and then a modest increase of 7.65% in 2014. These figures reflect not only the growing unavailability of investment resources (which, if obtainable, could theoretically improve the quality of prog-ramming or the technical quality of transmissions) but also suggest a decreased importance of the company in the eyes of the federal government. Admittedly, resources which are available for investment do not necessarily guarantee the success of a company; however, their unavailability ensures that the EBC will not have the basics to compete with other broadcasters. In short, this is yet another sign that the EBC has become less important to the federal government.

# VIII

Prior to the creation of the EBC and in the years immediately following its creation, the EBC found support in Secom-PR, an organ which it was affiliated with, and in MinC, which had participated in the project since its inception and had appointed some of the company's leaders. At times, it was supported by other government bodies, such as the Ministry of Education, whose participation was important in several of the Board of Trustees meetings.

Up until then, the Ministry of Communication was not as active as the other aforementioned organs in establishing the company, although it did not present any obstacles to its creation. Under new management in 2011, the ministry began to echo the discourse on the importance of public broadcasting and, more importantly, to seek solutions to its problems. The immediate goal of these initiatives was not to specifically strengthen the EBC, but to consolidate the field in which it was inserted. I was directly involved in these initiatives and held different positions in the ministry related to public service broadcasting until 2016.

The new management in 2011 already realized that the problems this segment was facing were very different from those in the private broadcasting system, and different solutions would have to be found. Building a new method of working was just as important as finding new solutions, a method that focused on the formulation and implementation of public policies, as well as reviewing the traditional processes inherent to the agency. In other words, it was not enough just to appoint and deal with the demands of the entities holding the grants; it was necessary to establish new rules, change the routine, and make it faster and more transparent. In the first few months, a new structure for the former Secretariat of Electronic Communication Services was developed that would separate private broadcasting systems from state and public broadcasting systems. This structure was consolidated in 2016.

The first major change was to make future grants more transparent and probable. The main instrument with which to do this was the National Grant Plans (NGPs), plans that contained lists of the municipalities that would be covered with qualification notices and public selection notices for different broadcasting services. The criteria for including municipalities varied with each plan, but were always disclosed. These included registered unmet demands, technical viability and locations without other grants. With NGPs, all interested parties could prepare for bids months in advance. The plans were initially conceived in February 2011 to meet the demand for new grants for community radios. Within a few months this same model was adopted for TV rebroadcasts and educational broadcasters, both partners of the EBC. Three NGPs were prepared for educational broadcasters: the first plan, for the 2011–12 biennium, included 475 municipalities, but was put on hold; the second, for the 2015–16 biennium, included 375 municipalities. All planned notices were published, except for the last one, which the Temer government did not publish. Lastly, the third plan for the 2016–17 biennium initially included 235 municipalities, but had not been implemented by the new government at the time this book was written.

Streamlining the granting process was essential, but it would not be enough. Some broadcasting services were subjected to an unnecessarily drawn out granting process with outdated rules; others were not even subject to clear rules. This was the case with educational broadcasting, and up until 2011 there were no public criteria for defining the winner of a public notice. The grant was discretionary and was awarded by the Executive Power to any entity that applied, met the minimum documentary requirements, and had a profile compatible with that defined by law. The following table shows the results of a lack of objective criteria:

**Table 6: Educational Broadcasting Grants (until 2010)**

| Classification | Total Number of Grants | Percentage |
|---|---|---|
| Public Universities (and support foundations) | 35 | 6 |
| States (direct and indirect administration) | 32 | 5.5 |
| Municipalities (direct and indirect administration) | 21 | 3.6 |

| Classification | Total Number of Grants | Percentage |
| --- | --- | --- |
| Public Universities (and support foundations) | 26 | 4.4 |
| Private Law Foundations | 472 | 80.5 |
| **Total** | **586** | **100** |

**Source:** PIERANTI (2016).

More than 80% of educational broadcasting grants were owned by private law foundations, which were not always affiliated with educational institutions. This scenario helps explain the high number of educational broadcasters with mostly religious programming, as these grants allowed various religious entities to operate on radio and TV.

From 2011 to 2015, the new educational broadcasting grants were regulated through a number of different ordinances from the Ministry of Communications. Some of these ordinances shared points in common, one of which is fundamental: a preference for public entities and, if those are not possible, for educational institutions, which in the medium term could lead to the effective installation of broadcasters with profiles that match the original vision of educational broadcasting:

**Table 7: Profile of educative broadcasting entities**

**(2011 to 2016)**

| Classification | Total | Percentage |
|---|---|---|
| Public universities, faculties (and support foundations) and technical schools | 59 | 62.8 |
| States (direct and indirect administration) | 4 | 4.2 |
| Municipalities (direct and indirect administration) | 4 | 4.2 |
| Private Universities (and support foundations) | 4 | 4.2 |
| Private Law Foundations | 23 | 24.6 |
| **Total** | **94** | **100** |

**Source:** PIERANTI (2016).

The previous table does not include those public notices which had no winners, or those which were abandoned. More than 70% of the other winners were public law entities, almost the reverse of the proportion from the previous table. These numbers, however, are an intermediate result: in order for these grants to materialize, the Ministry of Communications needs to end the bureaucratic routine and analyze the technical (engineering) design of the stations. However, most of the public notices were not completed under the Temer government by the Ministry of Science, Technology, Innovations and Communications (MCTIC), which absorbed the former ministry. In a previous book

(PIERANTI, 2017), I analyzed the interruption of this process. Here, it is worth noting that, if the public notices had been concluded, they could have generated another panorama in the public broadcasting segment, incorporating new public actors and enabling for the expansion of networks.

In that same book, I explained in detail the effort to regulate and implement public Digital TV channels. The first was the Citizenship Channel, which was to broadcast institutional programs from the state, municipality and community associations open to social participation. The Education and Culture channels were then regulated, in partnership with their responsible organs.

Other Executive Power TV channels were already operating in 2015, in addition to TV Brasil, but they were only broadcast on subscription, Internet or satellite platforms. The Ministry of Communications then coordinated a working group to migrate these channels to open digital TV. Thus, NBr, the institutional channel of the Executive Power; TV Escola, programmed by MEC, in partnership with ACERP; and Canal Saúde, an initiative of Fiocruz, would start broadcasting in multiprogramming with TV Brasil in Rio de Janeiro, São Paulo and Brasilia. As per the original plan, these four programs were then to be broadcast in municipalities with populations of over one hundred thousand using free frequencies or in places where analog TV was not in use, thus freeing up the broadcast frequencies. Once again, the Temer government stopped an important action in the field of public broadcasting and did not proceed with the project.

These actions were implemented after the necessary technical conditions had been assured. Municipalities were included in the PNOs after the channels had been studied and predicted. The processes for the Canal da Cidadania moved forward after the feasibility for their implementation in each municipality had been verified. A public test conducted in 2014, coordinated by the Ministry of Communications and Inmetro, and accompanied by several entities, the results of which were released later, led to Digital TV broadcasts on channels 7 through 13. This was then attributed to new public channels in municipalities where no other frequencies were available. Multiprogramming was also tested by the ministry, in partnership with the EBC, which allowed for the simultaneous broadcast of about seven separate programs on the same digital channel.

It is true, however, that more was expected from this same government in terms of broadcasting. In 2010, the Lula administration ended a successful biennium in broadcasting. Amid much dispute and criticism, his government managed to hold the First National Communication Conference was held, to organize and conduct a GT to draft a new regulatory framework for the sector, and completed his term with record popularity. The new government was expected to continue this process by finishing a bill, forwarding it to National Congress, and disputing its approval. This was not done. Even though the Ministry of Communications had taken important steps, like the ones we have presented here, the legal revision of the model was missing. Had it been legally revised, it would have been more difficult for major initiatives in public broadcasting to be interrupted.

Thus, the political will to expand public broadcasting was coupled with technical guarantees so that this movement would occur without directly harming the stations already operating in the country. Political will, in this case, is not to be confused with the uncertainties and discretion that marked broadcasting (not only public) in the country's new grants. It is actually a sovereign decision that led to the construction of a conscious public policy, although poorly explained in official documents at the time. We can say that this policy began to take shape during the First National Forum of Public TVs. It was presented and detailed in the creation of the EBC, and worked on further in the following years until 2016, even without the legal review of the general model for the sector, and was largely interrupted by the new government.

# THE BEGINNING

# IX

A booming new media market also began to take form in the new age of public service broadcasting in Central and Eastern Europe. Not only was there competition, but in many cases that competition was quicker to gain more audience and resources than the old broadcasters could.

There is an important difference between Central and Eastern Europe and Brazil. The private system in Brazil was fully consolidated at the time the EBC was created, with broadcasters and commercial networks having operated for decades. The response of public service broadcasting was different for radio and TV. Radio broadcasters continued to operate in the same manner after the EBC had been created; they just incorporated the legal principles of public service broadcasting. Their flagship cities continued to be Rio de Janeiro and Brasilia, in addition to operations along the Amazon border. For television, the change was significant: it had to merge TVE and TV Nacional together;

obtain a consignment in São Paulo to install the station; ensure the use of the name TV Brasil and disclose it; establish a network of new programming; and compete for audiences. It was, in practice, a new participant in the industry, and had to take on all the burdens that come with it.

The end of the socialist regimes in Central and Eastern Europe appeared to have been advantageous for previously established broadcasters. This view, however, is not completely true – after all, they were connected to a part of history that most of society regarded with contempt. Moreover, the idea of "democracy" and "democratization of media" at that time led to state broadcasters being replaced (HRVATIN, MILOSAVLJEVIC, 2003), and some countries quickly establishing new private broadcasters. The enthusiasm surrounding the autonomy from the state that this new open market represented was idealistic as many believed that it would lead to market demands which would be free from the political bias of media, that it would lead to guaranteed jobs, and that the competition it created would improve the quality of programming (PERUŠKO, 2008).

In Slovenia, grants were being issued prior to the publication of the new legal framework in 1994, and two broadcasters were launched the year after that framework entered into force. Similar to Slovenia, the Albanian government also did not wait for the new law to enter into force in 1998 before beginning private broadcasts. In Poland, an estimated 57 TV stations were already operating illegally by 1993. In Romania, the government precariously licensed twelve new TV stations before the Audiovisual Law was published. New channels were already being broadcast by cable or satellite in Bulgaria before the new law had been enacted. In Slovakia, in 1991, with the new law having been approved quite quickly, state broadcasters were officially made public, with six private broadcasters licensed within the first few years of the decade. On the other hand, in Lithuania, private broadcasters were allowed to operate in 1992, but the transformation from state to public broadcaster only officially took place as of 1996 (MARINESCU, 1995; HRVATIN, MILOSAVLJEVIC, 2003; OPEN SOCIETY INSTITUTE, 2005; LOND, 2006; DASKALOVA, 2017).

In addition to allowing for the creation of new channels, governments also focused on privatizing part of the infrastructure available to them. Like East Germany with its *Treuhandanstalt* (THA), other countries such as Romania set up specific structures for transferring over state-owned enterprises to its employees or to private enterprises. The end of the DFF state television broadcaster was looked at in a previous chapter of this book. Among the East German companies were 14 regional newspapers, formerly owned by the SED party. In 1990, two of these newspapers were sold; in April 1991, another 10. Although efforts were made to deconcentrate the market (each entity was only permitted to buy one newspaper) for Western investors (potential Eastern investors were restricted from buying particular companies, including newspapers), a public policy for print media was being designed specifically for the right to purchase specific publications. In practice, the state, via THA, chose who would occupy the new market. In Poland, the overthrow of the socialist regime led to 71 out of the 170 political publications being handed over to its staff, although those publications later became private enterprises. Hungary privatized two of its national TV channels at the same time, one of which had been previously used by the Soviets. Each competitor became a consortium, in which a company could hold up to 49% of the shares, and Hungarian entities could hold at least 26% of the shares. In Slovenia, all daily newspapers (with the exception of one) were privatized by distributing its shares among its employees. Three new newspapers, which had been created after 1990, went bankrupt. In 2003, there were four companies which controlled 90% of the daily newspaper market (HOFFMANN-RIEM, 1991; HRVATIN, MILOSAVLJEVIC, 2003; SPARKS, 2008; COMAN, 2009).

Even though there was a national economic elite which was getting stronger in the months after the end of socialist regimes, their investment capacity was limited. The established rules even provided a certain space for the national bourgeoisie in the new enterprises. However, the most significant role was played by large foreign groups, notably those already operating in Western Europe. In other words, official democracy brought many economic opportunities to Central and Eastern Europe.

The 1994 law in Croatia allowed for a maximum of 25% of broadcaster capital to be owned by foreign investors; however, this restriction was changed in 2000. In Romania, entities and individuals could not hold a majority stake in two media companies; they could not own more than 20% of the shares for the second media company, and the media owners had to be Romanian. In Poland, foreigners could buy up to 33% of companies holding public broadcasting licenses. At the beginning of the new century, it was estimated that over 50% of the daily newspapers in Hungary, Poland and the Czech Republic were controlled by foreign capital. One daily newspaper (Pravo), one weekly magazine (Respekt), and public TV and radio stations in the Czech Republic had no connection with outside investors. In 1997, one foreign company (CME – Central European Media Enterprises) controlled several broadcasters and content producers in former East Germany, the Czech Republic, Slovakia, Slovenia, Hungary, Romania, Poland and Ukraine. In 1999, CME tried to merge with SBS, another foreign media controlling company in Central and Eastern Europe. If the initiative had been successful, it could have led to monopolies in several countries as this newly-formed company control more than just small local commercial broadcasters (with largely imported content) and public media. The deal did not come to fruition. International investments being used to rebuild Bosnia in 1996 led to the creation of the OBN, an independent (and private) TV station that affiliated other similar broadcasters in the country to replace government-controlled broadcasters. The OBN received more than US$20 million in foreign funding and broadcast to 70 percent of the country, but was shut down due to low audience numbers at a time when the underutilized local workforce and journalists who gained prominence during the war were not given key positions (SPLICHAL, 2001; HRVATIN, MILOSAVLJEVIC, 2003; HOZIK, 2008; PERUŠKO, 2008; COMAN, 2009). The following table summarizes the arrival of various foreign groups in the mass market in Central and Eastern Europe.

**Table 8: Initial operations of major international media groups**

| Country | Group | Channel | Inauguration Year |
|---------|-------|---------|-------------------|
| Bulgaria | News Corporation | bTV | 2000 |
| Croatia | Central European Media Enterprises (CME) | Nova TV | 2000 |

| Country | Group | Channel | Inauguration Year |
| --- | --- | --- | --- |
| Slovakia | Central European Media Enterprises (CME) | Markiza TV | 1996 |
| Slovenia | Central European Media Enterprises (CME) | Canal A | 1991 |
| Estonia | Modern Times Group (MTG) | TV3 | 1993 |
| Hungary | RTL Group<br><br>SBS Broadcasting | RTL Klub<br><br>TV2 | 1997 |
| Latvia | Modern Times Group (MTG) | TV3 | 1998 |
| Lithuania | Modern Times Group (MTG) | TV3 | 1992 |
| Czech Republic | Central European Media Enterprises (CME) | TV Nova | 1994 |

| Country | Group | Channel | Inauguration Year |
|---|---|---|---|
| Romania | Central European Media Enterprises (CME) | PRO TV | 1995 |



Another mark of the opening process (quite predictable in fact) was the increase in the number of available media. This was already happening in Western Europe: in 1980 there were 40 public and 5 commercial channels; in 1999, there were 60 public and 70 private ones (MIHELJ, 2012).

In Romania, there was an increase in the number of daily newspapers and magazines between 1989 and 2005, from 36 to 80 newspapers and 459 to 2044 magazines. The number of private radio and TV stations jumped from 4 and 2 in 1993 to 443 and 158 in 2006, respectively. In 1992, public notices were being held for grants to new private broadcasters. In this year, there were public notices for 147 new radio stations in 70 locations and 74 TV stations in 65 municipalities; in 1993, those numbers were 142 for radio, 93 for TV and 298 for cable TV and radio; in 1994, 110 for radio, 73 for TV and 351 for radio and cable TV; and in 1995, 212 for radio, 155 for TV, and 518 for radio and cable. New private networks soon began to form. In 2006, in Albania, there were already 66 local TV stations, two national, two satellite, 40 cable channels, 46 local, and two national radio stations, with 72% of radio stations and 75% of TV stations located in the capital Tirana. At the time, two private TV stations covered 43% and 30% of the national territory, respectively. 1995 saw the addition of another national broadcaster, three regional broadcasters and twelve local broadcasters in Slovenia, that was in addition to the two public broadcasting TV channels which already existed. In 2008, Bosnia had 43 public and private TV stations, 142 radio stations, and seven newspapers in circulation, and there are many doubts about the sustainability of these media in a market of this size. Russia became one of the four fastest growing advertising markets in the world in the 1990s, hovering around 30% per year. In 2003, there were nine channels available to over 50% of the population. The number of private broadcasting licenses had increased considerably: in 2002, 1276 television licenses were issued and 1002 radio licenses. In 2008, Russia had an average newspaper circulation rate of 7.8 billion copies per year. However, the steady decrease in circulation and the increase in the number of TV sets (99% of households owned at least one set) eventually defined television as the most important medium, watched by 94% of Russians on a daily basis. In 2015, there were 20 national TV networks dominating the market, in addition to regional and local broadcasters. Moscow had 21 open broadcast channels, and the 200 largest cities in the country had about 15. Additionally, about 100 subscription channels reached about 30% of the population. There were also around 30,000 print titles and 2,500 Russian-language websites (MARINESCU, 1995; SPLICHAL, 1995; VARTANOVA, ZASSOURSKY, 2003; LONDO, 2006; HOZIC, 2008; COMAN, 2009; VARTANOVA, 2012; VARTANOVA, 2015).

As the market grew, problems arose – more than just a few. Competition between public and private broadcasters was not just about capturing audiences: private broadcasters looked to the successful formats and established professionals in public broadcasters to start their operations. The new channels transmitted with teams – which represented fixed costs – far lower than those of public TV, which in the new century already employed between 1,500 and 3,000 people. That number varied from country to country: in Hungary it reached 1,600; in Romania, more than two thousand; in Poland it reached 4,600; in Germany, it amounted to 25,000 (that number includes the ARD and ZDF workforce). The expansion of the market stimulated the training of new professionals. For example, in Romania, there were 2,060 registered journalists in 1989; 6,909 in 1992; and by 2000 there were estimated to be more than 20,000 registered journalists in the country – an increase of about 870% in the span of a decade. On one hand, the supply of new jobs in countries with shaky economies is encouraging, yet on the other, the rapid and dizzying growth in the number of professionals has led to debates on inadequate training without any stable and precise mechanisms to punish errors of conduct (OPEN SOCIETY INSTITUTE, 2005; COMAN, 2009; BRIKŠE, 2010).

There were also loopholes in regulatory systems, which then raised questions about who was actually in control of important media. For example, a lot of debate was generated around the New Bulgarian Media Group in the first decade of the new millenium and its acquisition of a number of media outlets, including, as of 2011, a TV channel, five national newspapers, one weekly, and two regional newspapers. In fact, in 2010, the Union of Publishers in Bulgaria accused the group of being in practice financed by the state since its capital was provided through bank loans by the Corporate Commercial Bank, in which 48% of the funds of Bulgarian state-owned companies were kept. Earlier, the German group WAZ had acquired various mediums. The Bulgarian antitrust agency did not see any risk of a monopoly here, but even so, the group chose to sell its operations and leave the country. Small radio stations were eventually bought by large groups. In Poland, Hungary, and Croatia, the media market evolved to the level of a duopoly. In Croatia, it was estimated that EPH and Styria controlled about 80% of the market despite legal restrictions on concentration. One of these restrictions was that a company could not purchase new media if that purchase would result in a concentration of more than than 40% of the newspaper market. In Slovenia, the supposed invasion of large foreign media companies (perhaps due to the size of the country and its potential market) did not happen in the 1990s. The first private broadcaster in old Yugoslavia, Channel A, was constituted in 1989, but only started transmitting two years later. It was controlled by 150 shareholders. Delo, one of the country's leading newspapers, stopped its employee management system and started to sell its shares on the stock exchange. This led to a decrease in the number of smallholders and the state was unable to immediately check the new corporate structure. Small radio stations were largely family-run businesses, and since each relative was treated as an individual, it was difficult to characterize violations of cross-ownership restrictions. In the Balkans, however, media owners also controlled companies outside the countries, making it difficult to monitor the corporate chain of the entire economic group. In Serbia, in 2004, information on which mediums were still controlled by the state was not made public. In the same year, economic data on the media sector in Albania were not disclosed - it is worth remembering that information on those who controlled companies with broadcasting licenses began to be systematically disclosed at this same time in Brazil (SPLICHAL, 1995; HRVATIN, MILOSAVLJEVIC, 2003; HRVATIN, PETKOVIC, 2004; LOZA-NOV, 2011; KREŠIC, 2012).

Not everything was so mysterious in the new Central and Eastern European private media landscape – the close relationship between politics and communication was, for example, much more explicit. There are some cases of successful entrepreneurs in the field of communications who took up politics, and vice-versa. Pavol Rusko, one of the owners of Markíza, became Minister of Finance of Slovakia. Dan Voiculescu, founder and owner of a controlling group for several TV and radio grants, has been elected Senator in Romania three times. Dan Diaconescu ran for president. Dinu Patriciu was elected deputy. Several other politicians and businessmen in Romania have become mayors, presidents of legislative assemblies and city councils, among other positions. Lastly, the political parties in some countries, such as Yugoslavia, controlled broadcasters. In Slovenia, between 1990 and 1994, the rules on self-management in TV stations began to be abolished and the three main ones were controlled by political parties (SPLICHAL, 1995; GROSS, 2008; ŠKOLKAY, 2008; COMAN, 2009). When analyzing this scenario, Splichal (2001) concluded:

"In almost all former socialist countries, broadcasting laws brought an end to state monopoly and the beginning of private enterprise. However, the end of monopoly alone is not equivalent to media diversity and democratization of the communication sphere. The ruling coalitions and opposition parties, as well as other political actors such as the Catholic Church, still seem to see the media (especially public broadcasters) as a corporatist 'democratic' organ of the new 'pluralist' state, that is, they hold the same perspective as the previous authorities. This old and authoritarian conception of politics, practiced for decades in the old socialist regimes, can also be found in other activities such as appointing leaders in educational, cultural and health institutions, or

It cannot be said that the state has not tried to respond to this situation, at least in some countries at some point in time. Despite all the sales, regulatory fragility, legal inaccuracy, and lobbying of private companies already operating in the broadcasting industry even before the rules for the sector had been fully defined, the state in Central and Eastern Europe still played an important role in the communications sector. Even the privatization of the telecommunications sector continued to transmit signals from all public and private broadcasters – it is worth remembering that, in several European countries, the transmission of TV signals is handled by a single company, one which is contracted by all broadcasters. In addition, the state had a monopoly on postal services, which is important for the written press, and had significant advertising funds.

In some countries (like Germany) the state exercised greater discretion in who could buy its assets. The model adopted in Slovenia was different: there was the possibility of "internal" privatization, subject to specific legislation. In short, the company announced it wanted to be "controlled by society" and submitted its privatization plan to the regulatory agency. This process might have involved methods like allocating shares to three state funds, distributing local shares, purchasing employee shares, and more. The shares represented the difference between a company's assets and its liabilities. One of the state funds used was the Development Fund, which re-sold shares at a 25 percent discount to employees – it was expected that at least one-third of all employees would buy shares. The fund itself could later sell the unsold shares to other buyers (HRVATIN, MILOSAVLJEVIC, 2003).

In Russia the state played a very distinct role in the communications sector. Even after the media was opened up to private enterprise, the state resumed its leading role. It still continued to own several major broadcasters such as Rossia, Kultura and Vesti-24. Magnates and public or private government-related companies started to take control of other companies. In addition, the state distributed resources directly to broadcasters. Some broadcasters were exempt from certain fees, and investments were made in publishers and newspaper infrastructure. Since 1995, a total of 1,950 publications have received such resources without having very objective criteria. In 2005, widespread aid began to decline and the state announced that it would only grant subsidies to publications aimed at the disabled, the elderly, and the young, as well as provide publications for cultural, educational, literary and artistic purposes, which allowed for discretion. If support policies had no effect on affiliation, other means could be employed such as tax enforcement, fire insurance and sanitation rules; imposing restrictions on access to press conferences; court disputes over possible defamation; purchasing competing media and investing directly in them; investigating the privatization process of a particular newspaper or broadcaster; and filing complaints for violations of anti-terrorism laws. The case of the Media-Most holding company, which acquired the national state-independent broadcaster (NTV) was a popular one. Actions such as imposing extra fees, criminal charges, and police raids on group property ate away at finances and led to transferring the grant to the state-owned company Gazprom (BECKER, 2004; SPARS, 2008; KYRIYA, DEGTEVERA, 2010; VARTANOVA, 2012; VARTA-NOVA, 2015).

And how did public broadcasters react to this competition? One aspect worth reiterating is the expansion of public channels. With the end of the socialist regime, public broadcasters began to launch new programs to reach specific audiences or to focus on certain themes, maintaining the generalist nature of their main programming. Even before digitization – and the range of optimization possibilities it provides – public broadcasters were already betting on new channels. In 2010, TVP in Poland operated three national channels (TVP1, 2 and Info), one focused on migration, one high-definition channel and three satellite channels (culture, history, and sports). The PR, responsible for public radio broadcasters, operated four national channels, Radio Parliament, an overseas broadcaster, and 17 regional stations. The public system in Hungary (in the same year) consisted of two national TV channels (one via satellite), one international satellite station dedicated to migration, three national radio stations, one on local and regional legislative activities, and one channel for ethnic minorities (LENGYEL, 2010; STĘPKA, 2010). In April 2017, TVP broadcast 12 national and 16 regional programs; PR broadcast seven national programs, one international program, and regional programming; and the Hungarian system had seven national and international TV programs and seven radio programs, as well as regional stations.

In Europe, most researchers agree that the key indicator of the performance of public broadcasters is still quantitative; i.e., the verification of market share (percentage of devices tuned in to broadcaster channels). With the exception of a few rare cases, public broadcasters have lost their status as audience leaders in television, but tend to maintain larger audiences in radio.

## Table 9: Market share percentage for public television broadcasters (1995-2015)

| Country | 1995 | 1998 | 2000 | 2003 | 2007 | 2015 |
|---|---|---|---|---|---|---|
| Albania | n.a. | n.a. | n.a. | 17.1[11] | n.a. | n.a. |
| Germany | 40.1 | 42.5 | 43.1 | 44.4 | 44.6 | 44.8 |
| Azerbaijan | n.a. | n.a. | n.a. | n.a. | n.a. | 3.9 |
| Belarus | n.a. | n.a. | n.a. | n.a. | n.a. | 28 |
| Bosnia | n.a. | n.a. | n.a. | 31.8 | 23.7[12] | 5.3 |
| Bulgaria | n.a. | 76 | 66.5 | 24.8 | n.a. | 8.1 |
| Croatia | n.a. | n.a. | 94.3 | 72.9 | n.a. | 28.4 |
| Slovakia | 73.7 | 24.3 | 18.4 | 21.8 | n.a. | 12.7 |
| Slovenia | 61.5 | 32.4 | 32.9 | 34.7 | n.a. | 21.7 |
| Estonia | 28 | 22.4 | 16.6 | 16.7 | 16.4 | 18.4 |
| Georgia | n.a. | n.a. | n.a. | n.a. | n.a. | 4.7 |
| Hungary | 79 | 25.5 | 13.6 | 17.5 | n.a. | 16 |
| Latvia | n.a. | n.a. | 18.2 | 18.4 | 15.3 | 12.4 |
| Lithuania | n.a. | 16.3 | 10.2 | 11.8 | 14.3 | 10.3 |
| Macedonia | n.a. | n.a. | 37.6 | 21.2 | n.a. | 4.5 |
| Moldova | n.a. | n.a. | n.a. | n.a. | n.a. | 6 |
| Poland | 80 | 52.6 | 46.2 | 51.2 | 41.2 | 31.2 |

---

[11] According to data from 2002.
[12] According to data from 2006.

| Country | 1995 | 1998 | 2000 | 2003 | 2007 | 2015 |
| --- | --- | --- | --- | --- | --- | --- |
| Czech Republic | n.a. | 33.3 | 31.2 | 30.2 | n.a. | 30.4 |
| Romania | n.a. | 46.4 | 40.4 | 35 | n.a. | 4.7 |
| Russia | n.a. | n.a. | n.a. | n.a. | n.a. | 20.5 |
| Serbia | n.a. | n.a. | 26.4 | 35.5 | n.a. | 20.8 |
| Ukraine | n.a. | n.a. | n.a. | n.a. | n.a. | 0.8 |

**Sources:** OPEN SOCIETY INSTITUTE, 2005; HOZIC, 2008; D'HAENENS; SOUSA; HULTÉN, 2011; EBU, 2016a.

The numbers in the table represent the total audience numbers for national channels transmitted by public broadcasters. Five years after the end of socialist regimes, the market share of public broadcasters exceeded 60% in some cases. Some countries did not even have functioning broadcasters at the time. In 2000, after new commercial broadcasters had already begun to operate, this percentage (considering the countries listed in Table 9) dropped to 35.4%; in 2007 that percentage dropped again to 25.9%; and in 2015 to 15.9%. That means the market share of broadcasters fell by 55% over the span of 15 years.

The situation in Germany is atypical as its market share for public broadcasting has gradually increased – in Europe, it ranked behind only Iceland, where the market share for broadcasting reaches 55% (EBU, 2016a). Then, according to the data in Table 9, there are countries such as Poland, the Czech Republic, Croatia and Belarus where percentages are high, but are in a steady decline. From 2000 to 2015, Croatia and Poland experienced a drop of almost 66% and 15%, respectively. Slovakia's audiences were increasing at the time of this survey, reaching 16% according to official station data (MIKA, 2017). Slovakia, historically covered by Austrian and Hungarian broadcasters, is one of the countries where foreign channels are watched the most (SKOLKAY, 2017). There is another group of countries which have experienced a much more drastic decrease, and whose public broadcasters do not offer much competition. This is the case in Bosnia, Macedonia and Romania, whose percentages dropped by 83.3%, 78.7% and 86.5% during the period from 2003 to 2015, respectively. In Bosnia and Romania, this decrease was linked to a major crisis with the model which left stations on the verge of bankruptcy (ROMINA, 2017).

The situation is much worse in Brazil. Publicly available audience data is collected differently from European countries. The television network TVE, based in Rio de Janeiro, was quite relevant up until 2007, although there is very little objective data available on its actual audience numbers. In the first half of April 2017, the five highest-rated programs on TV Brasil (successor to TVE) had less than 1% viewership. This continued into the first few months of this year, with the exception of special programs. The samba schools that parade in Carnaval registered 1% viewership. The five most-watched TV Cultura programs during the same period in the state of São Paulo registered 2% or 3%, however, this broadcaster transmits to a much larger audience than other states (IBOPE, 2017).

The Central and Eastern European radio scenario is depicted in the table below:

| Country | 2015 |
|---|---|
| Germany | 55.7 |
| Bulgaria | 19 |
| Croatia | 18.9 |
| Slovakia | 33.1 |
| Slovenia | 24.4 |
| Estonia | 34.1 |
| Hungary | 31.6 |
| Latvia | 37.5 |
| Lithuania | 18.1 |
| Poland | 18.3 |
| Czech Republic | 22.5 |
| Romania | 30.2 |
| Russia | 12.7 |
| Serbia | 7.5 |

**Source:** EBU, 2016b.

We were unable to find a history of radio audience data. Even still, there are a few references we can look at: the public broadcaster in Poland had an audience of 25.2% in 2009, and in Romania it was 36.9% in 2008 (COMAN, 2009; STĘPKA, 2010). It is worth remembering that, due to the larger number of broadcasters, the market share leaders in radio tend to have lower numbers than television. We were also unable to find a history of public information on radio in Brazil.

At the beginning of this chapter, I pointed out an important difference between the formation of the broadcasting sector in Central and Eastern Europe and in Brazil. Commercial broadcasters were newcomers to the Central and Eastern Europe market and competed for audiences with the pre-existing public broadcasters. That is exactly the opposite of what happened in Brazil. Some might say that the new broadcasters in Central and Eastern Europe were much more successful in their mission than the EBC in Brazil was since TV Brasil's new programming was unable to win over the audiences of most of the country's pre-existing broadcasters.

I will state that one of the criteria for assessing the success and relevance of public broadcasting in each country is the objective measurement of market share. It is an important issue, but not the only issue. The structure of public broadcasting and its importance to society are related to aspects that go beyond the total number of viewers and listeners.

**X**

In a study supported by UNESCO, Mendel (2000) agreed with Eric Barendt and the English government (in their assessment of the future of the BBC) in terms of what the essential characteristics of public broadcasting are. These elements are: being available to all of society; having a concern for national identity and culture; having objectiveness in programs; having a variety of programming; and being structured on a funding model based largely on collections from the public. Five years later, in a new publication on the same topic supported by UNESCO, Banerjee and Seneviratne (2005) recognized that there is not a single ideal model of public broadcasting, but did stress that there are a set of characteristics that are central to it, those being universality, diversity (in terms of program genres, audience, and topics discussed), independence, and differentiation from other broadcasters.

It is important to explain these characteristics. The 21st century has seen some of them cross the boundaries of public broadcasters. There are objectives and they are easy to measure. One central example is universalization: every national network – public, private or state – is understood or intended to be universal either by belief in the public service model or by market reasons.

*Being understood* or *intending to be* is obviously not the same as *being universal*. For example, based on the regulatory criteria established by Anatel Resolution No. 581/2012, none of the 16 Brazilian national networks, other than TV Brasil, is or will be effectively universal due to the fact there are isolated communities and indigenous tribes in the country that do not make use of traditional technologies. Even so, for reasons already mentioned, this should not prevent them from trying to extend coverage as much as possible.

A second group of characteristics essential to public broadcasting are programming, directives, and not being dissociated from the private broadcasting system. One example is a concern for national culture. And what exactly is national culture? Moreover, how does one measure this characteristic, in other words, how does one measure if national culture is, in fact, being valued? Since there is no single consensual way to do this, how could one argue that the private system does not value it as well? Considering that this was the first system to assert itself in the country and that television, even today, still has much higher audience levels, can we actually say that this medium has not been concerned with national culture over the decades? And if this concern did not exist, if the medium was detached from national culture, how did it seek to connect with society and how did it take root in the life of the country so deeply? Just as there is no single consensual method of measuring national culture, there is also no way to defend it as being something exclusive to the public system.

Universalization and valorization of national culture are characteristics of the public system, but also of other systems. I understand that the real element of differentiation between the systems is independence from government and the market: it is up to public broadcasters to adopt critical behavior on both, and must therefore be editorially independent. Along these same lines, the Council of Europe states that openness and transparency, editorial independence and autonomy, and leaders being independent from political interference are all principles of public broadcasting that should be maintained (ABASHINA, 2016). Kops (2001) summarized this understanding:

> "Public broadcasting, in its most genuine form, must first be non-governmental, i.e., decisions about tasks, content, organization and funding must be made publicly, and not by governmental political institutions, but by non-governmental public institutions. To this end (...) these institutions must be controlled by politically independent staff, who should be recruited by citizens, who feel responsible for the political, social, and cultural effects of the programs they watch and listen to, and who are therefore able to directly influence these schedules (...). Such political independence and neutrality of public broadcasting are difficult to put into practice, as there is great interest from governments and individual politicians in governing parties to control it" (KOPS, 2001, p. 4).

There is a slight caveat concerning Kops' definition. In a previous article (PECI, PIERANTI, RODRIGUES, 2008), I tried to point out that the opposition between administration and politics was common in earlier theoretical discussions about public administration, but since the 1950s, literature has pointed to the link between them as being parts of an indissoluble whole. Although New Public Management and similar approaches in the last decades of the twentieth century sought to rescue this dichotomy, it is not sustained or justified – at least not in the Brazilian context. More than a decade into writing that article, and unable to explore the idea further (which would have ended up being quite a departure from the objective of this book) I still hold the conviction that administration (or 'technical') and politics are two sides of the same coin.

This does not mean we do not value the need for technical solutions, quite the contrary; it means that technical referrals are sought after more and more in the political scenario. But we also must remember that these same solutions are often built on their agents' political perception of the world. In other words, since they are indissoluble, permeating the policies of technique and recognizing the policy that exists in technique are more efficient as well as sincere and honest approaches. In light of this theoretical comment, we need to understand that the degree of permeability between politics and technique differs depending on the national context. And the level of institutionalization of German public broadcasting, something which Kops has experienced (2001), may help explain his approach.

Broadcasters being independent from governments and the market may seem like a utopian concept – and it is. But it does not mean that it should not be pursued and fought for. This, in fact, is another element that unites the establishment of public broadcasting in Brazil with the process observed in the other countries studied in this book: broadcasters are targets of political pressure everywhere, and the declaration and defense of independence are the only possible ways to resist it. And how is this independence characterized? I understand it to be built from four elements, as shown in the figure below:

**Figure 10. Public broadcasting independence model**

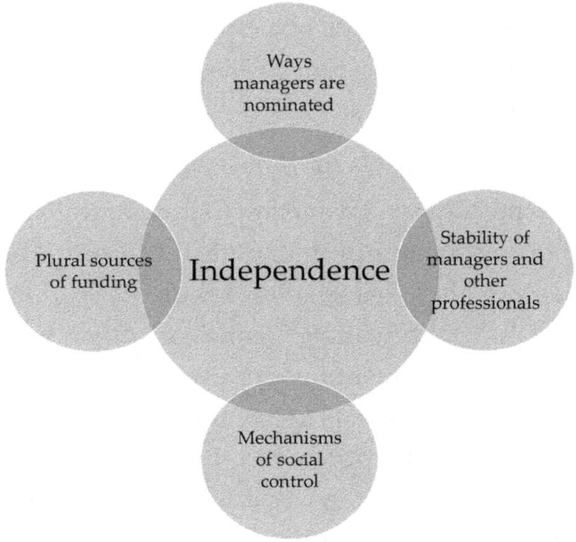

Ways managers are nominated

Plural sources of funding

Independence

Stability of managers and other professionals

Mechanisms of social control

**Source:** Prepared by author.

These four elements need to be examined in theory, as they the analysis in this book is based around them. A side note: these four elements are not part of the broadcast programming, but they ensure its independence. These are what I consider to be structuring elements yet are more linked more directly to broadcaster management.

The first element is the complex form in which managers are appointed. It is complex because it involves the official and legal inclusion of a larger number of actors into the selection process. For example, at the international level, it is common for leaders to be appointed by a Prime Minister (in parliamentary governments), a President, regulatory bodies, or Parliament – often all at the same time. Thus, in theory, public broadcasting managers are no longer chained to a single authority or trend, thereby reducing and sometimes dissolving political influence and pressure.

The second element deals with the stability of managers and important professionals. Managers and professionals who can be dismissed without notice by their critics tend to weaken or even undermine independence. This, of course, should not be confused with the inability to respond to criticism – after all, the manuals ensure that the rights of all parties and different points of view are to be heard (in theory, but not always in practice).

The third element is the mechanisms of social control, being the incorporation of society into the daily routine of public broadcasting and that broadcaster's openness to and awareness of the opinions of its viewers and listeners. These mechanisms can – and should – be extended to all public broadcasting plans: to their programming, by scheduling programs produced by and intended for specific segments; to their structure, by creating deliberative and permanent institutional spaces, occupied mainly by capable representatives of civil society; and to the regulation of the system itself, by regulatory agencies which are fully committed to the legal mission of public broadcasters.

Lastly, the fourth element involves various sources of funding. If the system relies solely or largely on contingent resources from the government – a model adopted in many countries, as we shall see below – then programming tends to yield more to the demands of broadcasting managers. In the best case scenario, managers feel a sense of obligation to try to measure criticism by mitigating budgetary risks; in the worst case scenario, they keep quiet so as not to compromise resources. Expanding the sources of funding reduces the chance of broadcasters being influenced and allows them to continue with their activities, even if one source happens to be temporarily or unexpectedly lost.

These elements are not absolute: there is ample space between their implementation and their absence for affirmation, hesitations, difficulties, disputes, attempts and exceptions. I focused more on the theory in the preceding paragraphs; in the next few sections I shall look at the practical side.

**XI**

Adhering to the four elements of independence for public broadcasting in socialist countries meant new laws had to be passed. There are two key aspects involved in this process. The first aspect is a quick search for international cooperation. East Germany was one of the first to do this, a result of the reunification process in 1990 when it joined the European Economic Community. Other bloc countries would join the community in the following years, ultimately leading to them joining the European Union.

Joining the community was voluntary and dependent on political and economic changes. One of these changes included the incorporation of supranational guidelines and treaties. One of the major directives for this in the field of broadcasting was Directive 89/552/ECC, better known as "Television without Borders", which was adopted by country members of the community in 1989. Afterwards, the directive was changed and renamed "Audiovisual Media Services" has since been revised to incorporate the Internet content. By the early 1990s, it had already been centered on two principles: to ensure the free distribution of European television programs among the associated countries and to provide these programs, wherever possible, with a minimum amount of air time, which could exceed more than half of the total transmission time. It was no coincidence that the directive was renamed "Television without Americans", which came to be the object of formal protests in the U.S., with the House of Representatives labelling it a protectionist and unreasonable restriction on trade (SCOTT, 1992).

National borders were no longer an obstacle to TV stations in countries that adhered to the new forms of European cooperation. Citizens of the old socialist countries were excited about installing antennas and receiving satellite channels, a feeling that was illustrated in the movie "Good Bye Lenin!" The directive allowed for signals from other member countries to be blocked but only in situations where rights violations were an issue. Thus, these new laws, coupled with the technology of the time, led to cultural integration and an increase in the number of viewers and, as a result, the market (SCOTT, 1992; MICHALIS, 2010).

These new open borders were met with resistance by some. Member countries were accused of trying to remove competences in sensitive areas such as safeguards of pluralism and control from European regulation. They won, in part, and they were more freely regulated by each country (MICHALIS, 2010). This preserved the second defining feature after the overthrow of socialist regimes: the rapid openness to private enterprise, notably to foreign groups, which often occurred before new legislation had been enacted and regulatory structures had been established.

A comparison of the specific aspects of public broadcasting legislation in Brazil and in 19 Central and Eastern European countries will be presented in the following pages. Some of these comparisons will be looked at first.

The following table contains only the standards recognized by the European Broadcasting Union (EBU, 2015). The EBU is made up of broadcasters from all over Europe (including some from outside Europe), particularly public ones. In addition to performing the kind of activities expected of representative entities, the EBU also produces and collects a series of studies, statistics and documents on the sector, including a list of existing legislation. Thus, the translated files referenced by the association – usually located on the platforms of national regulatory bodies – went through a double screening process; they were promoted by the countries and accepted by the entity that unites the broadcasters. We chose not to use the original language versions because first, I do not speak most of those languages, and second, because current automated translators are still not accurate or reliable enough. The only exceptions to the list are the laws from Brazil, Slovenia and Estonia: the last two are indicated in the EBU document, but the document's link to the Brazil laws was not working and there was no link to an English version. Since these documents can be found in Portuguese on official local government websites, I chose to use them. Brazilian law is available in the federal government's law archives.

Opting for a safer version of the legislation does present a disadvantage: the document is not always up to date. I tried to make this clear by mentioning the legislation and the year it was last updated. I do not believe this will present much of a problem considering the scope of this work, and since this book discusses the transition from state to public model, it is interesting to understand the process which that entails. In other words, the valid legislation in this phase brings together important elements to the analysis made in this book. In addition, I presented updated information for some of the aspects included in Table 11.

The comparison should not be seen as a finished portrait of each country's regulatory model as part of the subject matter deals with infra-legal rules (not included in the table), the legal provisions mentioned have not always been implemented, and real-world procedures are not always supported by legislation. The comparative should be seen as the will of the Legislator, who, in turn, is influenced by the social and political agreement on the debate about the possible rules for public broadcasting.

Another problem to be faced concerns the nomenclature used in the English versions of the laws. The term *"Board"*, for example, may refer to an entity's supervisory board, board of administrators or board of directors. I analyzed the competences of the organs in these specific cases and, in order to facilitate the reader's understanding, I standardized the nomenclature of the different organs and instances according to their attributions. I chose to standardize the terms "regulatory body", "Board of Administrators" (BA, supervisor of management activities), "Board of Directors", "CEO", "Managing Director" (MD), and "Fiscal Council" (FC, with competences including monitoring the financial activities of public broadcasters). Obviously, these expressions were adopted not only based on the translated nomenclature for each country, but on the competences attributed to each of the mentioned instances.

Lastly, I would like to point out that the categories of analysis in the table seek to highlight the central elements to building independence, already illustrated in Figure 10. The analysis on the following pages is centered on the categories of social participation, managers' terms of office, funding sources, and others.

Table 11: Comparative analysis of legal framework regarding PSB

|  | Albania | Armenia |
|---|---|---|
| Referred legislation | Audiovisual Law - Law nº 97 of 2013 | TV and Radio Law of 2000, alterations up to 2015 |
| Supervision | n.a. | Board of Trustees reports to the president of the republic, who can forward on his decisions, if necessary, to the Legislative Power as a new bill. |
| Appointing managers | Parliament elects Board of Trustee members, who in turn hold a secret ballot vote to elect the CEO; the candidate with 2 out of 3 board member votes is elected as CEO. The CEO suggests management, which is elected by at least 10 Board of Trustee members by secret ballot. | President of the Republic appoints 5 Board of Trustee members, who in turn appoint CEOs for the two broadcasters (radio and TV) and approves managers appointed by both CEOs. |
| Leader mandates | The Board of Trustees and the CEO both have 5-year mandates. Parliament can dismiss Board of Trustee members before their mandates are up based on legal scenarios which are not always exact. The CEO can be dismissed early on two-thirds of Board of Trustee votes. Managers have 4-year mandates and can be dismissed early if suggested by the CEO and the Board of Trustees majority. | Board of Trustee members have 6-year mandates and can only be dismissed under special circumstances such as nomination to other position or by law. |
| Other managerial features | Board of Trustee members must have more than 10 years' experience in the field of law; and managers must have a specialization in management, finance or business. Members cannot be managers of political parties, cannot have held a recently elected position or have run for one, cannot be a shareholder or a media company employee, among others. | Board of Trustee members cannot be political party leaders, foreigners, or managers in other broadcasting stations. |
| Social participation bodies | Bodies nominate candidates to the Board of Trustees. Viewer and Listener Council must have 15 of its members elected by the Board of Trustees, broadcaster journalists and at least two-thirds of external representatives, including people with deficiencies. Advisory committee rules must be established in the body's statute. | n.a. |
| Funding | *Licence fee*, public budget, advertising, service provision and content licencing, among others. | Commercial advertising (total time may not exceed 5% of total programming time and advertising cannot be run during programs), content licencing, sponsors, renting program space and other sources provided for by law. |

Source: Prepared by author.

Table 11: Comparative analysis of legal framework regarding PSB

| | Azerbaijan | Bosnia |
|---|---|---|
| **Referred legislation** | Public Service Broadcasting Law of 2004 | Public Service Broadcasting Law nº 78/05, alterations up to 2010 |
| **Supervision** | Law mentions which state authority will legally control the station, questioning its leaders in case of apparent violation of the rules. | Law provides for a single Board of Trustees for all four bodies (a national one, one for the Federation of Bosnia and Herzegovina, one for the Srpska Republic and one called "Corporation" of public service broadcasting, which coordinates the system and centralizes activities like content licensing and advertising sales). The Board of Trustees is made up of 12 members from the three first bodies and monitors the Corporation's activities. |
| **Appointing managers** | "Appropriated" public organ chooses 9 Board of Trustee members. The CEO is elected by votes from at least 6 board members. The CEO appoints 5 managers. | Board of Trustees appoints CEO of the Corporation. Gender equality is respected in appointments. |
| **Leader mandates** | Board of Trustee members have mandates of 2, 4 and 6 years. They can be dismissed early on legal grounds and the approval of 6 Board of Trustee members. The CEO has a 4-year mandate. Managers have 4-year mandates and can be dismissed by the Board of Trustees. | The CEO of the Corporation has a 5-year mandate and can be dismissed by the Board of Trustees. |
| **Other managerial features** | Board of Trustee managers cannot belong to political parties, work in public organs or broadcasting stations. Managers must be specialists in production, administration or finance. | The CEO of the Corporation cannot hold another public position, own a media company or be a shareholder in one. |
| **Social participation bodies** | NGOs, civic associations, unions and universities, among others, nominate candidates to the Board of Trustees. | n.a. |
| **Funding** | *Licence fee*, which must be the principal source of revenue, renting programming space, advertising (only between programs, with the exception of very long programs or programs with mandatory breaks, like sports programs), sponsors, other resources provided for under law. *Licence fee* must be provided in public budget for funding activities. | Advertising, content licencing, licence fee. A percentage of advertising must be split 25-25% (for subnational stations) and 50% (for national stations). |

Source: Prepared by author.

Table 11: Comparative analysis of legal framework regarding PSB

|  | Bulgaria | Croatia |
|---|---|---|
| Referred legislation | Radio and Television Law of 1998, alterations up to 2011 | Law nº 28 of 2001 |
| Supervision | n.a. | The CEO can suspend management decisions and inform the government of any possible breach of the law. |
| Appointing managers | The CEO appoints 5 Board of Trustee members for each public company (radio and TV). These board members must be approved by the regulatory body. | Management is appointed by parliament. The CEO is appointed by management, and agreed on by the council of civil society representatives. |
| Leader mandates | Board of Trustees and the CEO have 3-year mandates, which can be extended. | Management has 4-year mandates and can be dismissed at any time for a number of reasons, one being parliament decision. |
| Other managerial features | Board of Trustee members must be graduates and have professional experience in public service broadcasting or in cultural activities, among others. The CEO must have a minimum of 5 years' professional experience with a radio or TV broadcaster. | Management is composed of one employee representative and six specialists in the fields of economy, finance, law, culture and media. They cannot be members of a public administration or perform activities for political parties or competing companies. The CEO must have 5 years' experience speaking English or another universal language, must be Croatian, and must have a university degree. |
| Social participation bodies | n.a. | Board made up of 25 members appointed by acting bodies, most of which are civil society. Assesses programming and participates in appointments and dismissals. Has a say on who will be appointed CEO. |
| Funding | Resources from TV and radio fund, comprised of *licence fee*, public budget, advertising and sponsors, among others. | Advertising (maximum 9 minutes per hour between programs), *licence fee* (1,5% of the country's average salary from previous year) and public budget. |

Source: Prepared by author.

Table 11: Comparative analysis of legal framework regarding PSB

| | Czech Republic | Estonia |
|---|---|---|
| Referred legislation | Public Service Broadcasting Law of 1991, alterations up to 2005 | Law nº 88 of 2007, alterations up to 2014 |
| Supervision | Regulatory body appoints 5 supervisory board members, each with four-year mandates. | Board of Trustees carries out monitoring activities. The Law provides for internal auditing. Monitoring is completed by other public organs. |
| Appointing managers | Regulatory body appoints and dismisses the CEO and regional studio managers. | Parliament must nominate a representative for each bench and four public service broadcasting specialists to the Board of Trustees, who in turn nominates a CEO, who must have two-thirds of the council votes. Management is composed of five members, appointed by the Board of Trustees based on CEO proposals. |
| Leader mandates | The CEO has a 6-year mandate. | Specialist members of the Board of Trustees have 5-year mandates. They can be dismissed by parliament. Management has 5-year mandates and can be dismissed by the Board of Trustees for a number of reasons, including serious management mistakes and legal infractions. The CEO can be dismissed on the approval of two-thirds of the Board of Trustees. |
| Other managerial features | The CEO must be legally capable, reside in the country and have no criminal record. | Board of Trustee members cannot be broadcasting managers, members of government or affiliated with media companies. Most of these prerequisites apply to management positions. The same occurs if a family member is an employee or a broadcasting partner. Similar situations in the 5 years prior must be reported in writing. |
| Social participation bodies | Board has 15 members elected and dismissed by the Chamber of Deputies, nominated by cultural, regional, and social organizations. Mandates are for 6 years and are nonconcurrent. They cannot be political party leaders, elected politicians or public servants. | Advisory board is made up of 9 to 15 members appointed by management for a term of 5 years. Its members must be representative of the different segments of society. |
| Funding | *Licence fee* and commercial activities, among others. | Public budget, others. Broadcasters are prohibited from broadcasting advertising or infomercials, unless related to events promoted by the EBU or large sporting events. |

Source: Prepared by author.

Table 11: Comparative analysis of legal framework regarding PSB

|  | Georgia | Hungary |
| --- | --- | --- |
| **Referred legislation** | Broadcasting Law of 2004, alterations up to 2013 | Media Law, implemented in 2015 |
| **Supervision** | Provides annual external audit recognized internationally. Parliament is the regulatory body that assesses annual report. | Public Foundation controls the public company responsible for the PSB. Foundation management (also referred to here as Board of Trustees) monitors. Additionally, this law provides for an auditor and a Fiscal Board of 5 members responsible for economic-financial monitoring. |
| **Appointing managers** | Board of Trustees is composed of 9 members, elected by parliament, which must include public defenders (2), parliamentary majority (3), parliamentary minority appointed by at least 25% of parliamentarians (3), and the Supreme Council of the Autonomous Republic of Adjara. One-third of the Board of Trustees is changed every 2 years. The CEO is nominated by the Board of Trustees after public competition. | 6 Board of Trustee members are nominated by parliament, half by the ruling government and half by the opposition. The company's CEO responsible for broadcasters is selected by the Board of Trustees, based on two-thirds of the votes for the list of names sent by the regulatory body. |
| **Leader mandates** | Board of Trustee members have 6-year mandates and can be dismissed early without cause based on conflicts of interest, on failure to perform duties for a period of 2 months, and others. The CEO has a 6-year mandate and can be dismissed for similar reasons, or if the Board of Trustees deem him/her incapable of performing duties, a process which must be approved by two-thirds of Board of Trustee members, the end result determined by simple majority. | If the annual report is rejected, the board of civil society representatives can submit a proposal to dismiss the CEO to the Board of Trustees, which needs two-thirds of board member votes to go through. |
| **Other managerial features** | Board of Trustee members must hold a Master's degree, and have a minimum of 10 years' experience in public service broadcasting. Prerequisites for the CEO are the same, including 3 years' prior experience in management. They cannot be affiliated to political parties, members of public administration, or partners with or employees of other broadcasting stations. | Board of Trustee members cannot be hired by the foundation, nor by the company that manages the PSB for a period of one year after their mandates. The CEO must be Hungarian, have a university degree, and a minimum of 5 years' professional experience in media. Furthermore, the CEO cannot have held public office or been a political party leader in the two years preceding his/her election. |
| **Social participation bodies** | Law provides for public councils which can make recommendations to the broadcaster. Its creation, activities and functions depend on the broadcaster's statute. | Company board responsible for broadcasters is made up of 14 members, elected by civil society organizations. President is selected from the 14 members. |
| **Funding** | *Licence fee* and public budget. Advertising is only allowed if related to sponsored international events or sporting events. | Broadcasters are run on fund which receives public resources, among others. In addition, the law provides for a fund to run public broadcasters whose resources come from commercial broadcasting grants, fees, bidding, state resources, and others. |

Source: Prepared by author.

Table 11: Comparative analysis of legal framework regarding PSB

| | Latvia | Lithuania |
| --- | --- | --- |
| **Referred legislation** | Law nº 118 (4310) of 2010, alterations up to 2014 | Law nº I-1418 of 1996, alterations up to 2010; Law nº I-1571 of 1996 |
| **Supervision** | Regulatory body for monitoring public service broadcasting. | n.a. |
| **Appointing managers** | Each public media is managed by a board of directors, appointed by the regulator according to public competition. | Board of Trustees is appointed by parliament. The president of the Board of Trustees is chosen by the board itself. The CEO is appointed by the Board of Trustees based on public competition. |
| **Leader mandates** | n.a. | Board of Trustee members can only be dismissed on legal grounds. The CEO has a 3-year mandate and can be dismissed, by the Board of Trustees, on the approval of 8 of its members. |
| **Other managerial features** | Members of management must have a university degree and a minimum of 5 years' experience in broadcasting or management. They cannot belong to political parties or have stocks in communication media. | Board of Trustee members cannot be parliamentarians, members of government or private broadcaster shareholders. The CEO and other managers must cease their political activities, if they have any. |
| **Social participation bodies** | Advisory board is affiliated with regulatory body and other competences. It outlines guidelines for public broadcasters. The board is made up of civil society representatives. | n.a. |
| **Funding** | Public budget, revenue from its economic activities, donations. | Advertising (restrictions on products and type of content). |

Source: Prepared by author.

Table 11: Comparative analysis of legal framework regarding PSB

| | Macedonia | Montenegro |
|---|---|---|
| **Referred legislation** | Media Law and Audiovisual Law, both implemented in 2013 with alterations up to 2014 | Lawnº 79/2008,alterations up to 2012 |
| **Supervision** | Fiscal Board made up of 7 members. Responsible for monitoring the organ's finances. | n.a. |
| **Appointing managers** | Programming Council is appointed by parliament. Programming Council nominates Fiscal Board and PSB board of directors after public selection process. | Parliament appoints the Board of Trustees, who in turn appoint the CEO. The CEO appoints the director of TV and Radio. |
| **Leader mandates** | Programming Council members and Fiscal Board members have 5-year mandates. The CEO and his assistant have 3-year mandates. They can be dismissed early on legal grounds. | Board members have 5-year mandates. Parliament can dismiss them early on legal grounds. The CEO and radio and TV managers have 4-year mandates and can be dismissed early on non-compliance with PSB norms or in cases of negligence or misconduct. |
| **Other managerial features** | Programming Council members must have a university degree, cannot be parliamentarians, members of government, and cannot have held public office or been political or religious leaders within the last 5 years. Fiscal Board members must have a university degree and 5 years' experience in financing. Current Programming Council member restrictions apply to them as well. The CEO and his/her assistant must have a university degree, including 5 years' experience in communication, broadcasting, culture, law, among others. | Board members must have a university degree and be specialists in one of the PSB areas of activity. They cannot be political party leaders, hold an elected position, be shareholders of media companies, among others. The CEO and radio and TV managers must have a university degree and a minimum of 5 years' professional experience. |
| **Social participation bodies** | Programming Council is made up of 13 members, nominated by civil society bodies. | Civil society bodies nominate the 9 members of Council. |
| **Funding** | Advertising (outside of prime time hours, no more than 8 minutes per hour between programs and, in the case of sports and entertainment, between blocks), *licence fee*, public budget and donations. | 1,2% of the country's total public budget, advertising, production and content licencing, among others. |

Source: Prepared by author.

**Table 11: Comparative analysis of legal framework regarding PSB**

| | Poland | Romania |
|---|---|---|
| **Referred legislation** | Broadcasting Law of 1992, alterations up to 2012; *Licence Fee* Law of 2005, alterations up to 2012. | Law nº 41 of 1994, alterations up to 1998 |
| **Supervision** | Supervisory bodies are made up of 7 members appointed by the regulatory body (5) and the Ministries of Culture and Finance. | Parliament monitors broadcaster activities, able to fire Board of Trustee members. |
| **Appointing managers** | Regulatory body appoints Board of Trustee members (from one to three) according to selection process outlined in regulation. | All 13 Board of Trustee members are elected by deputies and senators, 8 representing parliament, one representing the president, one representing the prime minister, one representing employees and one representing parliamentary minority. The President of the Board of Trustees is the CEO, who works with an executive committee of 7 members. |
| **Leader mandates** | Board of Trustee members have 4-year mandates. | Board of Trustee members have 4-year mandates. They can be dismissed by parliament. |
| **Other managerial features** | Managers must have experience in communication management. Selection process is carried out by regulatory body. | n.a. |
| **Social participation bodies** | Programming Councils are established by a regulatory body of 15 members: 10 government representatives and 5 with experience in culture and mass communication. Mandates are 4 years. | n.a. |
| **Funding** | *Licence fee*, public budget, program sponsors, advertising and other sources. | Public budget, *licence fee*, own revenue and other sources. |

Source: Prepared by author.

Table 11: Comparative analysis of legal framework regarding PSB

| | Serbia | Slovakia |
|---|---|---|
| **Referred legislation** | Public Service Broadcasting Law of 2014 | Law nº 532 of 2010, alterations up to 2012 |
| **Supervision** | Monitoring is responsibility of the Ministry responsible for the PSB. | Appoints a specific Fiscal Board, responsible for monitoring the organ's finances. |
| **Appointing managers** | Regulatory Board appoints, based on two-thirds of the votes, the 9 Board of Trustee members according to public selection process. The Board of Trustees appoints and dismisses the CEO on two-thirds of the votes. | Regulatory body elects 9 Fiscal Board members. The CEO must apply to regulatory body for the position and appoint one manager for TV and another for radio. |
| **Leader mandates** | Board of Trustee members can be dismissed on legal grounds, on the approval of two-thirds of Regulatory Body votes. The CEO has a 5-year mandate and can be dismissed early on non-compliance of norms. | Fiscal Board members have 6-year non-concurrent mandates. They can be dismissed by the regulatory body under special circumstances. The CEO has a 5-year mandate and can be dismissed by the regulatory body, including on grounds of mistrust by the Fiscal Board. |
| **Other managerial features** | Board of Trustee members must be specialists in PSB areas and cannot hold a position with an elected mandate, be a political party leader or media company employee. The same conditions apply to the CEO (with the exception of being a media employee). The CEO must have a university degree and a minimum of 10 years' experience in management. | Fiscal Board members must hold Master's degrees, have at least 5 years' experience and 3 years' experience in management. The CEO must have 5 years' experience in management and hold a Master's degree. Appointment of the CEO is preceded by a public audience. |
| **Social participation bodies** | Programming Council is consultive in nature. It is made up of 15 members elected by the Board of Trustees. Mandates are for 4 years. Most members are civil society representatives. | Civil society bodies nominate Fiscal Board candidates. Nomination process is preceded by announcing on communication media. |
| **Funding** | Advertising, *licence fee* and public budget, among others. | *Licence fee*, public budget and advertising,  others. |

Source: Prepared by author.

Table 11: Comparative analysis of legal framework regarding PSB

| | Slovenia | Brazil |
| --- | --- | --- |
| **Referred legislation** | Law nº 96 of 2005 | Law nº 11.652 of 2008, changed by Provisionary Measure nº 744 of 2016, converted into Law nº 13.417 of 2017. |
| **Supervision** | Fiscal Board of 11 members; 5 appointed by parliament, 4 by government and 2 by employees. | Performed by a Board of Trustees composed mostly of ministry-appointed representatives. The Fiscal Board, composed of 3 members appointed by the President, monitors the EBC's financial activities. |
| **Appointing managers** | The CEO is appointed by the Programming Council after public selection process. The CEO appoints directors for radio and TV after public competition, with approval from the Programming Council. Employees are able to appoint a different editor-in-chief if they do not agree with previously appointed radio and TV directors. The CEO, together with the Programming Council, has the final choice. | Up until 2016, the chief executive officer and the CEO were appointed by the president. The provisionary measure of 2016 reduced the number of directors and required the president to appoint the chief executive officer, the CEO, and 4 directors. |
| **Leader mandates** | CEO has 4-year mandate. | Up until 2016, the chief executive officer's mandate was for 4 years. Any director could be dismissed if received 2 votes of non-confidence from the Board of Trustees within the span of 12 months. The provisionary measure of 2016 removed fixed mandates for directors, who can be dismissed at any time by the president. |
| **Other managerial features** | Programming Council members cannot be, nor have been in the 5 years prior to their election, managers of political parties, a politician with a mandate, a media company employee, among others. The CEO must be Slovenian, have a university degree and have experience in broadcasting, among others. Fiscal Board members must have a university degree and 5 years' experience. | The Law of 2008 did not establish prerequisites for directors. Law no 13.303 provides general prerequisites for public companies, such as a minimum of 10 years' professional experience and a minimum time period holding a management position. |
| **Social participation bodies** | Supreme body is the Programming Council, which monitors programming and is made up of 29 members, some of which are civil society representatives and others are appointed by parliament. A programming committee made up of civil society is to be created. | Up until 2016, the Board of Trustees was mostly composed of civil society, appointed by the president. This year's provisionary measure removed the board and created an Editorial Committee and a Programming Committee, with fewer attributes. This body started operations in 2017. |
| **Funding** | *Licence fee*, public budget, advertising and service provision. | Contributions to Public Service Broadcasting Development, public budget, institutional advertising, service provision, and others. |

Source: Prepared by author.

# XII

There are a few general characteristics which should be emphasized when comparing legislations. Many of them allow public broadcasters to transmit different programs. For example, in Albania, a country with a population of less than 2.9 million, the law provides for at least two national TV programs, two radio programs, one foreign language radio program, one diaspora radio program, regional channels, one satellite program and one which offers live coverage of Parliament. In Macedonia, whose population barely exceeds the 2 million mark, the law provides for one TV channel and two radio channels in Macedonian, and one TV channel and one radio channel in languages spoken by at least 20% of citizens. There are other stipulations, such as a legislative channel and a radio and TV channel for immigrants. It is worth remembering that it is common in a number of Central and Eastern European countries, regardless of the legal provisions, to transmit a larger number of programs from public broadcasters. In Brazil, where legislation also does not guarantee for a minimum of programs to be transmitted, the variety of programs is considerable, but it is not comparable, in quantitative terms, to these aforementioned nations. In 2017, the EBC was responsible for one TV channel (TV Brasil), one international channel (TV Brasil Internacional) and eight radio programs, as well as producing the federal government news channel, the NBr. The EBC relayed the signals from NBr, Canal Saúde and TV Escola to Sao Paulo, Rio de Janeiro and Brasilia (Canal Saúde and TV Escola were not produced by the EBC). The company also ran two news agencies.

In some cases, the legislation is also designed to safeguard the differences of each national context. In Bosnia, there are three different public broadcasters: two entity broadcasters, one in the Federation of Bosnia and Herzegovina and the other in the Republic of Srpska. The third one is a countrywide public broadcaster. There is an entity called "Corporation" which operates the transmissions for the three public service broadcasters and focuses on specific activities such as selling advertising space. In Georgia, the law provides the Autonomous Republic of Adjarawill with its own public broadcaster. Programs are also to be produced in four of its official languages, including Abkhaz and Ossetian. In Serbia, the law provides for two entities, one for Serbia and one for the autonomous province of Vojvodina, each of which must broadcast at least two TV channels and three radio channels. Some of these legal frameworks reflect a concern over dialoguing with territories from the old separatist struggle. The self-declared sovereign state of Abkhazia in northwestern Georgia is one case in point.

One point that stands out in terms of regulation are the laws concerning regulatory structures for an entity which has a range of managerial responsibilities: new grants are mostly subject to these authorities and – key to the issue discussed here – some of them have gained specific competencies in relation to public broadcasting. To put it another way, some of the new legal frameworks focus on protecting structures that adhere to the activities of public broadcasters, thereby guaranteeing that they are, in fact, preserving characteristics inherent to this model.

A brief return to the discussion on policy vs. technical is interesting here: are regulatory agencies, totally independent of government, able to fully perform their technical activities in relation to public broadcasting? In theory, the answer is no, but if the adverbs (totally, fully) are removed from the question, the answer might be different. Although not totally independent of governments, the rules applicable to regulatory agencies usually provide a reasonable degree of autonomy. Moreover, less political influence in decision-making is seen as a positive, as we shall see below.

Another important aspect highlighted by researchers concerns the regulatory agencies in the sector: would they be stricter with public broadcasting or private broadcasting? There is another underlying question here, one that is common in debates on Regulatory Theory and that concerns private agents acquiring public ones. According to Marinescu (1995), public broadcasters in the Romanian model were more regulated than private ones, perhaps because they were regulated by political agents which had an interest in them. Jakubowicz (1998/1999) notes that the regulatory bodies in countries such as Lithuania, Macedonia, Slovakia, Slovenia and Ukraine (apart from Romania) did not even have the competence to deal with public broadcasting. This demonstrates the fragility of the public system in these countries which, Jakubowicz believes, would still be flying the flag of state broadcasting.

The efficiency of regulation is also put in check. Splichal (2001) pointed out that violations were common in the Balkans for political reasons or because of a lack of staff and the technical means to ensure compliance with the law. In Bosnia and Herzegovina, communications were regulated through the support of the international community, a situation that was repeated in other economic sectors of the country's complex reconstruction process after the war in the 1990s. Hrvatin and Petkovic (2004) point out that the CRA/RAK regulatory agency was influenced by the local political elite and could not provide efficient action. These authors' criticisms extended to other organs in the region, such as Albania, Macedonia, Serbia and Croatia, accusing them of being too passive with broadcasters. Criticisms against regulatory efficiency can also be found on an international level: the European Commission has called for more transparency and accountability in public broadcasting funding in Central and Eastern Europe (DRAGOMIR, 2010).

Some of the criticism towards regulation goes much deeper, as it operates according to the legislation passed in each country. Part of the problem lies in the broadcasting laws. It should be noted that the previous table only listed the laws regarding public broadcasting; the criticisms, however, cover the sector's entire regulatory framework.

Several authors were concerned about the delay in promulgating the new law in the 1990s, and its amendment in the following years. The Hungarian Radio and Television Broadcasting Act came into force in 1996 after years of debate in Parliament. Two commercial TV channels were established the following year (LENGYEL, 2010). Bulgarian legislation also dates back to 1996, but several aspects of it were declared unconstitutional. A new law was passed in 1998. Up until that time, only rules for grants existed. In 2010, the possibility of taking rules that apply only to print and broadcasting and extending them to the Internet was discussed, such as prohibiting the publication of anonymous material, guaranteeing the right of reply, and having penalties for anyone who defames electoral candidates, just to name a few. The amendment was not approved at that time (TSCHOLAKOV, 2000; LOZANOV, 2011).

Part of the legislation was incomplete in some cases. In the first decade of the new century, Romania's constitution provided for freedom of the press, with some of its rules were extended to the law on audiovisual, the law on public broadcasting, and the Penal Code, but not to press law, as it had not yet been promulgated (COMAN, 2009). At the same time in Russia, legislation had been unable to provide natural values for public broadcasting, despite attempts at drafting a number of new laws for the sector (VARTANOVA, 2012; 2015). Lastly, there were some cases where principles and rules might have been present, but they lacked enforcement, which led to them being legally ineffective (HRVATIN; PETKOVIC, 2004).

It is true that new broadcasting laws were enacted much faster in other countries. It is also true that, when compared to the legislative process in Brazil, these "delays" are not much of a hindrance. One only need to look at radio in Brazil, which started operating in the 1920s, although the first official law (the Telecommunications Code of Brazil) came into effect in 1962. Before this law, the sector was regulated by decrees. After so many years, governments and new law proposals, the code remains in effect, although it has gone through some amendments. There is also the Federal Constitution of 1988, which mentioned the public system, but only enacted it in 2007. Change in Eastern and Central Europe was quick and intense at that time, and a wait of six or eight years seemed too long. Jakubowicz (1998/1999) concluded that there was no real consensus among the political class, media and general public in that region on what the role of media was, which led to confusion, a failure to operate and a general dissatisfaction.

Another frequent consideration was the amount of national content in programs. Even though Central and Eastern Europe was opening up to Western European practices, there is a resistance to and fear of cultural substitution present in the texts of many authors. Admittedly, the decision to join the European Union meant adhering to the principles of internationalization contained in the abovementioned directives. Because of their geographical characteristics, many people in socialist countries were accustomed to watching programs from their capitalist neighbors. This was the case in northern Yugoslavia, where watching Italian and Austrian channels were commonplace (OPEN SOCIETY INSTITUTE, 2005), and in East Germany and parts of Czechoslovakia, where they were already accustomed to broadcasts from West Germany. The broadcaster in Slovenia (located in the far northwest of former Yugoslavia) even transmitted news from RAI Italia, the national public broadcasting company of Italy. When France Perovšek, considered the father of Slovenian TV and director of RTV Ljubljana at the time, was criticized by Yugoslav authorities for broadcasting foreign content. He responded by saying that Yugoslav viewers had enough common sense to receive foreign information, and they also had the right to be informed – and a system which was unwilling to respect this did not deserve to exist (PUSNIK, STARC, 2008).

Transmitting foreign content really appeared to be the only option for broadcasters in countries who produced very little themselves but wanted to increase the number of programs, as Romania did in the early 1990s. Foreign content was in demand in Romania and thus gained prominence among its population.

Legislation and directives varied in terms of how to deal with a possible "foreign invasion", even for countries that joined the European Union. Some legislations, such as in the Czech Republic and Slovakia, required that a significant percentage of their programs reflect their cultural identities. Other legislations, such as those enacted in Poland, Romania and Hungary, set broadcasting quotas for public broadcasters, where 30 to 50 percent of their programs must be nationally produced (MUNGIU-PIPPIDI, 2003). There were also laws that set broadcasting quotas for public broadcasters where a certain percentage of content had to be independently produced, as in the case of Georgia, where this percentage was 25% (ABASHINA, 2016).

There were also the challenges of economic regulations. Splichal (1995) and Hrvatin and Milosavljevic (2003) made interesting analyzes of the 1994 mass communication law of Slovenia, a country formed after the break up of former Yugoslavia and was therefore accustomed to practicing self-management. The public broadcaster had its own managing body and was not subordinate to the regulatory agency operating in the broadcasting sector. New private broadcasters had to fit into a system which now had rules for hiring professionals, for dismissing the editor-in-chief (by recommendation from the editorial board, which is made up of journalists' editors and delegates), and for restrictions on cross ownership. For example, the law prevented daily newspaper publishers from holding more than 10 percent of shares in another daily newspaper publisher or public broadcasting company. Non-compliance with this law would result in broadcasters losing their licenses.

Even still, the law was criticized for not preventing the transfer of channels, the sale of grid space, and for not providing parameters of internal pluralism in programming. A new law came into force in 2011 and, once again, rules were put in place to prevent market concentration: a single person or company could not simultaneously control broadcasters and publishers, unless authorized to do so by the Ministry of Culture. However, expectations on how effective these laws would be were not high: Hrvatin and Milosavljevic (2003) believed it would be difficult to maintain the percentages of capital described in the law given the lack of data and the lack of transparency on the real owners of broadcasters.

The situation in Slovenia was unusual. As a rule, states initially chose to interfere less and privatize or disrupt much of their operations in the media sector, even though they ended up adopting a more interventionist policy years later. This was the case, for example, in Russia (VARTANOVA, 2015). This option could be linked to the de-regulation of the sector, to the delay in passing new laws or, as in Serbia, to the encouragement of self-regulation (PERUŠKO, 2014), however fragile its bases may be.

The state had its own time and customs, and it did not always correspond with the frenetic pace of change in Central and Eastern Europe in the 1990s. In general, the dynamics and speed of the market were not ceremonious in relation to the slowness or hesitation of rulers and parliamentarians, or the rearrangement of public broadcasting in that region.

# XIII

What kind of media should each country seek? This was one of the questions asked – and the construction of public broadcasting itself depended on the answer. The issue has generated a long debate.

Two elements seemed to converge toward a natural solution that could simplify the problem for the transitional political forces in Central and Eastern Europe. The first element being that governments and parliamentarians had no experience dealing with the inherent problems of capitalism, and were involved in a number of debates on various areas, the consequences of which were far more evident to society: unemployment, the economic crisis, the lack of basic consumer goods, and the guarantee of political rights. The second element is in reference to the communications landscape of neighboring European countries that were beginning to become partners in the same economic bloc. To integrate this landscape each candidate country had to commit to the pre-defined guidelines. Adherence to this model either by inexperience or by necessity would therefore be the only possible way. Or would it?

This fatalistic concept was partly justifiable, especially in terms of the structuring elements of this process. However, the answer should start with the fact that there was some scope for creativity. Discussions about the future of media in socialist countries gained momentum in the academic environment.

Karol Jakubowicz played an important role in this debate. Every researcher devoted to the broadcaster transitions in Central and Eastern Europe refers to his reflections; it is no stretch to consider him as one of the pioneers in this discussion. While Poland was still under socialist rule, he participated in the first debates on a new law for mass communication. It is worth remembering that the democratic opposition was already advocating the "socialization" of Polish mass communication at round table meetings with the government between February and April 1989. Public broadcasters were established as per the Broadcasting Act of December 1992, one of the longest debated acts in the history of parliament so far (STĘPKA, 2010). A journalist, Jakubowicz worked at state broadcasters as a journalist during the country's socialist era, and pursued an academic career. He held various public positions in sector regulation following the end of socialism, including director of the Polish regulatory body and chairman of the supervisory body of the public television broadcaster, TVP. He is recognized internationally as an expert in the field of public service broadcasting, having worked for the Council of Europe and UNESCO, and others. He received the second highest government award bestowed on Polish civilians. He died in 2013, tributes in his memory are available to this day on the Internet, such as the one made by the European Broadcasting Union.

Some of the works mentioned in this book are from him. In one, Jakubowicz and Sükösd (2008) discuss twelve concepts that marked the evolution of the region's media system in the transition promoted in the 1990s. Among them are three orientations in terms of communication policies. The first, called the "idealist," was based on the concept of democracy that intellectuals and opponents of communism hoped to build. There was a fascination with the Western concepts of 'access', 'participation' and 'social control' of media, as well as the guarantee of rights. The second orientation, recognized as 'mimetic', presupposed the transposition of 'free and democratic' Western models, which often went uncriticized, without much regard given to whether this freedom was so complete. Within a few years this practice led to a growing disappointment in Central and Eastern Europe with these models in view of the shortcomings they presented. They were presented as "free and democratic" when, in fact, the reality may have been different in these countries. Lastly, we have the "atavistic" orientation. Jakubowicz and Sükösd believe that what emerged from post-communism was not civil society, but a political one; the fruit of a system centered on the ruling party. They argued that the political elites wanted to imitate Western Europe, yet at the same time stick to the controlling elements of the previous model. Journalists and public broadcasters should "cooperate" with the government in this system.

They finished by agreeing, at least in part, with the thesis of Daniel Hallin, Paolo Mancini and Slavko Splichal (also references in dealing with public broadcasting) which says that the result of these approaches pointed toward the "Italianization" of the media (prior to the 1992 model) in the countries that had been under socialist rule. In short, this metaphor epitomized a scenario in which political, commercial, and professional interests were intertwined with the dissolution of boundaries between state, market, and civil society. The media was controlled by the state, either directly or through economic subsidies; the media were subordinate to political parties, which were even responsible for editorial choices; the elites of the media and political fields were similar and no precise ethical guidelines were in place (SPLICHAL, 2001). Jakubowicz and Sükösd (2008) concluded: if Spain, Portugal and Italy could not guarantee the independence of their public mediums by that time, it would be unrealistic to expect countries in Central and Eastern Europe to accomplish the same endeavor in less time.

Thus, the trend of imitating the Western European model was real, but it does not paint the whole picture. The media in Central and Eastern Europe became a place where politics and the market merged and were welcomed, despite the fact that formal and official guidelines of the international plan did not provide for it.

And what was the role of public broadcasting in this scenario, as unexpected (at least officially) as it is dynamic? At this point, there were all types of opinions. Broadcasters could specialize their programming, but then focusing on minority and elitist interests hurts the central features of the Western European model, being that public broadcasting has always been generalist and has always spoken to the largest possible audience (BARDOEL, D'HAENENS, 2008). In order to increase audiences, it would be necessary to broaden the discussion of public policies not only to one medium (public broadcasting), but to all of them, and to do so in a unified way (D'HAENENS, SOUSA, HULTÉN,

2011). At the same time, it would be necessary to integrate public broadcasting with public policies and regulations throughout the sector. There were those who advocated for the adoption of single regulatory bodies for the entire sector which would appoint the leaders of the broadcasters (MUNGIU-PIPPIDI, 2003). Also on the agenda were discussions about redesigning the accountability model for public broadcasting in order to make it more up-to-date, and to make it so that the actors involved could reach a consensus on what was expected of these broadcasters, what kinds of services they should provide, what audiences they should reach, and what mechanisms should be in place in order to monitor whether these measures are reached or not (JAKUBOWICZ, 2003). There was even a defense of public broadcasting because of a supposed market failure: if commercial broadcasting offers more popular content, it is up to public broadcasters to ensure that informational, educational and cultural content is not underrepresented (D'HAENENS, SOUSA, HULTÉN, 2011). In Latvia, commercial and public broadcasters transmit such similar content that it has even led to discussions on whether the latter is actually necessary (BRIKŠE, 2010).

Lastly, in the midst of this debate, Jakubowicz (2008) tried to systematize what, in his view, had gone wrong with the transition towards public broadcasting. Broadcaster structures were poorly designed, which made decision-making processes slow. Political control prevailed, highlighted by broadcasting directors being appointed by the government or Parliament. Leadership issues were resolved by managers or directors being replaced, yet done so through political interference, not by voting. There was a lack of financial resources and programming *know-how*. Professionals had to censor themselves as they could not expect their superiors to protect them in the event of clashes of political interest.

The debate was undoubtedly intense. The keen reader will notice that most of the references used in this book were published between the late 1990s and the end of the first decade of the new millenium. The number of publications on the transition in Central and Eastern Europe to public broadcasting has considerably decreased after this period. This reflects, at least in academia, that the debate has slowed over the last few years. This idea was echoed by interviewees for this book and by public broadcasting researchers in Central and Eastern Europe.

Amid the profusion of topics included in public debate in the early 21$^{st}$ century, the main elements of public broadcasting stood strong, at least in terms of the ideal to be pursued. In this context, I highlight the four main elements of the independence model summarized in Figure 10: complexity in appointing leaders; stability of managers and critical professionals; social control; and plural sources of funding.

This stream of ideas that do not always converge, the need for rapid implementation of changes, the search for reference in Western countries, available infrastructure, the growing bourgeoisie, and the imprecise limits of state action were able to produce unique and uncommon solutions. Azerbaijan had chosen a three-way broadcasting model which preserved the state system and added the public one to it. The media in Turkmenistan (a country where a "lifetime" President of the Republic was recognized by Parliament) is still under state control.

Then we also have the unusual Russian model of public broadcasting, presented in an earlier chapter. The initial public offering of Ostankino led to the creation of the ORT ("Public Russian Television"), which operated between 1994 and 2002 as a public broadcaster, yet this concept differed from those employed on the rest of the continent. Its philosophy, obligations, values and funding were different from other public broadcasters. Public bodies and entities held 51% of the shares; the other 49% were transferred to private banks, insurance companies, and to parts of the industry. The station was said to be controlled by Boris Berezovsky, a businessman who owned only 36% of the shares. The ORT supported Yeltsin's re-election and was seen as the country's official television station. Despite the attempts to strengthen public broadcasting in Russia previously mentioned in this book, setbacks were a commonplace up until the creation of the aforementioned OTR in 2013, not to be confused with ORT (VARTANOVA, ZASSOURSKY, 2003; VARTANOVA, 2015).

We shall now evaluate the four elements from Figure 10.

# XIV

The majority opinion is that the heads of public broadcasting companies should be appointed differently than they were prior to the transition. If the Council of Europe allows governments to be involved in appointing the heads of public broadcasters then other actors must also be involved in this process, such as Parliament. In addition, legislation must clearly lay out the rules for appointing and dismissing, as well as leaders' mandates and other obligatory conditions (ŠIMUNJAK, 2016). We can separate the analysis into three aspects: (a) the involvement of different actors in the appointment process; (b) the definition of a fixed term of office; and (c) other requirements for company positions.

It is only logical to assume that the participation of different political bodies, powers and groups tends to lessen the influence on leaders of broadcasting stations, and may prevent them from being subordinate to any one specific actor. Several authors have devoted themselves to studying and researching the appointment process since the socialist regimes came to an end, they also express their approval of the plurality of actors in this process. From the late 1990s to the beginning of the 21$^{st}$ century, these studies showed that, even with broadcasters which were still transitioning to the public broadcasting model, there was concern about adopting a plural model for appointing its directors and managers. Depending on which governing body a particular director works for, his or her appointment might have involved the regulatory body for the sector, the Parliament, the President, the government, civil society, and the broadcasting company's employees. Part or all of these actors have been included in studies conducted over the years by Jakubowicz (1998/1999), who analyzed 13 models from Central and Eastern Europe, and Mungiu-Pippidi (2003), who focused on the situation in Poland, Hungary, Czech Republic, Romania and Bulgaria.

Adopting a complex appointment model was a quicker transition in some countries than in others as the removal of previous governments took longer in countries such as the Soviet Union, Albania and Yugoslavia. For example, the political situation in the countries of former Yugoslavia was defined only in the second half of the 1990s. Splichal (2001) pointed out that these countries continued to use policies from the old socialist regime, such as directly appointing directors and publishers, and the availability of public budgets or government advertising, which could be used to maintain control over broadcasters. At the time Splichal wrote his article, the heads of public broadcasters were appointed by the government (Serbia, Vojvodina, Kosovo, and Croatia) or by the Parliament (Bosnia). As Table 11 illustrates, the way in which heads of public broadcasters were appointed in these countries began to change in the years following the publication of Splichal's article.

The governance of public broadcasters in Central and Eastern Europe, and in Brazil, usually involves at least two individual bodies. A model which is used fairly frequently is one that is comprised of a Board of Directors or an Executive Board and a Chief Executive Officer. An example of this can be seen in Albania, Armenia and Lithuania. In some cases, a fiscal board may be added to this model (as is the case in Slovakia and Brazil) or well-defined supervisory practices may be added, such as the internationally recognized annual external audit provided for under Georgia law. There are other cases where legislation provides for a social participatory body with decision-making powers, which we shall look at in a further chapter.

There is an interesting shift in Slovenia, one that is compatible with the tradition of self-management presented in this book. After going back and forth on the issue of how public broadcasting managers should be appointed (SPLICHAL, 2001; HRVATIN, MILOSAVLJEVIC, 2003), the 2005 law provided that employees could appoint another editor-in-chief if they disagreed with the appointment made by the radio or TV director (who, in turn, was appointed by the CEO). If this did occur, the final decision would be made by the CEO in concert with the Programming Council.

There was a period of five years in Brazil where the regulatory body for the communications sector employed a complex model for appointing managers. From 1962, when Law No. 4,117 was created, to 1967, when the Ministry of Communications was created, the president of the National Telecommunications Council (Contel) had been appointed by the President of the Republic and integrated by the director of the Department of Post and Telegraphs. Also, three members were appointed by the military ministries, one by the Joint Staff of the

Armed Forces, four by the listed ministries, three by the major political parties as represented in the House of Representatives, one from a public company that would operate the National Telecommunications System, and by the CEO for the National Department of Telecommunications.

In terms of public broadcasting, the appointment model established by Law No. 11,652 of 2008 was not as complex as the previously mentioned ones. Up until 2016, it was incumbent upon the President of the Republic to appoint the Chief Executive Officer and the Managing Director of the EBC, and the Board of Directors was responsible for approving the other managers (in practice, these are normally appointed by the Chief Executive Officer). In theory, a greater independence was enjoyed thanks to the mandate and the fact that these leaders could not be dismissed by the President of the Republic. After Provisional Measure N°. 744 of 2016 (which was later passed to become Law No. 13,417 of 2017) the Managing Director, the Chief Executive Officer, and other directors at the EBC were all appointed exclusively by the President of the Republic; the Board of Trustees was thus dissolved. This referral system strengthens the necessary ties between the President of the Republic and EBC directors, subordinating, at least in theory, the direction of the company to the ruling government. In short, out of all the models studied here, the current Brazilian model is the worst in terms of appointing managers. It compromises the independence of these professionals and, consequently, of the broadcasters themselves.

Even though legislation officially guarantees a high level of independence by incorporating different actors into the appointment process, this does not always occur in practice. A good example is Romania. The Audiovisual Law of 1992 set the parameters for private broadcasting grants, for the CNA regulatory body, and for the operation of public stations. It also prohibited political parties, other political groups or public authorities from obtaining grants (COMAN, 2009). However, as previously presented in this book, several of the country's important politicians came from broadcasting stations, or began to control them. The Law of 1994, which regulates the selection process for public broadcasting directors, contained a complex rule for defining the Board of Directors: eight of its representatives are directly chosen by Parliament, one chosen by the President of the Republic, one by the Prime Minister, one by employees, and one by the minority party in Parliament. The chairman of this board is chosen by the CEO. The model is, in theory, compatible with "good practice" because the selection process involves several political actors, mitigating the possibility of direct government interference in this process. Of course, this is all in theory:

> "The ruling political party always has someone in mind who they wish to be appointed to the Board of Directors. The idea is that this person will later be elected president. In 2016, the Board of Directors elected another person. The Board of Directors was chosen by Parliament, held a meeting to choose the CEO, and selected another person. Parliament rejected this choice. The Board of Directors held another election and, once again, named another person different from the one that was expected. This happened about three times, until Parliament finally appointed the individual the Social Democratic Party wanted as President" (SURUGIU, 2017).

The second aspect related to the appointment process concerns establishing a fixed mandate for public broadcasting managers. There are countries whose laws have provided a fixed mandate for managers of organs, such as Romania and Croatia, and there are other countries where this provision extends to more than one body, even to the supervisory board, as is the case in the Czech Republic. Although establishing a fixed mandate is important, the central point here should be the cases in which this institute can be shortened. This will be looked at in the next chapter.

The third aspect of the appointment process concerns the requirements required of each candidate to occupy a managerial position within the organization. Managers are normally required to be national citizens of the country they reside in. University education is also a common requirement, this includes having a Master's degree in countries like Slovakia (for Supervisory Board members and the CEO) and in Georgia (for Board of Directors members and the CEO). The laws often require managers to have experience in the field of public broadcasting or in other fields related to public entities such as law, management or finance. Eleven countries have a fixed period of minimum experience ranging from 3 to 10 years. The laws in Albania, Brazil (in this case, the general law applicable to appointing directors of public companies), Bulgaria, Slovakia, Slovenia, Georgia, Hungary, Latvia, Macedonia, Montenegro, and Serbia all state that prior experience is necessary. Similar prerequisites may also in public notices that guide public competition aimed at choosing such professionals, such as in the Czech Republic (SEDLÁČEK, 2017). It can be said that the requirements presented here aim to qualify the search for leaders, making it difficult to appoint persons who have no background in the field of broadcasting.

There are also some manager actions which may be seen as conflicts of interest, and are therefore prohibited. To start, public broadcasting managers are prohibited from controlling or owning a private broadcaster. In Estonia, this limitation extends to the managers' family members. Then there are some leaders who are prohibited from holding public office (Azerbaijan, Bosnia, Georgia and Lithuania). In even more complex models, such as the Hungarian one, broadcasters are prohibited (for a pre-defined time period) from employing heads of supervisory entities once their mandate is over. Lastly, it is quite common to prohibit broadcasting managers from being affiliated with political parties (to a certain degree). Sometimes, as is the case in Albania, Armenia and Serbia, they are prevented from being party leaders. And in other cases, the prohibition may be more restrictive, like in Latvia, where the law prohibits any involvement with political parties. Brazilian Law N°. 13.303 of June 30, 2016, prohibits any person who had been a political party leader in the previous 3 years, who had been active in an electoral campaign over the same time period, or who had held public office but was not permanently linked to the public service and union leader to be appointed to the Board of Directors or to any public company management position. Some of these restrictions also extend to their family members, even up to third-degree relatives.

Even with all these restrictions, government or parliament are often criticized for the fact that managers – and consequently the broadcasters and their programming – are subordinate to them. In Romania, shortly after the collapse of socialism and before the 1994 law was enacted, the "Free TV" channel was accused of being a staunch supporter of the governments at that time and of its new leaders who would later go on to form the Social Democratic Party. Parliament was accused of still trying to control the station, which was reflected in the choice of the CEO

(MUNGIU-PIPPIDI, 2003; DRAGOMIR, 2010; SURUGIU, 2017). The whole media system in Russia, and how it went back and forth to the public system, is seen by some authors as the result of the Putin government (KIRIYA, DEGTEVERA, 2010). The broadcaster's subordination to political parties in Slovenia was criticized in the first half of the 1990s (SPLICHAL, 1995).

# XV

The legal provision for fixed mandates alone shows intent to give leaders stability which, in theory, strengthens the possibility of independence. However, what's more important than these terms are the conditions for their early termination.

A number of laws provide for very objective penalties for early dismissals. These include criminal conviction, loss of nationality or being appointed to another position. Hungarian legislation states that the council of civil society representatives may call for the CEO to resign if the annual report is not approved. Up until 2016, Brazilian law stated that any director may be dismissed on two votes of distrust from the Board of Trustees. Slovak legislation states that the CEO may be dismissed on one vote of distrust from the Fiscal Board.

Some laws, on the other hand, establish subjective or vague reasons for dismissals. In Estonia and Serbia, legislation requires that the CEO resigns for non-compliance with the rules.

Legislation is similar in Montenegro, but extends this resignation to negligence and irregular conduct. In Croatia, the Parliament may call for the resignation of a member of the Board of Directors without specific justification. Regardless of the legislation, the dismissal of managers – as well as other broadcasting professionals – occurs on a regular basis.

Recent events in Eastern and Central European history have served as the basis for an almost natural shift in the power structure of public broadcasters. Slovakia experienced a difficult phase in the 1990s. Vladimir Mečiar was Prime Minister of the country three times, the last of which, from 1994 to 1998, was the most contested because of its dictatorial nature and how he distanced the country from integration policies with capitalist countries. This period became known as "Mečiarizmus", a neologism that alludes to the socialist period and criticizes authoritarianism. An impressive story involving the prime minister was told in the movie "Unos" ("Kidnapping"). Prime Minister Mečiar was a political opponent to Michal Kovac, President of the Republic. In August 1995, Kovac's son was stopped in his car by gunmen who forced him to drink two bottles of whiskey. He tried to escape, but was beaten and shocked with a stun gun. His kidnappers left him in Austria where he was arrested by Austrian police for allegedly being involved in financial fraud in Germany. The Austrian court released him and rumor has it that all of this was done with the intention of embarrassing the President of the Republic, Michal Kovac. During the investigations, a police officer, who maintained contact with a key witness in the case, was killed in a car bomb explosion. The police still managed to uncover a connection between the criminals and the Slovak secret police, at the time led by Ivan Lexa, a close ally of Mečiar's. Before investigations came to an end, however, a new law was enacted, supported by the Prime

Minister, which granted amnesty to the others involved in the case (ECONOMIST, 2017).

It would be very difficult for public broadcasting to gain any strength under these circumstances. At the time, some of the local media was accused of focusing on government propaganda (SKOLKAY, 2017). Replacing their leaders after this period was almost natural.

Not any less natural were the changes that came to Central and Eastern Europe years earlier with the downfall of the socialist regimes. In East Germany, key employees at the DFF (currently being incorporated into the West German public system) were replaced by West German professionals. In Bulgaria, at least half of the radio announcers and journalists left quickly. In addition, the broadcaster had to deal with large numbers of professionals leaving to go to private broadcasters. In 1991, the broadcaster lost four of its anchors at the same time. The solution was to look to young graduates. In Czechoslovakia, mass layoffs began as early as 1989. In Romania, the changes to television were just as swift: in November 1989 – weeks before Ceauşescu was overthrown – secret tests were carried out to hire new professionals, but these professionals only joined in January, once the government had changed. Some former professionals were just removed and ended up making public apologies. The timing of the tests led to suspicions: were station managers privy to the plans for overthrowing the government (MUNGIU-PIPPIDI, 2003; KON-STANTINOVA, 2017; NISTOR, 2017; SEDLÁČEK, 2017)?

For many countries, these changes seemed to be less about the law of lustration and more about natural substitutes for the leaders, voices, and faces of the old governments that new governments wanted to move away from. In Poland, the lustration process was not an important variable in layoffs following the fall of the regime in the 1990s. In Bulgaria, legislation even stated that anyone who had connections with the secret police could not become a head of a public broadcaster, however this was declared unconstitutional. The files from that period have been released slowly over the years and, as a consequence, not everyone who was involved with the secret police has become public knowledge. In Romania, several public figures from the Ceauşescu government initially went into hiding and then gradually started to reappear and articulate themselves in the political scene. In Czechoslovakia, journalists covering sports events were immediate suspects – after all, they were able to travel and report on events beyond the country's borders. About 3,000 journalists are estimated to have been affected by the lustration process because they worked at government-affiliated broadcasters. About 10% had to leave their jobs, but many had already left the stations once the government changed (DASKALOVA, 2017; JĘDRZEJEWSKI, 2017; KRAJEWSKI, 2017; MIKA, 2017; SKOLKAY, 2017).

Once the great political transformation had concluded, new laws were approved to create mechanisms for protecting the stability of leaders and professionals who speak out against the government. In practice, however, this protection does not always exist and the strategies employed to ensure that the interests of governments are preserved are numerous. One such strategy is to put so much pressure on a station's chief executive until he or she finally agrees to resign.

Another more explicit strategy is to change the law so that the government can appoint anyone it wants. This happened in Brazil in 2016 through a Provisional Measure which was later approved by the National Congress. Poland had a similar experience at the same time. In December 2015, members of the

Board of Directors and the Fiscal Council were temporarily appointed by the Minister of Finance, who promoted the first changes to directors. In June 2016, Parliament approved the creation of the National Media Council, which had the power to organize the auction and appoint heads of public broadcasters. Up until that time, this ability was exercised by the Polish National Broadcasting Council (KRRiT). The leaders of the new council were appointed by the Sejm, the lower house of the Polish parliament, and the President of the Republic. Its creation allowed for leaders of public broadcasters to be replaced or changed. The international backlash was sizeable: the Council of Europe spoke out against the new law, stating that it compromised the broadcasters' independence. The government also intended to pass new legislation to address other aspects related to public broadcasting, such as the funding model. Changes applied to Polish public broadcasting rules were frequent; the legislation was amended 19 times between 1992 and 2015 (KLIMKIEWICZ, 2016; ŠIMUNJAK, 2016; KRAJEWSKI, 2017).

Changes made to legislation in order to ensure that the new appointed leaders of public broadcasters were more closely aligned with government was a practice employed in other Central and Eastern European countries, even before the Polish episode. This has happened numerous times in Macedonia since the country gained its independence. In Slovenia, in the first half of the 1990s, the law was amended to give the government power to appoint station leaders. It did not take long for criticism of the station's intense gerrymandering to surface, and a new law was passed which re-introduced the idea of social institutions and organizations having direct representation in the council. A law was enacted in Georgia which led to some of the members of the Board of Directors to be dismissed, but the Supreme Court ruled that their mandates were still valid and they could only be dismissed under very specific situations (SPLICHAL, 1995; HRVATIN, PETKOVIC, 2004; ABASHINA, 2016).

There are also those who are dismissed on the grounds of political and ideological differences, which do not depend on existing mandates. Public broadcaster employees in Bulgaria do not hold secure jobs, and are subject to dismissal. The layoffs of critical journalists at BNT shed doubt on the station's independence (PETKOVA, 2011). In 1995, the Bulgarian public radio station (BNR) went on strike which resulted in at least eight dismissals, a decrease in listeners, and a stop to broadcasts that protested against the government. One of the eight employees who were dismissed was associate director Raina Konstantinova, who was publicly accused in a newspaper article of being a CIA spy. She even sent a letter in response to the newspaper, but it was never published:

> "Two or three days later, they came to me and fired me. I asked why. 'I can't explain'. The director's driver sat down next to me, I wasn't allowed to touch anything anymore and I was fired after 25 years on radio (...). I couldn't get a job because no one wanted to hire me. People stopped calling" (KONSTANTINOVA, 2017).

Bulgaria's annual inflation rate rose to over 2,000% in the second half of the 1990s, and a part of the population lost all their savings, swallowed up by bank fraud and investments unprotected against price increases. Konstantinova would be rehired years later, only to face another strike in 2001. At the time, she was running for office in radio management with support from civil society organizations, but Ivan Borislavov ended up being elected as Director General. The company's employees did not agree with the election result and consequently held a protest in front of the building, preventing the new CEO from entering the building. This ended up becoming the longest strike in the history of Bulgarian media up to that moment – 58 days. The CEO suffered a heart attack and was replaced by Alexander Brazitsov, who went on to dismiss 38 employees, setting off a new crisis at the station. He too ended up being replaced. His replacement rehired the 38 dismissed employees and Konstantinova left the station to be head of the EBU radio department (DASKALOVA, 2017; KONSTANTINOVA, 2017).

The Slovakian government was pushing for a friendlier journalism in the beginning of the 21$^{st}$ century when Radim Hreha was appointed as the new director of the public service television broadcaster. A number of important journalists were fired or quit as a result of his election. The head of the coalition government publicly stated that the station would be controlled by different spheres of influence. He said that he wanted his party to be responsible for the newscast, offering the guarantee to make "programs that should be on public television" (SKOLKAY, 2008).

The Prime Minister of Hungary, in 1991, decided to dismiss public service radio and TV station managers and replace them with pro-government professionals. The President did not agree with this decision, arguing that it undermined democracy. He was supported by the opposition in Parliament. The Prime Minister and his government appealed to the Supreme Court, claiming the president had broken the law which would lead to grounds for *impeachment*. The Supreme Court determined that there was a conflict of principles. The situation was partially resolved when the two station managers handed in their resignations. A new problem presented itself in 2000: the government and the opposition did not agree on the allocation of seats on the Board of Directors as provided by legislation at the time. The Board ended up being composed only of representatives from the governing party (SPLICHAL, 2001).

In Romania, the lack of independence for public broadcasters, which has even received criticism from Reporters Without Borders, and the threat of firing professionals have always gone hand in hand. Those who were against journalistic independence pointed to the inexperience of journalists and how they would abuse their right to express opinions and write inaccurate reports. It's no coincidence that two-thirds of journalists (depending on the study) believed that political pressures have made their profession insecure (MUNGIU-PIPPIDI, 2003; GROSS, 2005; GROSS, 2008).

In 2007, the independence of the Romanian broadcaster and the stability of its professionals were once again tested. A TVR team was able to secretly record a video of Agriculture Minister Decebal Traian Remes allegedly accepting a bribe of 15,000 euros, 20 kilos of sausages and 100 liters of spirits. He resigned shortly after and declined to release a statement. The prime minister and other politicians criticized the broadcaster for this "public execution" of his colleague and for tarnishing his plea of innocence. Media organizations and the regulatory body came in defense of the broadcaster. Station managers opted to restructure the broadcaster into two departments – one in charge of news and sports and the other dedicated to conducting research for journalistic programs. Rodica Culcer, one of the more important journalists, was asked to supervise both departments. Other important journalists were then removed from primetime programming and sent to present programs at other time slots; a more subtle solution than firing them or censoring topics (DRAGOMIR, 2010).

Layoffs and temporary dismissals in these and other countries are part of the history of public service broadcasting. Not surprisingly, the number of broadcasting managers and directors who have come and gone in the little over a quarter of a century between the end of the socialist regimes and the publication of this book is high. From the end of 1989 to 2017, Bulgarian National Television (BNT) had 13 different CEOs and Bulgarian National Radio (BNR) had 14, several of whom were affiliated with political parties at the time they were appointed or during their time in office. The TV broadcaster had only 8 different directors between 1959 and 1989. In post-socialist Romania, no CEO has ended his or her tenure at TVR. By local standards, the network is large and operates on a large budget, making it very interesting to political parties. In Slovakia, between 1992 and 2012, the year in which broadcasters merged, radio was run by four different CEOs and television by 17 (DASKALOVA, 2017; MIKA, 2017; SURUGIU, 2017).

The cases and numbers presented here demonstrate that legal provisions are not enough to protect leaders and professionals who speak out against the government. A study conducted on public media in European countries, eight of which are covered in this book, found that six of these eight have medium to high risks of independence (Romania, Slovenia, Latvia, Lithuania, Poland, and Slovakia) and only two (Croatia and Czech Republic) have low risks. In fact, the Latvian law analyzed in this book even promoted "a patriotic attitude towards the independent state of Latvia and its democratic system" as being one of the guidelines for public service broadcasting.

Apart from these, there were other apparently similar cases: the different Russian governments, for example, were accused of controlling private and state media, and firing critical leaders and professionals. Some electronic media were still being controlled by the Kremlin, while others were bought by large government-allied companies, compromising the independence of the media as a whole. Thus, local media are often accused of following the same pattern of political polarization and government adherence as before (BECKER, 2004; SPARKS, 2008; ŠIMUNJAK, 2016).

Sometimes the link between government and public service broadcasters becomes almost natural, as was the case in one episode broadcast on Romanian public TV: "One of the TV anchors was the wife of the Minister of Health. In one particular program, she interviewed her husband, which was anything but ethically standard. No one seemed to think anything of it" (SURUGIU, 2017). Not coincidentally, Coman (2009) found it correct and valid to a degree:

> "Romania's public radio and television are struggling with the same problems their brothers in other post-communist societies are facing. Public service institutions inhabit a space blurred between the public and state spheres, and enjoy only limited freedoms. They are caught between the control and pressure exerted by political institutions and the journalistic responsibility to the public that is idealistically defined in their mandates (...). Ironically, in the strange turns of the transformation that are still in full swing, regulations governing public service broadcasting guarantee the right to correction and response, while the commercial press and broadcasting media are not under such legal obligations" (COMAN, 2009, p. 3-4).

How does one handle this kind of situation? One answer may be to seek a better conceptualization of public service broadcasting and to redefine the role of its professionals so they meet the real objectives of these media. In Poland, for example, attempts were made to consolidate self-regulatory mechanisms, such as establishing codes of ethics and good practices which media professionals are subordinated to, as well as reflecting on media *accountability*. In this sense, public service broadcasters argued that how they are controlled, the publication of links to original sources, and the organization's mission should all be transparent (GŁOWACKI, URBANIAK, 2011; GŁOWACKI, 2016).

In a country that has just changed its legislation to allow for managers to be dismissed and replaced by more satisfactory ones, this action strategy may be important; but it is not enough. If we consider that initiatives to change law and the simple dismissal of critical professionals are common in Central and Eastern Europe and Brazil, then the solution will necessarily have to be balancing mechanisms: inserting other actors into the model who, through the operation of well-defined institutional mechanisms, may advance governments. The solution necessarily therefore requires securing power for civil society.

# XVI

The incorporation of civil society into public broadcasting management or supervision is provided for in most of the legislations studied in this book. This participation usually takes place in the form of councils, and in three distinct forms.

The first form involves creating specific organs for representatives nominated by civil society, for monitoring programming and making sure it meets the legal responsibilities of broadcasters. This is provided for in legislation for countries such as Albania, Croatia, Georgia, Macedonia and Serbia. A similar model was also adopted in Brazil, before the law changed in 2016. The EBC's Board of Trustees went beyond monitoring programming as its members could dismiss managers on feelings of distrust. The Programming Committee, created under Law N°. 13,417 of 2017, is a pale successor to the former council, with limited powers. What's more, this committee had not been implemented at the time this book was concluded. The participation model may also include mediators and ombudsmen as bodies that support the councils by analyzing public statements. This occurs in Brazil through the EBC ombudsman.

The second form concerns the appointment of broadcasting managers by civil society entities, sometimes explicitly defined by law. As a rule, these managers are the Board of Directors for the organs. This model is included in the legislation for countries such as Albania, Azerbaijan, Hungary and Montenegro. Lastly, the third form of participation is civil society bodies that indicate representatives for the supervisory body of the organ that maintains the public broadcasters. This is the case with Slovakia. There are also councils which were not created under law, but through a public broadcaster's internal rule. Bulgaria is an example of this.

Civil society participation in public broadcasters has encountered limits. Jakubowicz (1998/1999) reminds us that about a decade after the end of socialist rule, the empowerment of civil society was struggling in most Central and Eastern European countries because it was proving to be weak and passive. Jakubowicz believed it to be weak because a number of new organizations did not meet social needs; many institutions and organizations were just remnants of the past, and the state was still seen as being able to meet the needs of the population. It has been almost two decades since Jakubowicz's analysis; certainly enough time to build stronger entities, ones which are prepared for debates and public policy making. However, political instability in the region, while they do uphold a formal democracy, can make this process difficult.

There are other transparency mechanisms, outside of councils, that facilitate a greater participation by civil society. Since 2010, the Bulgarian regulatory organ has provided for live broadcasts of the hearings that appointed the directors of the BNT and BNR. In Slovakia, all contracts signed by broadcasters have to be published in full, much to the displeasure of major foreign studios. Entities that act like *media watchdogs* were created in Croatia (and in other countries in the region); they monitored media activity, ensuring they complied with the codes and ethics councils (PERANIC, 2006; SPASSOV, 2010; MIKA, 2017).

The councils are still the main space for civil society participation in public service broadcasting. Many of them are large and cover more segments of civil society (possibly even government). Councils of 9 to 15 members became common, but there were, and are, much larger ones. The EBC Board of Trustees, disbanded in 2016, had 22 members. In Hungary, prior to legislation being published, MTV and DunaTV were governed by a large number of *trustees* (a total of 60 for both stations), which included NGO representatives. There was no objective rule for choosing NGOs. The Slovenia council, in the early 1990s, was composed of 25 members: 5 from Parliament, one from the Italian minority, one from the Hungarian minority, 15 from civil society associations and other institutions, and three elected by the employees. The new Programming Council went on to include 29 members. Croatia tried to design a civil society appointment model for the council, similar to the one used in Germany and the Netherlands, which would include representatives from political parties, from unions, industry, churches, universities and non-governmental organizations, among others. A Croatian law passed in 2001 provided for a 25-member council. The German council already had 77 members (SPLICHAL, 1995; OPEN SOCIETY INSTITUTE, 2005; WOLDT, 2010; PERUŠKO, 2014).

The makeup of the boards is constantly criticized. Peruško (2014) pointed out that, contrary to expectations in the German and Dutch models, nominees for the council in Croatia mostly came from poorly represented entities, which led to a preponderance of informal political influences. Sedláček (2017) and Skolkay (2017) estimate that appointments to councils in the Czech Republic and Slovakia, which include representatives from civil society, were also permeated by political relations. Since these appointments (even those made by civil society) are subject to approval from public officials, one may naturally assume that some kind of political relationship exists between candidates. This does not mean, however, that these candidates, or the council, are subject to the government. Another criticism concerns how these bodies operate, the Polish council being one example:

> "I was vice president of the TV Programming Council. It was a joke. Its composition was not a joke, because it was composed of members who were appointed by political parties, representing each party in Parliament; five were on TV and are now on the new council. And there were five from civil society; I was one of them. The composition was reasonably ok, but the influence on programming was zero. We received several spreadsheets containing the names of the programs ... in case you weren't aware of them all... and, since the station worked with advertising, they told us that nothing could be changed; they had to honor the contracts (... ) It is an illusion to say that the committee has power over programming, it is an artificial waste of time" (KRAJEWSKI, 2017).

There is a further form of common social participation in the media sector in Eastern and Central Europe – protests. Big ones. Communication and freedom of expression are issues that have been fought over, and for, in most countries. In Brazil, a few dozen protesters stood out front of the EBC headquarters in Brasilia in opposition to Provisional Measure N°. 744 in September, which disbanded the Board of Trustees. People in Europe learned to take to the streets to defend their public broadcasters. The most significant protest, in this sense, occurred in the Czech Republic.

On December 20, 2000, Jiří Hodač was hired as Director General of Česká televize, the public television broadcaster in the Czech Republic, and he appointed Jana Bobosikova as Head of News. A former BBC journalist and Česká televize director himself, Hodač was criticized by broadcasters for his alleged affiliation with the main opposition party, and its leader Vaclav Klaus, who had served as Prime Minister of the Czech Republic. The unlikely situation of a government appointing a person who supposedly had close ties with the main opposition party to a senior post seemed to be the result of a larger agreement between Prime Minister Milos Zeman's party and his opponents in an attempt to ensure governability. This agreement led to discussions on making amendments to the Constitution, there were rumors of changes being made to the freedom of expression, there were protests from other opposition parties, and Czech public television soon found itself at the center of the dispute. Professionals at the station criticized Hodač's choice, occupied the station and began producing and broadcasting anti-decision programs via satellite and cable (signals which they had control of). Meanwhile, the unions called for a strike, and the resistance was supported by the President of the Republic, Václav Havel. The new leadership responded by firing the strikers and threatened to use force in order to make them leave the station. Strikers tried to transmit the newscast, but their broadcasts were often interrupted by a slide announcing technical problems at the station. Viewers could only watch the news content produced by the strikers via satellite or cable, or by the team formed by the new direction which broadcast on an open signal.

The people then took to the streets: it is estimated that more than 100,000 people, in support of Czech television employees, participated in the country's largest demonstrations since the fall of socialism. On January 3, 2001, approximately 100,000 people took to the streets of Prague in winter, when the average temperature in the city is around 0°C. Strikers could not leave the station as security would not let them back in, so they started receiving supplies and basic hygiene products through the windows. In January 2001, the Prime Minister and the Parliament publicly defended Hodač's resignation, which he eventually agreed to on reasons of poor health. Parliament elected Jiri Balvin as the network's interim director the following month. He had worked at the broadcaster for 25 years, and proceeded with a legislative amendment to incorporate organized civil society into the board member selection process. Instead of appointing board members directly, Parliament had to elect one from a list of civil society nominees (MILLER, 2001; PARTRIDGE, 2001; RSF, 2002; OPEN SOCIETY INSTITUTE, 2005; SEDLÁČEK, 2017).

Protests also broke out in Slovenia in 2005 when the government presented a new emergency bill to shut down the public broadcaster, without holding any public debate. The proposal meant Parliament would have more say in appointing council members. Thousands of people protested in January 2016 against the Polish government's proposal to change how the heads of public broadcasters were selected. Some demonstrations were even held in the freezing snow. This was just another demonstration out of many which had occurred in the country over the years. Public broadcasting was sometimes not even the main reason for protesting, but it was always a part of it. This was the case in Hungary, in 2006, when a taped conversation was leaked in which Prime Minister Ferenc Gyurcsány confessed that his party had lied in order to win that year's elections. Protesters stormed MTV in Budapest to try to broadcast their outrage. The target was not always public broadcasting: people took to the streets in Slovakia in the late 1990s in protest against the new owner of private broadcaster *Markíza*; it was suspected that this new owner was actually a member of the government party. Some of the more critical journalists began to be fired, which led to hundreds of people protesting in Bratislava and seven other cities in the country. Thousands of people took to the streets in Georgia, in 2015, to protest what they believed to be a threat to their freedom of expression: the new owner of Rustavi 2, the country's leading private broadcaster, who ended up having connections with the government. The Supreme Court of Georgia declared who the owners were, and in March 2017, the European Court of Human Rights suspended the Supreme Court's decision. Changes to broadcast ownership and attempts by the government to reduce its activities had already generated controversy in previous years. The most controversial circumstance occurred in 2001, when Giorgi Sanaia, one of the country's most popular journalists and government critic, was murdered. His death was widely believed to be politically motivated. Months later, the secret police stormed the station. Both of these cases led to protests in the streets, ultimately forcing then-president Eduard Shevardnadze to dismiss all his ministers. That same year, thousands of people took to the streets of Moscow in protest against Gazprom, a state-owned gas company, and its initiative to take over NTV, Russia's leading independent broadcaster. Some of these protests were effective, Georgia being one example in point; however, other protests were not as effective, such as in Poland (RADIO FREE EUROPE, 1998; MCLAUGHLIN, 2001; SAMARDZIJA-MATUL, 2005; JAKUBOWICZ, 2008; WELT, 2015; GREENSLADE, 2016; SKOLKAY, 2017; RADIO FREE EUROPE, 2017).

Protesting for communication rights and for specific public or private broadcasters in Central and Eastern Europe may be related to the fact that for decades it was not something that the people were allowed to do. Even still, these demonstrations were held by young people who did not live during that time period. Brazil also did not have public broadcasters or fundamental rights such as freedom of expression and freedom of the press for more than two decades. Nevertheless, doing away with the fixed mandate of EBC leaders and disbanding its Board of Trustees did not lead to similar protests.

Here lies the second criterion which highlights the importance of public broadcasting to society. The first and most objective criterion, pointed out in the previous chapter, is audience – programming is only important if it is watched or listened to by large numbers of people. The second criterion is related to how established a public broadcaster is in the everyday life of society. If it is seen as an essential institute for building local democracy and if its programming is viewed as important and independent of governments and the market, then it's more likely for demonstrations in its defense to occur, even in the snow.

# XVII

The fourth essential element for the independence of public broadcasting is funding. Economic crises were a common occurrence for these broadcasters in the early 21st century, including countries that were not studied for this book. For example, the Greek government decided, in 2013, to discontinue the ERT's activities for a period of about two years as part of its cost containment policy.

Problems are more frequent in Eastern and Central Europe. Hungary completely revised its public broadcasting model when broadcasters were on the verge of financial collapse. By the end of the 1990s, the country had 3 public channels: Magyar1 (broadcast to 100% of the population), Magyar2 (55%) and DunaTV (45.3%), which is geared more towards Hungarians residing outside the country. These last two channels were transmitted by cable and satellite only. Funding sources for the channels were unstable: by the end of the 1990s, the direct budget, including the obligatory taxes paid by the public, made up the bulk of the budget (54.4%), with advertising making up the rest of it (45.6%). Less than a year earlier, however, advertising revenue accounted for 63.3% of the total budget. Maybe this inconsistency in budget totals helps toward explaining the crisis (CSEH, 2000).

While I was writing this book, I took some time to follow similar uncertainties in two other countries. I will start with Bosnia. The country's model (which I alluded to earlier in this book) is fragmented, complex and would need effective coordination in order to be successful. However, what we have seen over the years has been the failure of key elements of the system. No more than 65% of the public paid for the *license fee*. Croatian politicians recommended not paying the fee because, in their view, the public system would not meet the interests of this part of the population. Consumers were legally allowed to not pay the fee. And even though this funding was lower than planned, the way it was redistribution among public system broadcasters was flawed (HOZIC, 2008).

The economic problems increased mainly in BHRT, the national public broadcaster in Bosnia. In 2016, after years of finanacial losses, the network announced that it would discontinue its activities. Since then, several entities have appealed to government to keep the station on air and to Parliament to vote on new legislation capable of making the model more sustainable. The EBU has, on more than one occassion, publicly criticized the closure of the station. Not only is there the obvious negative impact that comes with bankruptcy, there is also a symbolic importance – after all, various governments and entities have committed themselves to rebuilding war-torn Bosnia.

The crisis in Romania's TVR was similarily painful. Annual losses are constant. Surugiu (2017) points out that the company's inability to pay its debts even led to discussions about minimizing interest rates, but the EBU would have condemned the idea. In 2016, the EBU prevented TVR from participating in the *Eurovision Contest*, a popular song competition representing primarily European countries. Meanwhile, problems in management were beginning to increase. One example can be found with two journalism teams which traveled to other countries: one team spent 2 weeks in Thailand recording a documentary; the other spent one month in South Korea to record a documentary on that country. None of the two teams, however, volunteered to travel to other Eastern European countries to cover the collapse of socialist regimes a quarter of a century later.

A more obvious problem, however, was the increased payroll: TV channels employed over 2,300 employees. This number is well below the approximately 13,000 employees in the last few years of the DFF in East Germany, and more than the 1,370 employees at the Slovakian public broadcaster, including TV, radio and the Philharmonic Orchestra (MIKA, 2017). The Romanians refer to the relationships among station employees with a dry sense of humor: "We have a joke, which goes: if you go to the front door of the station and shout 'Mommy', all the women employees will show up to see which one of their children is calling them" (SURUGIU, 2017).

A cost-cutting effort was even attempted: Surugiu (2017) states that the first Council on which he served had the backing of Parliament and the government to reduce the number of employees in the company. About 600 people left, some of whom applied for retirement, and received a year's salary as compensation. Several people appealed to the courts and managed to get their jobs back.

Apart from the costs, which the broadcasters can theoretically reduce themselves, there are other factors which they cannot control. As was the case in much of Europe, including the still socialist Eastern and Central part, the production and programming infrastructure of broadcasters did not belong to the same organization (state) that owned the transmission infrastructure and telecommunications networks. These networks were sometimes connected to the Armed Forces, as they were seen as as strategic to national security. This was the case, for example, in Poland. With the fall of European socialist governments, transmission infrastructure was privatized, sold and re-sold, and is currently contracted by all the broadcasters in each country. The margin for negotiating these costs is small: broadcasters that cannot take on these costs may have to stop broadcasting, and there are usually no other companies that provide the same type of service. Václav Mika (2017) also points out another important difference between public and private broadcasting funding models:

> "Private media is a business, public media is a mission. It is not just about different types of content, nor about focusing on private media performance or having more audience with less investment (...). There is a big difference in management objectives: At *Markíza*, I focused on annual or periodic results in my management, in presenting results to the company, which would then present them to the group and shareholders. I was not concerned about issues that were two or three years down the road. Here we have long term investments in co-productions, in cartoons – 5 years

until they are shown, 3 years for co-productions. That would make no sense for private TV. Its focus is on itself, the company and its shareholders. And the difference with the mission is that most of the projects we have invested in this year, or in the past, will be on screen within a year or two, after the end of my term. We acquired the rights to sports content for the period between 2018 and 2020" (MIKA, 2017).

The economic difficulties are also related to public broadcasters' different budgets. It would be unhelpful to compare their budgets in absolute terms, as each country's political, geographical, and economic conditions have different impacts on their public broadcasting. A more useful indicator is the total invested per capita, which also reveals disparity, as shown in the following table:

**Table 12: Public Broadcasting Budget Per capita**

| Country | Budget per capita (€) | Year |
|---|---|---|
| Norway | 155.49 | 2011 |
| Germany | 118.53 | 2011 |
| Sweden | 97.98 | 2011 |
| United Kingdom | 87.96 | 2011 |
| Japan | 37.48 | 2015 |
| Canada | 27.46 | 2013 |
| Czech Republic | 23.98 | 2016 |

| Country | Budget per capita (€) | Year |
|---|---|---|
| Estonia | 18.04 | 2009 |
| Hungary | 16.31 | 2015 |
| Poland (TV) | 10.88 | 2011 |
| Bulgaria | 7.66 | 2016 |
| Latvia | 7.02 | 2009 |
| Albania | 6.56 | 2015 |
| Romania (TV) | 5.23 | 2016 |
| Lithuania | 4.01 | 2009 |
| United States | 2.92 | 2012 |
| Brazil | 0.84 | 2016 |

**Source:** Prepared by author, based on JÕESAAR (2011); IFM (2011); RTSH (2015); MINISTRY OF FINANCE (2016); BALOGH (2016); ČT (2016); ROMANIA INSIDER (2016); BENSON; POWERS; NEFF (2017).

The budget for Bulgarian broadcasters only accounts for resources from the government; other sources have not been found and therefore represent only a small part of the total amount. At first glance, one might think that the low per capita budgets correspond with low audience ratings. This would be premature; however, the sample size is insufficient to warrant such a statement. It is true though that public broadcasters in Lithuania, Romania and Brazil have low *market shares* and per capita budgets, different from Germany and the United Kingdom.

The difference between resources spent on costs and investments in Brazil is worth looking at: after all accounts have been paid, there is a low percentage of resources left to invest in the EBC, which harms the quality of programming and competition for *market share*. Moreover, if we take into account the educational broadcasters with links to state governments and their respective budgets, the per capita index previously presented would rise slightly. Even so, the public broadcasting budget per capita in Brazil is noticeably low.

Although there is no ideal theoretical model for public broadcasting funding, there is one aspect considered essential: a diversity of sources. The more avenues for financial resources that broadcasters have, the less they have to depend on just one agent to support them. Legislation for all the countries studied in this book provides for diversified sources of funding. The budgets for public broadcasters in European countries in 2005 are divided as follows:

**Table 13: Public broadcaster funding sources (2005)**

| Country | *Licence Fee* | Public Budget | Advertising and Endorsements | Others |
|---|---|---|---|---|
| Albania | n.a. | 58 | 8.6 | 33.4 |
| Germany (ARD) | 94 | 0 | 6 | n.a. |
| Croatia | 57.4 | 0 | 36 | 6.6 |
| Slovakia | 60.2 | 16.8 | 18.8 | 4.2 |

| Country | *Licence Fee* | Public Budget | Advertising and Endorsements | Others |
|---|---|---|---|---|
| Slovenia | 72.8 | 0 | 16.5 | 10.7 |
| Estonia | 0 | 93 | 0 | 7 |
| Latvia | 0 | 57 | 43 | |
| Lithuania | 0 | 176 | 23 | 1 |
| Macedonia | 80.2 | 0 | 12.1 | 7.7 |
| Poland | 31.9 | 0 | 56.3 | 11.8 |
| Romania | 75.5 | 14.3 | 8.38 | 0 |
| Czech Republic | 66.7 | 0 | 29.1 | 4.2 |
| Serbia | 0 | 75.2 | 24.8 | |

**Source:** OPEN SOCIETY INSTITUTE (2005).

There are extreme cases involving diversity of funding sources. Ten years after the study on which table 13 was based, the *licence fee* for Albanian public broadcaster RTSH totalled 45% of its total budget, 14% towards public budget and 2.37% to advertising, with other sources accounting for more than 38% of the total budget (RTSH, 2015). Such a high percentage is unusual. Table 13 presents the three main sources of public broadcasting funding in the world, which we shall look at below.

The first main source of funding is the *licence fee*. The term "licence fee" in Portuguese is actually technical jargon used to refer to a specific amount of money paid by each broadcaster to give them the right to operate. In English, however, licence fees refer to the amount of money paid by anyone who owns a TV or radio to public broadcasters in order for them to operate, excluding special circumstances provided for under law. In some countries, retirees, children and people with disabilities are exempt from the fee.

When fully implemented, licence fees tie the broadcaster (in theory) to the public interest, thus avoiding pressures from the market and government. After all, this resource comes directly from society, to whom the broadcaster should ultimately serve:

> "In European tradition, the best model is the license fee. In Slovakia, we have *license fees*, combined with the public budget, advertising and commercial activities. The ratio is very important: if the total budget is made up of almost 30% of the public budget, there is no way to keep the public media. Sustainability goes hand in hand with funding. After last year's election, the Minister of Culture proposed an increase to *license fees*, to com into effect 12 years from now. The reason was not only to improve funding, but to increase the independence of public media in Slovakia (...). We say that we not only have to increase the total budget, but also change the ratio. For me, the ideal model would be 90% license fees, 5% public budget, and 5% others" (MIKA, 2017).

It is worth briefly examining the German model, in which the budget comes primarily from the *licence fee*. The structure of German public broadcasting is complex and quite different from the other models studied here. The ARD is a joint organization of 8 regional broadcasters, which also includes the international broadcaster Deutsche Welle, and others. It operates regional and local radio channels, including one national channel. The ZDF, another public service broadcaster, and runs at the federal level. The ARD and the ZDF have been, and are, partners in specific initiatives such as the *KI.KA* children's channel and the Phoenix news channel. The combined public broadcasting system transmitted 115,000 hours in 2007, compared to about 50,000 hours for the BBC. Every two years an independent commission, with state representatives nominated by local governments, assesses the needs, budgets and plans of the German public system and recommends a value for the licence fee to all the states. In 2004, some state governments did not follow said recommendation because they wanted broadcasters to cut costs. The ARD and the ZDF took the case to Federal Constitutional Court which, in 2007, ruled that the state governments deciding on the value of the licence fee was a violation of the principle of the freedom of broadcasting. The court also decided which states would fund broadcasters appropriately. On the other hand, it recognized that it was the right of states to define the scope of the broadcasters, but not according to the political procedure and argumentation used (HOLTZ-BACHA, 2003; WOLDT, 2010; WIMMER, 2014).

For a number of countries, the first obstacle in the way of implementing this source of funding (licence fee) is cultural reasons. Not every society would accept "paying for a TV or radio channel". Obviously, this perception is fallacious: if public service broadcasting is understood as a public service and, in this case, helps toward building democracy, then there is nothing more natural than it being funded directly by society. Even when the public budget is the main source of funding, these broadcasters are still being indirectly funded by society. Even though provided under law, the licence fee was not adopted in Bulgaria

(DASKALOVA, 2017; KONSTANTINOVA, 2017). Economists in Slovakia even held a referendum to decide whether to continue paying the fee or not (DRAGOMIR, 2010). In Brazil, the former governor of São Paulo, Mário Covas, even mentioned the possibility of adding an extra tax to the electricity bill for every residence in the state in order to fund TV Cultura. The proposal was publicly criticized and was thrown out before it could even be discussed. When the EBC was being created, a decision was made to impose a tax on telecommunications service providers and broadcasters called the Promotion of Public Broadcasting Tax (CFRP). This was challenged in court in a battle that had already been going on for at least ten years at the time of writing this book. Another issue being discussed is the annual fee:

**Table 14: Annual licence fee amount (2006)**

| Country | Amount (€) |
| --- | --- |
| Denmark | 294 |
| Norway | 248 |
| Sweden | 221 |
| Germany | 204 |
| United Kingdom | 196 |
| Slovenia | 132 |
| France | 117 |
| Croatia | 108 |
| Italy | 104 |

| Country | Amount (€) |
| --- | --- |
| Macedonia | 64 |
| Poland | 49 |
| Czech Republic | 44 |
| Slovakia | 35 |
| Romania | 14 |
| Albania | 4 |

**Source:** DRAGOMIR (2010).

Few countries have licence fee pricing systems with checks and balances similar to those in Germany. What normally happens is that the government or parliament decides on the value, and they do so without necessarily relying on any technical criteria, which means that value is often lower than it should be in order to avoid any public outcries to lower taxes. This problem tends to be more serious in Eastern and Central Europe (according to the information in Table 14) where the last six positions are occupied by countries in this part of the continent.

This is not a new problem. As early as the 21st century the purpose of licence fees has been questioned, as low value amounts could not cover the costs of broadcasters. Hyperinflation had just ended (or was still present) in some of the Eastern and Central European countries at the time, making for more difficult economic conditions for their populations. In Romania, the licence fee reached up to around US$1 per month. In Bulgaria, the value for the licence fee was equivalent to the price of a single newspaper. The fee was also announced as being equivalent to 0.6% of minimum wage for individual persons and 2.5% of minimum wage for legal entities, but this would only come into force in 2003, so the budget for broadcasters was complemented by appropriations from another fund which was created (TSCHOLAKOV, 2000; MUNGIU-PIPPIDI, 2003).

Even once the hyperinflation stage was over, the reality was cruel. In Bulgaria, neither a fund nor a licence fee has been implemented. In Romania, licence fees were removed as a source of funding in December 2016, and were replaced by the public budget. At the time, its value was very low: 4 LEI per month (equivalent to less than € 1 per residence). This monetary amount could buy you 4 small baguettes and was less than the 5 LEI charged for a round-trip subway ticket. The government refused to increase the licence fee for political reasons, which ultimately contributed to the TVR's debt of about €160 million. Similar reasons had led the Hungarian government at the beginning of the century to also consider maintaining its licence fee (LENGYEL, 2010; DASKALOVA, 2017; KONSTANTINOVA, 2017; SURUGIU, 2017).

If low values weren't enough, evasion is a big problem. Not all models collect the fee from electricity bills. It is common for TV and radio sets to be registered with a specific entity which in turn becomes responsible for collecting the fee. This entity could be the Post Office, as was the case in the Czech Republic and Poland; it could be the station itself, as was the case in Slovakia; or it could be another entity (BANAZINSKI; GÓRKA, 2000; LANDOVA, 2000; SMATLAK, 2000). If the devices are not registered, then there is no way to collect a fee. Even if they are registered, tax evasion still occurs.

In Hungary, in 2002, tax evasion reached an estimated 60% of the public (LENGYEL, 2010). The most symbolic case, however, is that of Poland. One of the largest countries in Central and

Eastern Europe in terms of population, Poland has had a complex media system ever since the end of socialism. By 1993 there were already 60 commercial broadcasters, 14 of which were television. They operated illegally, but several of them received grants in 1994. There were already 3 national commercial networks by the year 2000. The public broadcaster was expanding, becoming responsible for two national channels (TVP1 and 2), an international satellite channel (*TV* Polonia) and 12 regional channels. Most of the television budget (67%) came from advertising, and less than 30% came from licence fees. In 2009, the fee applied to owning a radio was about € 13 per year, and the fee applied to owning both a radio and a TV set was € 42 per year. At the time, tax evasion was close to 50%. Even public organizations did not pay the fee; only 5% of them had registered their radio and TV sets. From 1994 to 2007, the amount collected fell by 25%. About 60 percent of the total went to public radio, which earned less from advertising than public TV did. Even the Prime Minister said this fee was a joke and it should be abolished, which motivated people not to pay. Tax officials were not allowed to enter homes to check for radio and TV sets, so anyone who did not want to pay the fee would be, in practice, exempt from doing so simply by not declaring the equipment. Out of the 13 million Polish households in 2017, only 750,000 paid the licence fee (BANAZINSKI; GÓRKA, 2000; STĘPKA, 2010; JĘDRZEJEWSKI, 2017; KRAJEWSKI, 2017).

This erratic behavior regarding licence fees, which did not cover all the costs of broadcasters in Central and Eastern Europe, has generated all kinds of reactions. In the United Kingdom, the communications regulator Ofcom even suggested using part of the BBC's funding to subsidize public content from other broadcasters, including commercial ones. This would guarantee pluralism in these broadcasters' programming. There are others across Europe who advocate expanding the fee to cover all devices capable of receiving public media (such as cell phones), and others still who wish to abandon it altogether and find a new source or change it to a mandatory tax collected from all households and citizens (DRAGOMIR, 2010; IOSIFIDIS, 2010). While it may not be the best solution for public broadcasters, it does allow them to enjoy less interference from governments and the market.

Now, the public budget is a very different situation, usually seen as being more committed to the independence of public broadcasting. There is an obvious risk involved should this source of funding prevail: the government and parliament would be able to influence broadcasters even more. In addition to the harm this can do, there is also the argument, presented by private broadcasters in some countries, that this source of funding would be anti-competition by the fact it privileges only one entity (or possibly two) in this economic segment. In 1998, the European Union decided to address the issue and set limits on the allocation of public resources to public broadcasting, only allowing for the amounts necessary to meet their public service obligations (WHEELER, 2010).

In Eastern and Central Europe, however, the tendency is for there to be a lack of resources, even for the public budget. In Bulgaria, in 2016, BNT requested a budget of 95.5 million leva (€48.8 million), but only received 65.2 million (€33.3 million) from the government – about 32% less than requested. In addition, the dynamics of the public budget process create uncertainties: it is possible for some European countries to implement a fixed budget for three years, which further reduces the possibility of political interference. However, in Bulgaria – and in Brazil, where the public budget is also the predominant source of funding – there is no guarantee that the values will remain the same (DASKALOVA, 2017; KONSTANTINOVA, 2017).

Even still, several governments and parliaments have opted to reduce access to other sources, meaning the broadcasters have to depend more on the public budget. I mentioned earlier about how Hungary, Bulgaria and Romania are hesitant to collect licence fees. In Albania, at the beginning of the 21st century, rather than being immediately redirected to the broadcaster, the amount collected from the licence fee was placed in the Treasury. In Georgia and Azerbaijan, the law provides for a licence fee which, if not implemented, is replaced by the public budget (HRVATIN; PETKOVIC, 2004; ABASHINA, 2016).

One of the more symbolic cases is Estonia. The Broadcasting Act of 1994 has been amended 33 times. In the late 1990s, commercial broadcasters were required to pay fees in order to maintain the ETV, the country's public broadcaster. The model began to crumble, however, when private broadcaster TV1 stopped paying its annual contribution. As of 2002, the ETV was prohibited from selling advertising. In 2007, the government gave in a little more: the licence fee paid by commercial broadcasters was abolished and they were granted €4 million to help them with the transition to digital. At the same time, public radio and TV broadcasters were unified into one company, with the public budget as their main source of funding (OPEN SOCIETY INSTITUTE, 2005; JÕESAAR, 2011).

The third most common source of funding is commercial advertising. The more of this kind of funding a budget has, the more public broadcasters, in theory, have to structure their commercial departments, align with market practices, and compete for advertisers. The larger the audience, the more advertisers are willing to pay for advertising space. When the competition for audiences is a broadcaster's means of survival, they tend to move slowly away from the supposed ideal of what public broadcasting is. Restructuring programming and making it more pleasing and agreeable – or in other words, adopting a format similar to the one practiced by commercial broadcasters – seems to be the logical way to go.

It seems reasonable to assume that by relying more on advertising, public broadcasters tend to include content which has the potential to reach a higher audience. Authors such as Benson, Powers and Neff (2017) conclude that commercial advertising is responsible for making public and private broadcaster programming more homogeneous.

In some countries, where advertising makes up a significant sum of revenue from public broadcasters, the audiences tend to be higher. In the Czech Republic in the early 1990s, the two national channels, ČT1 and ČT12, were accessible to 98% and 89% of the audience, respectively.

In 1991, the cost of the licence fee was doubled and, in 1993, broadcasters stopped receiving direct public budget. Up until 1993, most of the broadcasters' budgets came from commercial advertising, but in 1995 that percentage dropped to 15.7% due to competition with commercial broadcasters. This competition led to a crisis, and broadcasters began to cover their costs by saving money and selling property. In 1998, 22.8% of broadcasters' budgets came from commercial advertising and 65% from the licence fee. During the same period, ČT1's market share fell from 60% to 28%. This drop is likely to be associated with the entry and strengthening of new competitors. In Poland, where its public system has a higher audience, the programming is similar in structure to commercial broadcasters. In the second week of March 2017, TVP aired eleven of its twelve highest nationally-rated programs on channels 1 and 2: six drama-based channels, including soap operas; two sports channels; and one newscast channel (LANDOVA, 2000; KRAJEWSKI, 2017).

Alternatives have been attempted in some countries where commercial advertising has gained relevance so that programming continues to meet the expectations of a public broadcaster. In 1988, the public broadcaster of New Zealand (which went through an intense neoliberal reform process at the end of the 20th century) was restructured and is mainly funded by advertising. In 2004, 70% of the station's budget came from this advertising. A fund was then created to produce content that was in danger of being removed from the programming schedule. The fund established the percentage of resources to be allocated to each format, mainly funnelled towards independent production (BARDOEL, D'HAENENS, 2008).

The political decision to leave the fate of public broadcasting to commercial advertising, however, generates resistance. This resistance comes from academia, from social movements, and especially from commercial broadcasters. The World Trade Organization has even argued that the public broadcasting funding system is representative of unfair competition since it seeks public funding while also resorting to the advertising market, which is the main (if not the only) source of private broadcasting. In Brazil, due to the regulations established for educational broadcasting in the 1960s, these broadcasters were not able to use commercial advertising. These regulations were extended to public service broadcasting decades later. Commercial advertising by public broadcasters in Europe was restricted. In Romania, even with the crisis, parliament protected private broadcasters by stating that TVR could only broadcast advertising between programs, and less than commercial broadcasters. In Germany, advertising on public channels was restricted to 20 minutes a day on weekdays, and only before 8 p.m. In Georgia, in 2014, the public broadcaster stopped transmitting commercial advertising. Other countries have similar restrictions, as previously mentioned in this book (HOLTZ-BACHA, 2003; MUNGIU-PIPPIDI, 2003; DRAGOMIR, 2010; ABASHINA, 2016; SURUGIU, 2017).

Efforts have been made to secure other sources of funding with varying degrees of success. Sponsorship, cultural support, commercial agreements with foreign broadcasters, and donations are all viable alternatives, but they do not replace the others. Slovenia once again decided to go beyond public broadcasters and support the "public field". In 2013, 3% of lottery revenue went to non-commercial media published by civil society organizations. In addition, a pilot investigative reporting project was created. These measures followed previous initiatives, such as the 28 million dinar budget for democratizing media and launching new media in 1991 (HRVATIN, MILOSAVLJEVIC, 2003; HRVATIN, PETKOVIC, 2004).

# EPILOGUE

# XVIII

It was a cold morning in March in Bratislava. The lecture at the journalist union headquarters was coming to an end. A white-haired man, who looked to be in his sixties, asked the question, "Why do you think our Public TV criticizes the government as much as it does?" I hesitated to answer because I had already heard a number of allegations, on this trip and others before it, about how submissive public broadcasters are to Central and Eastern European governments. A few weeks earlier, I was studying the Slovak case and came across a statement from then Prime Minister Robert Fico I thought surprising (at least by Brazilian standards). He spoke at length about journalists who have deliberately compromised national interests, citing tabloid journalists, professionals from two other newspapers, and professionals from public radio and TV stations.

On that same day, in the afternoon, I interviewed Václav Mika, Director General of Slovak Radio and TV. He was a manager who had worked in private media, defended the importance of public broadcasting, presented improvements to broadcasters, and showed pride in the work he was doing. Near the end of the interview, I mentioned how I found Fico's statement and the question I heard at the end of the lecture surprising. I pointed out that this could suggest that the broadcaster was moving towards an editorial line which was independent from government, which in fact is a principle of public service broadcasting. Mika mentioned the report to his advisers and recalled that, on the eve of the interview, the Prime Minister had stated that Mika was more concerned about his reinstatement than he was the broadcasters. This statement made it clear that Mika was not the government's candidate for the upcoming RTVS board election, which was to take place in a few months' time.

Even still, Mika ran in the election. He obtained some unlikely votes from parliamentarians belonging to other parties, but none from the government. He lost the election to Jaroslav Reznik, who had been director of Slovak Radio for eight years (before the company merged with the TV station), and before that was the director of the Slovakian News Agency.

The discussion on independence on this side of the Atlantic Ocean continued years after the EBC had been established. Critics of public broadcasting called it a set of old state-owned broadcasters with a new guise – some called it "Lula's TV". In 2017, critics once again attacked public broadcasting. Regardless of the content, these critics chose to try and do away with the EBC rather than build it up together, or at least monitor and supervise its activities accurately and honestly.

I presented a defining model for the concept of public broadcasting independence in earlier chapters. That model was comprised of four elements: (a) complexity in appointing leaders, which alludes to how the different actors involved in the selection process help eliminate influence from certain political groups and opinions; (b) job stability for managers and important professionals, which helps to keep the team together, regardless of the positions expressed in the programming; (c) mechanisms of social control so society can monitor broadcaster activities; and (d) plural sources of funding, so that any resource which may happen to get cut or reduced does not compromise ongoing activities. These elements are present in public broadcasting at varying levels: the more present and preserved, the greater the independence broadcasters have from governments.

Independence is not the only element in the field of public broadcasting that brings countries and regions of the world together. Brasilia is more than 10,100 kilometers away from Bucharest. Daylight savings time begins in Sofia in March, which means there is a seven-hour time difference between the two cities. In 2017, it took about 24 hours to get to Warsaw from Brasilia: you would have to go from Brasilia to São Paulo or Rio de Janeiro; from there to either Paris or Frankfurt; and from Paris or Frankfurt to the Polish capital.

So close yet so far. In the late 1980s, TV and radio were extremely popular media everywhere. The first official demonstrations for public broadcasting came when countries were freed from authoritarian regimes. There was no prior knowledge in these countries of what public broadcasting was. Existing structures and their staff made the transition. There were not enough resources to really experiment with it. Civil society participation was limited in this process because it was not organized enough to follow the issue. In fact, public debate itself was limited.

The similarities continued in subsequent years. Government has maintained, or attempted to increase, its influence on broadcasters either by increasing the role of the public budget or by appointing leaders who are knowledgeable of the current government. Important professionals were fired. Not even social participation bodies, such as councils, were immune to political interference. In which country (in the months prior to this study) did the Executive Power take it upon themselves to change the law in order to replace the leaders of public broadcasters? There were two: Brazil and Poland. Before them, there were several other countries that did the same.

I would like to use the next two pages to highlight two points in Brazil. The construction of public broadcasting in Brazil does not, and never will, pass exclusively through the EBC. Due to political reasons, a lack of financial resources, and the absence of free radio frequencies throughout the country, the EBC will probably always have to rely on affiliated broadcasters in its network. Thus, the EBC's level of independence will always be related, to some degree, to the independence of its partners. In this sense, it is important that these broadcasters also migrate towards a model which is more compatible with public service broadcasting. Theoretically-speaking, there are a few options to help accelerate this migration, federal law being one of them; however, this option is unlikely to occur due to political reasons or because of the questionable constitutionality of the law, as it would mean interfering with the organization of state public administration. Another hypothesis would be a natural migration to the EBC model. This kind of transition was already stimulated by the company itself during the formation of its national network, but the migration did not occur. A third alternative would be to stimulate this transition through investment. For example, state broadcasters adopting governance compatible with the principles of public broadcasting could benefit from the possibility of resorting to specific federal funding sources. This solution has already been discussed and I understand that it is more feasible than the previous ones.

The second point concerns relevance. The EBC was built as a result of a building policy for public broadcasting, one which is maintained mainly by public resources, and therefore the EBC should be relevant. I believe this relevance can be measured in at least three different ways.

The first and most obvious way to measure its relevance is with audience: if the public watches or listens to the programming, we can consider it to be relevant. In this regard, the EBC-affiliated broadcasters, principally the television broad-casters, are very different from many of their European counterparts. At the beginning of this book, I argued about the importance of public broadcasting and how it is still a reference in society today. This can be evidenced, for example, by the high and growing percentages of the population who watched TV and listened to the radio between 2014 and 2016. Of course, Internet use has unquestionably increased over the years, and new forms of access to media have appeared with it. Thus, it is essential that older public broadcasting bodies go beyond the limits of TV and radio, and enter the world of digital. So, what I'm trying to say is that the concept of audience must expand to include the performance of these bodies on the Internet. There is a lack of concrete data for measuring, but I see no evidence to suggest that the EBC's situation is very different from other broadcasters.

Many people believe that public broadcasting audiences in Brazil should be "measured in another way". Those who defend this position often claim that the programming from public stations is "distinct" and is not able to compete with the audience numbers that commercial broadcasters have. There is a core problem with this argument: it assumes a necessary elitization of public service broadcasting which is inconsistent with how successful this system has been on an international level. Moreover, the problem tends to increase when considering the average socioeconomic indicators of the Brazilian population.

One could try to measure audiences "in another way", but what would this "way" be? I am unaware of any structured proposals which have been tested on a large enough sample size to be able to compare different broadcaster schedules. Until this "other way" has actually been implemented, the EBC can only measure audiences in the traditional way. Although it cannot compete with the major markets, its major relevance will be with the audience it can compete for, especially on TV.

The second way to measure relevance concerns how rooted public broadcasting is in a particular society. If it is defended explicitly and regularly, it may be considered relevant. Once again, the EBC's situation is quite different from Europe's. In the Czech Republic, people took to the streets, in winter, to support employees who were striking against a broadcasting manager who had been recently appointed by government. Similar situations have occurred in other countries, as this book has illustrated. There has never been a movement similar to these ones in Brazil.

Lastly, public service broadcasting is relevant if it is defended as being different from private broadcasters and if it is in line with clear democratic principles; a key element towards building a plural society. In this respect, yes, the EBC was extremely relevant: the narrative that supported its creation and the defense of that narrative by its managers reinforced this link during the company's early years. This discourse, however, diminished and faded over time.

Would the solution, then, be the disappearance of the EBC? Not a chance, at least for those who believe public service broadcasting is central to building democracy. The solution involves categorically recovering this defense, which includes reaffirming its role and its own raison d'être. It also involves seeking an audience and taking root in society.

The history of public service broadcasting in different countries is marked by resistance. This book relates a part of this history, and there are certainly many others in the world who have told this history. Resistance to political pressure. Resistance to pressure from governments. Resistance to attacks by private broadcasters. Resistance against a lack of resources, whether accidental or on purpose. Resistance to inept leaders, who are sometimes unable to understand the importance of public broadcasting itself. Is resistance not, in fact, a mark of the history of democracy?

# Afterword: Does Public Communication in Brazil resist?

In the second half of 2018 the subject of communication was once again a topic of intense public debate. One of the most polarizing electoral campaigns in the country's history took place. After the first round of elections, only two candidates remained. The first candidate, Fernando Haddad, was a member of the government which created EBC a decade earlier. He was supported by former president Lula da Silva (who launched his campaign but was prevented from running). Haddad's government program was geared toward regulating the sector and expectations were raised about possible advancements in public communication. His opponent was Jair Bolsonaro, an extreme-right candidate, who was elected at the end of October.

In an interview with a commercial broadcaster the day after his election, Bolsonaro announced that he would either privatize TV Brasil or shut it down (SOUZA, 2018). Rumors started circulating that this broadcaster would consume R$1 billion annually (about 231 million euros). This amount was unrealistic – as presented in this book, even at its peak, TV Brasil did not receive funding like this. Even still, Bolsonaro's decision was not a surprise: not only had he criticized the station's parliamentary activity, he had stated numerous times during his campaign that public companies would be privatized over the next few years.

The new government took office on January 1, 2019, but the president only mentioned privatizing the EBC at the end of May, during an interview with a second commercial broadcaster (SOARES, 2019). This break, however, was not a quiet time for the EBC. Amid the layoffs of managers and the promise to reduce the number of employees, a measure was adopted which had been used by the previous government: merge the NBr (institutional content of the Executive Power) and TV Brasil (public communication) and keep the name of the latter. It was supposed to be "more citizen-oriented" (LAUTERJUNG, 2019). In the beginning of 2020, the government announced a provisory schedule for privatizations. According to it, EBC would be sold in two years from then.

At the same time as the official speech, complaints about the direction of the company increased. Programming for the new TV Brasil began to be interrupted, even during children's cartoons, by live federal government broadcasts, such as the Armed Forces Day celebrations. In addition, the network was accused of censoring its own professionals in their coverage of certain subjects or their use of specific terms. For example, "military coup" and "dictatorship" were no longer used to refer to the political regime that ruled Brazil from 1964 to 1985. Institutional content was increasingly added to the broadcaster's main newscast. The CEO of the EBC stated, however, that there was no censorship, that the company based itself on parameters of neutrality and did not defend any ideology, and that institutional content was added to its newscast as a cost-saving measure (MADEIRO, 2019).

While merging the programs did bring new problems, criticism of the EBC's decline was something that started with the previous government. The Federal District Journalists' Union, a unit of the federation where the company's headquarters is located, listed more than sixty cases where news coverage was restricted from 2016 to August 2018. In addition, according to a study conducted this year, eight out of ten journalists were victims of moral harassment at the EBC, threatening to move them to another sector, municipality, or to change their function (MADEIRO, 2019).

In fact, the public broadcasting policy implemented by the Bolsonaro government in its beginning was a continuation of that adopted by the former interim president, Michel Temer. The merging of state and public station programming just leads to weakening public broadcasting even further. The removal of the EBC's Board of Trustees and of the fixed mandate for its CEO, initiatives of the Temer government previously reported on in this book, was an attack on the public broadcasting model and its structural elements that guarantee its independence, which is key to its survival.

This attack against EBC was upheld on weak grounds. One of the arguments was that TV Brasil's low audience numbers did not rationalize the investments it was receiving. However, from July 2016 to July 2018, the broadcaster's audience grew by 64%, jumping from 27th in the country to tenth. Its market share is low, continuing under 1%, but it's growing (FELTRIN, 2018). This time period coincides with the shutdown of Analog TV throughout much of Brazil – since the EBC was established only a few years earlier, it did not count on analog television channels in important municipalities in the country. The investments seemed to have had the greatest effect once Digital TV became the only option.

The argument that public communication in Brazil is too expensive is also false. The tactic of simply referring to absolute budget values, often employed by critics, ignores basic comparisons. I compared the budgets of other public broadcasters in the world in this book. The EBC consumes much less resources (per capita) than all other public broadcasters analyzed. This per capita indicator amounts to less than two bus tickets per year in some Brazilian capitals.

Equally questionable is the argument that merging state and public programming is "more citizen-oriented". There is no evidence that this merger provides any advantage to citizens, who now has to discern between what is institutional content and what is in line with public service broadcasting guidelines. It seems reasonable to suppose, based on the criticisms presented here, the historical context, and the examples of foreign broadcasters covered in this book, that government-critical content tends to be increasingly restricted. If this assumption is true, then the misrepresentation of the purpose of public service broadcasting is obvious.

It is worth asking if public service broadcasting in Brazil resists – as the title of this book suggests – and will continue to resist. I believe so, for a number of reasons. The first is the existence of a complex and intricate legal and regulatory framework that, even if altered, continues to be relevant. After all, the constitutional provision of public broadcasting, according to the Brazilian legal system, makes it difficult for this system to be simply abolished.

The second reason is the capillarity of public service broadcasting in Brazil. The EBC is an important part of this system – and ideally should be one of the organs responsible for its leadership and articulation – but it goes far beyond the company. There are about 4,600 community radios in the country and nearly 600 educational radio and TV stations. There are also community and university pay-TV channels. And the Citizenship Channel, which allows community channels to be broadcast on open TV, was regulated under Dilma Rousseff's government, but did not receive any grants after her tenure in government.

Lastly, the current media ecosystem in Brazil means that the concept of independence inherent to public service broadcasting has spread, and serves as a foundation for a number of media that do not depend on public resources or are mainly funded by commercial advertising. In fact, this book points to the plurality of funding sources as a key element to independence from governments and the market. This reality has led to the creation of initiatives, especially on the Internet, that can be embedded in the traditional concept of public communication, or if not, seem to force a broader interpretation of it.

# References

## Interviews

CRUVINEL, Tereza. **Tereza Cruvinel (statement, 2013)**. Brasilia-DF, February 12, 2013. Interview given by Octavio Penna Pieranti.

DASKALOVA, Nikoleta. **Nikoleta Daskalova (statement, 2017)**. Sofia, March 27, 2017. Interview given by Octavio Penna Pieranti.

JĘDRZEJEWSKI, Stanisław. **Stanisław Jędrzejewski (statement, 2017)**. Warsaw, March 16, 2017. Interview given by Octavio Penna Pieranti.

KONSTANTINOVA, Raina. **Raina Konstantinova (statement, 2017)**. Sofia, March 28, 2017. Interview given by Octavio Penna Pieranti.

KRAJEWSKI, Andrzej. **Andrzej Krajewski (statement, 2017)**. Warsaw, March 16, 2017. Interview given by Octavio Penna Pieranti.

MARTINS, Franklin. **Franklin Martins (statement, 2013)**. Brasilia-DF, April 6, 2013. Interview given by Octavio Penna Pieranti.

MIKA, Václav. **Václav Mika (statement, 2017)**. Bratislava, March 22, 2017. Interview given by Octavio Penna Pieranti.

NISTOR, Irina Margareta. **Irina Margareta Nistor (statement, 2017)**. Bucharest, March 24, 2017. Interview given by Octavio Penna Pieranti.

OLIVEIRA, Euclides Quandt de. **Euclides Quandt de Oliveira (statement, 2006)**. Petrópolis-RJ, October 7, 2006b. Interview given by Octavio Penna Pieranti.

______. **Euclides Quandt de Oliveira (second statement, 2006)**. Petrópolis-RJ, December 26, 2006c. Interview given by Octavio Penna Pieranti.

SEDLÁČEK, Pavel. **Pavel Sedláček (statement, 2017)**. Brno, March 20, 2017. Interview given by Octavio Penna Pieranti.

SKOLKAY, Andrej. **Andrej Skolkay (statement, 2017)**. Bratislava, March 22, 2017. Interview given by Octavio Penna Pieranti.

SURUGIU, Romina. **Romina Surugiu (statement, 2017)**. Bucharest, March 24, 2017. Interview given by Octavio Penna Pieranti.

## Publications

AGÊNCIA BRASIL. **Américo Martins deixa presidência da EBC**. Feb. 2, 2016. Available at: <http://agenciabrasil.ebc.com.br/geral/noticia/2016-02/americo-martins-deixa-presidencia-da-ebc>. Access on: Feb. 10, 2017.

ABASHINA, Ekaterina. **Public service media in Transcaucasian countries**. Strasbourg: European Audiovisual Observatory, 2016.

AGUIAR, Pedro. **Sistemas Internacionais de Informação Sul-Sul: do *pool* não-alinhado à comunicação em redes**. Rio de Janeiro: UFRJ, 2010. Master's Dissertation.

ALTHUSSER, Louis. **Aparelhos Ideológicos de Estado: nota sobre os aparelhos ideológicos de Estado (AIE).** 3. ed. Rio de Janeiro: Edições Graal, 1987.

BALANENKO, Yury, BEREZIN, Alexander. **Moscow.** Moscow: Planeta Publishers, 1975.

BALOGH, Eva S. The deadly embrace of Hungarian Television Propaganda. **Hungarian Spectrum,** Oct. 3, 2016. Available at: <http://hungarianspectrum.org/tag/magyar-televizio/>. Access on: July 3, 2017.

BAMBIRRA, Vania. **A Teoria Marxista da Transição e a Prática Socialista.** Brasilia-DF: Ed. University of Brasilia, 1993.

BANAZINSKI, Cezary, GÓRKA, Maciej. **The Financing of Public Service Braodcasting in Selected Central and Eastern European States – Poland.** IRIS – Legal Observations of the European Audiovisual Observatory, 2000, p. 16.

BANERJEE, Indrajit, SENEVIRATNE, Kalinga. **Public service broadcasting: a best practices sourcebook.** Paris: Unesco, 2005.

BARDOEL, Johannes, D'HAENENS, Leen. Reinventing public service broadcasting in Europe: prospects, promises and problems. **Media, Culture & Society,** v. 30, 3, p. 337-355.

BECERRA, Martín *et alli.* **Caixas Mágicas: O Renascimento da Televisão Pública na América Latina.** Madrid: Editorial Tecnos, 2012.

BECKER, Jonathan. Lessons from Russia: a Neo-Authoritarian Media System. **European Journal of Communication,** v. 19(2), 2004, p. 139-163.

BENSON, Rodney, POWERS, Matthew; NEFF, Timothy. Public Media Autonomy and Accountability: Best and Worst Policy Practices in 12 Leading Democracies. **International Journal of Communication**, 11, 2017, p. 1-22.

BEUTELSCHMIDT, Thomas. "Alles zum Wohle des Volkes?!": Die DDR als Bildschirm-Wirklichkeit vor und nach 1989. In: Heiner Timmermann (org.). **Die DDR in Deutschland – ein Rückblick auf 50 Jahre**. Berlin: Duncker und Humblot, 2001. Available at: <http://www.ddr-fernsehen.de/5literaturverfilmungen/ddralsbildschirm.pdf>. Access on: Oct. 10, 2014.

BEUTELSCHMIDT, Thomas, OEHMIG, Richard. Connected Enemies? Programming transfer between East and West during the cold war and the example of East German television. **Journal of European Television History & Culture,** v. 3, issue 05/2014.

BRIKŠE, Inta. Public Service Broadcasting in Latvia: Old images, new user needs and Market pressure. **Central European Journal of Communication,** 1, 2010, p. 67-79.

BRÜCHER, Lars. **Das Westfernsehen und der revolutionäre Umbruch in der DDR im Herbst 1989**. Bielefeld: Bielefeld University, 2000.

BUCCI, Eugênio. **Em Brasília, 19 horas: A guerra entre a chapa-branca e o direito à informação no primeiro governo Lula**. Rio de Janeiro, Record, 2008.

CASTRO, Daniel. Consumo de TV explode, e Globo e Record têm melhor ano desde 2011. **TV Newscast**, Sep. 5, 2017. Available at: <noticiasdatv.uol.com.br>. Access on: Oct. 17, 2017.

CEPIKU, Denita, MITITELU, Cristina. Public Administration Reforms in Transition Countries: Albania and Romania between the Weberian Model and the New Public Management. **Transylvanian Review of Administrative Sciences**, n. 30E, 2010, p. 55-78.

CHALABY, Jean K. Public Broadcasters and Transnational Television: Coming to Terms with the New Media Order. In: Petros Iosifidis (ed.). **Reinventing Public Service Communication: European Broadcasters and Beyond**. Hampshire, UK: Palgrave Macmillan, 2010, p. 101-113.

COMAN, Mihai. Press freedom and media pluralism in Romania: Facts, myths and paradoxes. In: Czepek, Andrea; Hellwig, Melanie; Nowak, Eva. **Press Freedom and Pluralism in Europe.** UK: Intellect, 2009, p. 177-196.

CSEH, Gabriella. **The Financing of Public Service Braodcasting in Selected Central and Eastern European States – Czech Republic.** IRIS – Legal Observations of the European Audiovisual Observatory, 2000, p. 18-9.

ČT. **History**. 2016. Available at: <http://www.ceskatelevize.cz /english/history-in-a-nutshell/>. Access on: July 3, 2017.

DAHL, Robert. **Sobre a Democracia**. Brasilia: UnB, 2001.

DEUTSCHER, Isaac. **Stalin: uma biografia política.** Rio de Janeiro: Civilização Brasileira, 2006.

D'HAENENS, Leen, SOUSA, Helena, HULTÉN, Olof. From Public Service Broadcasting to Public Service Media. In: Josef Trappel. **Media in Europe today**. Intellect Books, 2011, p. 187-218.

DITTMAR, Claudia. Television and Politics in the Former East Germany. **CLCWeb**, v. 7, issue 4, article 3, Dec. 2005.

DOHLUS, Ernst. In der Grauzone – Wie der Staatsrundfunk der DDR aufgelöst wurde, Phasen und Organisation. **Deutschland Archiv**. Available at: <http://www.bpb.de/191061>. 11.9.2014. Access on: Nov. 20, 2016.

___. In der Grauzone – Wie der Staatsrundfunk der DDR aufgelöst wurde, Menschen, Material und Programmvermögen. **Deutschland Archiv**. Available at: <http://www.bpb.de/191086>. 22.9.2014b. Access on: Nov. 20, 2016.

___. In der Grauzone – Wie der Staatsrundfunk der DDR aufgelöst wurde, Was geschah mit dem Geld und den Grundstücken? **Deutschland Archiv**. Available at: <http://www.bpb.de/193800>. 27.10.2014c. Access on: Nov. 20, 2016.

DRAGOMIR, Marius. Central and Eastern Europe. In: Pippa Norris (ed.). **Public Sentinel: News media & governance reform**. Washington, DC: The World Bank, 2010, p. 245-276.

EBU. Public Service Media Remits.
Available at: <http://www.ebu.ch>. EBU, 2015. Access on: May 12, 2017.
_____. Audience Trends Television 2016. EBU, July 2016a.

_____. Audience Trends Radio 2016. EBU, July 2016b.

_____. Audience Trends Television 2017 – Public version. EBU, July 2017a.

_____. Audience Trends Radio 2017 – Public version. EBU, July 2017b.

_____. Audience Trends Television 2019 – Public version. EBU, August 2019a.

_____. Audience Trends Radio 2019 – Public version. EBU, August 2019a.

ECONOMIST. Who kidnapped the son of Slovakia's president? The Economist, April 1, 2017.
Available at:
<https://www.economist.com/news/europe/21719759-political-mystery-unresolved-20-years-later-who-kidnapped-son-slovakias-president>. Access on: Jan. 7, 2018.

ELLIS, Mark S. Purging the Past: the Current State of Lustration Laws in the Former Communist Bloc. **Law and Contemporary Problems**, 59, Fall 1996, p. 181-196.

FELTRIN, Ricardo. Em 2 anos, TV Brasil dispara 64% no Ibope e vira 10ª emissora do país. **UOL**, Aug. 14, 2018. Available at: <https://tvefamosos.uol.com.br/noticias/ooops/2018/08/14/em-2,-anos-tv-brasil-dispara-64-no-ibope-e-vira-10-emissora-do-pais.htm> Access on: June 22,. 2019.

FUNDER, Anna. **Stasilândia: como funcionava a polícia secreta alemã**. São Paulo: Companhia das Letras, 2008.

GŁOWACKI, Michał. Inside the Polish media firms: Accountability and transparency in the newsrooms. **Środkowoeuropejskie Studia Polityczne**, 2, 2016, p. 91-105.

GŁOWACKI, Michał, URBANIAK, Paweł. Poland: Between Accountability and Instrumentalization. In: Eberwein, T. *et alli* (ed.). **Mapping Media Accountability in Europe and Beyond**. Köln: Herbert von Halem Verlag, 2011.

GRAMSCI, Antonio. **Cadernos do Cárcere – volume 2**. Rio de Janeiro: Civilização Brasileira, 2004.

GROSS, Peter. Dances with Wolves: a Meditation on the Media and Political System in the European Union's Romania. In: Karol Jakubowicz; Miklós Sükösd (ed.). **Finding the Right Place on the Map: Central and Eastern European Media Change in a Global Perspective**. Bristol, UK/Chicago, USA: Intellect, 2008, p. 125-143.

GORBACHEV, Mikhail. Perestroika: **Novas Idéias para o Meu País e o Mundo**. São Paulo: Ed. Best Seller, 1987.

GREENSLADE, Roy. Polish journalists protest at state control of public broadcasting. **The Guardian**, Jan. 11, 2016. Available at: <https://www.theguardian.com/media/greenslade/2016/jan/11/pol ish-journalists-protest-at-states-control-of-public-broadcasting>. Access on: May 26, 2017.

GROSS, Peter, TISMANEANU, Vladimir. The End of Post-communism in Romania. **Journal of Democracy**, Apr. 2005.

HEIMANN, Thomas. Television in Zeiten des Kalten Krieges. In: LINDENBERGER, Thomas (org.). **Massenmedien im Kalten Krieg: Akteure, Bilder, Ressonanzen**. Köln: Böhlau Verlag, 2006.

HICKETHIER, Knut. **Geschichte des deutschen Fernsehens**. Stuttgart: Verlag J. B. Metzler, 1998.

HOFFMANN, Ruth. Stasi-**Kinder: Aufwachsen im Überwachungsstaat**. Berlin: Propyläen, 2012.

HOFFMANN-RIEM, Wolfgang. The Road to Media Unification: Press and Broadcasting Law Reform in the GDR. **European Journal of Communication**, v. 6, 1991, p. 523-543.

HOLTZ-BACHA, Christina. Of Markets and Supply: Public Broadcasting in Germany. In: Gregory Ferrell Lowe; Taisto Hujanen (eds.). **Broadcasting & Convergence: New Articulations of the Public Service Remit**. Göteborg, Sweden: Nordicom, 2003, p. 109-119.

HOZIC, Aida A. Democratizing Media, Welcoming Big Brother: Media in Bosnia and Herzegovina. In: Karol Jakubowicz; Miklós Sükösd (ed.). **Finding the Right Place on the Map: Central and Eastern European Media Change in a Global Perspective**. Bristol, UK/Chicago, USA: Intellect, 2008, p. 144-163.

HRVATIN, Sandra, MILOSAVLJEVIC, Marko. Media Policy in Slovenia in the 1990s: Regulation, privatization, concentration and commercialization of the media. **Eurozine**, Sep. 7, 2003, pgs. 1-35.

HRVATIN, Sandra, PETKOVIC, Brankica. **Regional Overview. Media Ownership and Its Impact on Media Independence and Pluralism.** Ljubljana, Slovenia: Peace Institute, 2004.

IBOPE. **Audiência de TV RJ**. 2017. Available at: <https://www.kantaribopemedia.com/conteudo/dados-rankings/audiencia-de-tv-rj/>. Access on: Apr. 30, 2017.

______. **Audiência de TV SP**. 2017. Available at: <https://www.kantaribopemedia.com/conteudo/dados-rankings/audiencia-de-tv-sp/>. Access on: Apr. 30, 2017.

IFM. **Country Profile: Poland**. 2011. Available at: <https://www.mediadb.eu/en/europe/poland.html>. Access on: July 3, 2017.

IMRE, Anikó. Adventures in Early Socialist Television Edutainment. In: Timothy Havens, Anikó Imre, Katalin Lustyik.

**Popular Television in Eastern Europe During and Since Socialism**. New York: Routledge, 2012, p. 30-46.

INTERVOZES. **Sistemas públicos de comunicação no mundo: Experiências de doze países e o caso brasileiro.** São Paulo: Paulus, Intervozes, 2009.

IOSIFIDIS, Petros. Pluralism and Funding of Public Service Broadcasting across Europe. In: Petros Iosifidis (ed.). **Reinventing Public Service Communication: European Broadcasters and Beyond.** Hampshire, UK: Palgrave Macmillan, 2010, p. 23-35.

JAKUBOWICZ, Karol. Normative Models of Media and Journalism and Broadcasting Regulation in Central and Eastern Europe. **International Journal of Communications Law and Policy.** Issue 2, Winter 1998/1999.

___. Bringing Public Service Broadcasting to Account. In: Gregory Ferrell Lowe; Taisto Hujanen (eds.). **Broadcasting & Convergence: New Articulations of the Public Service Remit.** Göteborg, Sweden: Nordicom, 2003, p. 147-167.

___. Finding the Right Place on the Map: Prospects for Public Service Broadcasting in Post-communist Countries. In: Karol Jakubowicz; Miklós Sükösd (ed.). **Finding the Right Place on the Map: Central and Eastern European Media Change in a Global Perspective.** Bristol, UK/Chicago, USA: Intellect, 2008, p. 101-124.

___. PSB 3.0: Reinventing European PSB. In: Petros Iosifidis (ed.). **Reinventing Public Service Communication: European Broadcasters and Beyond.** Hampshire, UK: Palgrave Macmillan, 2010, p. 9-22.

JAKUBOWICZ, Karol, SÜKÖSD, Miklós. Twelve Concepts Regarding Media System Evolution and Democratization in Post-

Communist Societies. In: Karol Jakubowicz; Miklós Sükösd (ed.). **Finding the Right Place on the Map: Central and Eastern European Media Change in a Global Perspective**. Bristol, UK/Chicago, USA: Intellect, 2008, p. 9-40.

JAMBEIRO, Othon. **A TV no Brasil do Século XX**. Salvador: EdUFBA, 2002.

JÕESAAR, Andres. Different ways, same outcome? Liberal communication policy and development of public broadcasting. **Trames**, 15, 1, 2011, p. 74-101.

JOFFILY, Bernardo. **O Bastião Albanês**. São Paulo: Editora Alfa-Omega, 1990.

KIRIYA, Ilya, DEGTEVERA, Elena. Russian TV market: Between state supervision, commercial logic and simulacrum of public service. **Central European Journal of Communication**, 1, 2010, p. 37-51.

KLIMKIEWICZ, Beata. Poland: **The Public, The Government and The Media**. Available at: <http://blogs.lse.ac.uk/mediapolicyproject/2016/02/08/poland-the-public-the-government-and-the-media/>. 8.2.2016. Access on: Dec. 15, 2016.

KOCHANOWSKY, Katja, TRÜLTZSCH, Sascha, VIEHOFF, Reinhold. An Evening with Friends and Enemies: Political Indoctrination in Popular East German Family Series. In: Timothy Havens, Anikó Imre, Katalin Lustyik. **Popular Television in Eastern Europe During and Since Socialism**. New York: Routledge, 2012, p. 81-101.

KOPS, Manfred. **What is Public Service Broadcasting and How Should It Be Financed?** Cologne: University of Cologne, Sept. 2001. Working Paper.

KRASNER, Stephen D. Global Communications and National Power: Life on the Pareto Frontier. **World Politics**, v. 43, n. 3, Apr. 1991, p. 336-366.

KREŠIC, Hrvoje. **Croatia: the Price of Corruption**. Oxford, UK: University of Oxford, 2012.

LANDOVA, Marina. **The Financing of Public Service Braodcasting in Selected Central and Eastern European States – Czech Republic.** IRIS – Legal Observations of the European Audiovisual Observatory, 2000, p. 17.

LAUTERJUNG, Fernando. EBC une programação da TV Brasil e da NBR. **Telaviva**, Apr. 9, 2019. Available at: <https://telaviva.com .br/09/04/2019/ebc-une-grades-da-tv-brasil-e-da-nbr/>. Access on: June 20, 2019.

LEAL FILHO, Laurindo Lalo. **Vozes de Londres: Memórias Brasileiras da BBC. São Paulo**: EdUSP, 2008.

LENGYEL, Márk. From 'State Broadcasting' to 'Public Service Media' in Hungary. In: Petros Iosifidis (ed.). **Reinventing Public Service Communication: European Broadcasters and Beyond**. Hampshire, UK: Palgrave Macmillan, 2010, p. 245-257.

LENIN, V. I. **Prensa y Literatura**. Madrid: Akal, 1976.

LEUVEN, K. U *et al*. **Independent study on indicators for media pluralism in the member states – Towards a risk-based approach**. April, 2009.

Available at:
<http://ec.europa.eu/information_society/media_taskforce/doc/plu
ralism/pfr_report.pdf>. Access on: Jan. 19, 2017.

LIMA, Mauricio. Diretor da EBC pede demissão após ingerência
política. **Veja.com**, Feb. 2, 2016. Available at: <http://veja.abril.com
.br/blog/radar-on-line/diretor-da-ebc-pede-demissao-apos-ingeren
cia-politica/>. Access on: Feb. 10, 2017.

LONDO, Ilda. **Digital Television in Albania: Policies,
Development and Public Debate.** Albanian Media Institute, 26th
May 2006.

LOZANOV, Georgi. The Law: The Media's Good Grandfather. In:
Lozanov, Georgi; Spassov, Orlin (ed.). **Media and Politics**. Sofia:
Foundation Media Democracy/Konrad Adenauer Stiftung, 2011,
p. 8-18.

MADEIRO, Carlos. Nova TV Brasil é marcada por denúncias de
censura e "overdose de governo". **UOL**, Apr. 25, 2019. Available
at: <https://noticias.uol.com.br/politica/ultimas-noticias/2019/04/25
/nova-tv-brasil-e-marcada-por-denuncias-de-censura-e-overdose-
de-governo.htm>. Access on: June 21, 2019.

MARINESCU, Valentina. Romania: Private versus State
Television. **The Public**, v. 2, 3, 1995, p. 81-95.

MARX, Karl. **Crítica ao Programa de Gotha**. eBookLibris, 2005.

______. **Liberdade de imprensa**. Porto Alegre: L&PM, 2006.

MCLAUGHLIN, Daniel. Russia's NTV protests takeover, CNN
deal reported. **Reuters**, Apr. 4, 2001. Available at:
<http://www2.stetson.edu/~psteeves/relnews/ntvtakeover.html>.
Access on: May 26, 2017.

MELO, Débora. O que está por trás da saída do presidente da EBC? **Carta Capital**, Feb. 4, 2016. Available at: <http://www.cartacapital.com.br/sociedade/o-que-esta-por-tras-da-saida-do-presidente-da-ebc>. Access on: Feb. 10, 2017.

MENDEL, Toby. **Public Service Broadcasting. A comparative Legal Survey**. Kuala Lumpur: Unesco, Asia Pacific Institute for Broadcasting Development, 2000.

MICHALIS, Maria. EU Broadcasting Governance and PSB: Between a Rock and a Hard Place In: Petros Iosifidis (ed.). **Reinventing Public Service Communication: European Broadcasters and Beyond**. Hampshire, UK: Palgrave Macmillan, 2010, p. 36-48.

MIHELJ, Sabina. Television Entertainment in Socialist Eastern Europe: Between Cold War Politics and Global Developments. In: Timothy Havens, Anikó Imre, Katalin Lustyik. **Popular Television in Eastern Europe During and Since Socialism**. New York: Routledge, 2012, p. 13-29.

___. Understanding Socialist Television: concepts, objects, methods. **Journal of European Television History & Culture**, v. 3, issue 5, 2014, p. 7-16.

MIHELJ, Sabina, DOWNEY, John. Introduction – Comparing Media Systems in Central and Eastern Europe: Politics, Economy, Culture. In: John Downey; Sabina Mihelj. **Central and Eastern European media in comparative perspective: politics, economy and culture**. Farnham, UK: Ashgate Publishing, Ltd., 2012, p. 1-13.

MILANEZ, Liana. Primeiros Momentos – Uma Voz para a Ciência. In: MILANEZ, Liana (org.). **Rádio MEC: herança de um sonho**. Rio de Janeiro: Acerp, 2007a, p. 17-45.

______. **TVE: cenas de uma história**. Rio de Janeiro: Acerp, 2007b.

MILLER, Catherine. TV dispute focuses public anger. **BBC News Online**, Jan. 4, 2001. Available at: <http://news.bbc.co.uk/2/hi/euro pe/1100998.stm> Access on: May 24, 2017.

MINISTÉRIO DA FAZENDA. **Orçamento da BNT e da BNR**. 2016. Available at: <https://www.minfin.bg/bg/page/1150>. Access on: July 3, 2017.

MOTTA, Paulo Roberto. Autogestão: a experiência empresarial iugoslava. **RAP**, 14 (1), Jan - Mar. 1980, p. 7-24.

MUNGIU-PIPPIDI, Alina. From State to Public Service: the Failed Reform of State Television in Central Eastern Europe. In: Sükösd, Miklós; Bajomi-Lázár, Péter. **Reinventing Media: Media Policy Reform in East-Central Europe**. Budapest, Hungary: Central European University, 2003, p. 31-62.

MUSTATA, Dana. Television in the Age of (Post-)Communism. In: Timothy Havens, Anikó Imre, Katalin Lustyik. **Popular Television in Eastern Europe During and Since Socialism**. New York: Routledge, 2012, p. 47-64.

OLIVEIRA, Euclides Quandt de. **Renascem as Telecomunicações: Construindo a Base**. São José dos Pinhais, PR: Editel, 1992.

______. **Renascem as Telecomunicações: Construção e Operação do Sistema**. São Paulo: Landscape, 2006.

OPEN SOCIETY INSTITUTE. **Television across Europe: regulation, policy and independence – Volume 1**. Budapest: Open Society Institute, 2005.

PARTRIDGE, James. How to get ahead in TV Journalism. **Central Europe Review**, v. 3, n. 1, 8 Jan. 2001. Available at: <http://www

.ce-review.org/01/1/partridge1.html>. Access on: May 25, 2017.

PECI, Alketa, PIERANTI, Octavio Penna, RODRIGUES, Silvia. Governança e *New Public Management:* convergências e contradições no contexto brasileiro. **Organizações & Sociedade**, v. 15, n. 46, July-Sep. 2008, p. 39-55.

PERANIC, Barbara. **Accountability and the Croatian Media in the Process of Reconciliation: Two Case Studies**. Oxford, UK: Oxford University, 2006.

PERUŠKO, Zrinja. Great expectations: On experiences with media reform in post-socialist Europe (and some unexpected outcomes). **Central European Journal of Communication**, 2, 2014, p. 241-252.

PERUŠKO, Zrinjka, POPOVIC, Helena. Media Concentration Trends in Central and Eastern Europe. In: Karol Jakubowicz, Miklós Sükösd (ed.). **Finding the Right Place on the Map: Central and Eastern European Media Change in a Global Perspective**. Bristol, UK/Chicago, USA: Intellect, 2008, p. 165-189.

PETKOVA, Kalina. Bulgarian Television Publicity: The Rise of Tabloid Politics. In: Lozanov, Georgi; Spassov, Orlin (ed.). **Media and Politics**. Sofia: Foundation Media Democracy/Konrad Adenauer Stiftung, 2011, p. 55-66.

PIERANTI, Octavio Penna. **Políticas Públicas para Radiodifusão e Imprensa: Ação e Omissão do Estado no Brasil Pós-1964**. 1. ed. Rio de Janeiro: FGV, 2007.

______. **O Estado e as Comunicações no Brasil: Construção e Reconstrução da Administração Pública**. 1. ed. Brasilia-DF: Abras/Lecotec, 2011.

______. Mudança de rumo na radiodifusão educativa: estabelecimento de regras para novas outorgas e implementação de uma política de massificação do serviço (2011-2016). **Eptic Online,** v. 18, n. 3, Sep-Dec. 2016.

______. **Políticas Públicas de Radiodifusão no Governo Dilma.** Brasilia-DF: UnB/FAC, 2017.

PIERANTI, Octavio Penna; FERNANDES, Elza Maria Del Negro B. Radiodifusão Pública? A Programação das Emissoras de TV Educativa no Brasil. **Eptic Online,** v. 19, n. 3, Sep-Dec. 2017.

PIERANTI, Octavio Penna; MARTINS, Paulo Emílio Matos. A Radiodifusão como um Negócio: um Olhar sobre a Gestação do Código Brasileiro de Telecomunicações. **Eptic,** v. IX, p. 11, 2007.

PUSNIK, Marusa; STARC, Gregor. An entertaining (r)evolution: the rise of television in socialist Slovenia. **Media Culture Society,** v. 30, 6, 2008, p. 777-793.

RADIO FREE EUROPE. Slovakia: Protests continue over firings at private TV station. **Radio Free Europe,** Sep. 9, 1998. Available at: <https://www.rferl.org/a/1089505.html>. Access on: May 26, 2017.

______. European Court Suspends Georgian Court Ruling On Rustavi-2 TV. **Radio Free Europe,** March 3, 2017. Available at: <https://www.rferl.org/a/georgia-tv-station-rustavi-2-court-ruling-protests/28345305.html>. Access on: May 26, 2017.

RAMOS, Murilo César. Empresa Brasil de Comunicación (EBC): un análisis de su modelo institucional. In: Instituto de Estudios sobre Comunicación RTA (org.). **Pensar la Televisión Pública.** Buenos Aires: La Crujía Ediciones, 2013, p. 311-336.

RAYCHEVA, Lilia *et al.*. **Bulgaria: Childhood in Transition**. Available at: <http://www.sv.ntnu.no/noseb/costa19/nytt/welfare/vol%20II/bulgaria.pdf>. 2004. Access on: Nov. 16, 2016.

REED, John. **10 Dias que Abalaram o Mundo**. Porto Alegre: L&PM, 2002.

ROMANIA INSIDER. Romanian public television gets less money from the state budget. **Romania Insider**, 2016. Available at: <http://www.romania-insider.com/romanian-public-television-gets-less-money-from-the-state-budget/amp/>. Access on: July 3, 2017.

ROSENBERG, Tina. **Terra assombrada: enfrentando os fantasmas da Europa depois do comunismo.** Rio de Janeiro: Record, 1999.

RSF. Czech Republic – Annual report 2002. **Reporters without Borders**, 2002. Available at: <http://archives.rsf.org/article.php3?id_article=1798>. Access on: May 25, 2017.

RTSH. Struktura e te ardhurave te RTSH gjate vitit 2015. Available at: <http://rtsh.al/wp-content/uploads/Analiza%20vjetore%202015%20per_Publikim.pdf>. Access on: July 3, 2017.

SAMARDZIJA-MATUL, Ksenija. Slovenian government introduces controversial bill that tightens control over public brodcaster. **Radio Praha**, Apr. 15, 2005. Available at: <http://www.radio.cz/en/section/ice_special/slovenian-government-introduces-controversial-bill-that-tightens-control-over-public-broadcaster>. Access on: May 26, 2017.

SAROLDI, Luiz Carlos, MOREIRA, Sonia Virgínia. **Rádio Nacional: o Brasil em sintonia.** Rio de Janeiro: Jorge Zahar Ed., 2005, 3rd ed.

SCHNEIDER, Peter. **Berlim, agora: a cidade depois do muro**. Rio de Janeiro: Rocco, 2015.

SCOTT, Christopher B. European Unification – Broadcasting Law – Eastern Europe and the "Television without Frontiers" Directive: Radio freed Europe – Can Television unify it? **The Georgia Journal of International and Comparative Law**, v. 22, 1992, p. 547-566.

SECOM. **Pesquisa Brasileira de Mídia 2014**. 2014. Available at: <http://observatoriodaimprensa.com.br/download/PesquisaBrasile iradeMidia2014.pdf>. Access on: May 1, 2017.

______. **Pesquisa Brasileira de Mídia 2015**. 2015. Available at: <http://www.secom.gov.br/atuacao/pesquisa/lista-de-pesquisas-quantitativas-e-qualitativas-de-contratos-atuais/pesquisa-brasileira-de-midia-pbm-2015.pdf>. Access on: May 1, 2017.

______. **Pesquisa Brasileira de Mídia 2016**. 2016. Available at: <http://www.pesquisademidia.gov.br/>. Access on: May 1, 2017.

ŠIMUNJAK, Maja. **Comparative analysis of risks for political Independence of Public Service Media across 19 European Union Member States**. Badia Fiesolana, Italy: European University Institute, 2016. Working Paper. Available at: <http://www.eui.eu/RSCAS/Publications>. Access on: Dec. 11, 2016.

ŠKOLKAY, Andrej. Central European Media in Comparative Perspective. In: Głowacki, Michał. **Comparing media systems in central Europe: Between commercialization and politicization.** Wydawn: Uniwersytetu Wrocławskiego, 2008.

SMATLAK, Martin. **The Financing of Public Service Braodcasting in Selected Central and Eastern European States –**

**Poland.** IRIS – Legal Observations of the European Audiovisual Observatory, 2000, p. 16-17.

SOARES, Jussara. Promessa de campanha, EBC será extinta, afirma Bolsonaro. **O Globo**, May 31, 2019. Available at: <https://oglobo.globo.com/brasil/promessa-de-campanha-ebc-sera-extinta-afirma-bolsonaro-23708282>. Access on: June 21, 2019.

SOUZA, Gabriel. Bolsonaro diz que vai extinguir ou privatizar a TV Brasil, criada por Lula. **Notícias da TV**, Oct. 29, 2018. Available at: <https://noticiasdatv.uol.com.br/noticia/televisao/jair-bolsonaro-diz-que-vai-extinguir-ou-privatizar-a-tv-brasil-criada-por-lula-23012>. Access on: June 22, 2019.

SPARKS, Colin. After transition: The Media in Poland, Russia and China. In: Karol Jakubowicz; Miklós Sükösd (ed.). **Finding the Right Place on the Map: Central and Eastern European Media Change in a Global Perspective**. Bristol, UK/Chicago, USA: Intellect, 2008, p. 43-71.

SPASSOV, Orlin. Media and Politics: The Decline of the Fourth Estate?. In: Lozanov, Georgi; Spassov, Orlin (ed**.). Media and Politics**. Sofia: Foundation Media Democracy/Konrad Adenauer Stiftung, 2010, p. 174-189.

SPLICHAL, Slavko. Slovenia: The Period of "Capitalist Enlightenment". **The Public**, v. 2, 3, 1995, p. 97-114.

___. Imitative Revolutions Changes in the Media and Journalism in East-Central Europe. **The Public**, v. 8, 4, 2001, p. 31-58.

STĘPKA, Paweł. Public Broadcasting in Poland: Between Politics and Market. In: Petros Iosifidis (ed.). **Reinventing Public Service Communication: European Broadcasters and Beyond**. Hampshire, UK: Palgrave Macmillan, 2010, p. 233-244.

SURUGIU, Romina. Exploring the Role of Romanian Television in Public Sphere (1957-1989). **The European Proceedings of Social & Behavioural Sciences,** 2017b, p. 771-779.

TAYLOR, Frederick. **Muro de Berlim: Um Mundo Dividido 1961-1989**. Rio de Janeiro: Record, 2009.

TOCQUEVILLE, Alexis de. **A democracia na América**. São Paulo: Abril Cultural, 1973.

TSCHOLAKOV, Radomir. **The Financing of Public Service Braodcasting in Selected Central and Eastern European States – Bulgaria.** IRIS – Legal Observations of the European Audiovisual Observatory, 2000, p. 14-15.

UNESCO. **Um mundo e muitas vozes: comunicação e informação na nossa época.** Rio de Janeiro: FGV, 1983.

VARTANOVA, Elena. The Russian Media Model in the Context of Post-Soviet Dynamics. In: Hallin, Daniel C.; Mancini, Paolo (eds.). **Comparing Media Systems Beyond the Western World.** Cambridge, UK: Cambridge University Press, 2012, p. 119-142.

___. Media Pluralism in Russia: In Need of Policy Making. In: Valcke, Peggy; Sükösd, Miklós; Picard, Robert G. (eds.) **Media Pluralism and Diversity: Concepts, Risks and Global Trends**. Basingstoke, New York: Palgrave Macmillan, 2015, p. 193-210.

VARTANOVA, Elena, ZASSOURSKY, Yassen. Television in Russia: Is the Concept of PSB Relevant? In: Gregory Ferrell Lowe; Taisto Hujanen (eds.). **Broadcasting & Convergence: New Articulations of the Public Service Remit**. Göteborg, Sweden: Nordicom, 2003, p. 93-108.

VOLTMER, Katrin. The Media, Government Accountability, and Citizen Engagement. In: Pippa Norris (ed.). **Public Sentinel: News media & governance reform**. Washington, DC: The World Bank, 2010, p. 137-159.

WELT, Cory. The curious case of Georgia's Rustavi-2. **ODR**, Dec. 2, 2015. Available at: <https://www.opendemocracy.net/od-russia/cory-welt/curious-case-of-georgia-s-rustavi-2>. Access on: May 26, 2017.

WHEELER, Mark. The European Union's Competition Directorate: State Aids and Public Service Broadcasting. In: Petros Iosifidis (ed.). **Reinventing Public Service Communication: European Broadcasters and Beyond**. Hampshire, UK: Palgrave Macmillan, 2010, p. 49-62.

WIMMER, Miriam. **Direitos, Democracia e Acesso aos Meios de Comunicação de Massa: Um Estudo Comparado sobre Pluralismo Interno na Televisão**. Scotts Valley, CA: CreateSpace, 2014.

WOLDT, Runar. Public Service Broadcasting in Germany: Stumbling Blocks on the Digital Highway. In: Petros Iosifidis (ed.). **Reinventing Public Service Communication: European Broadcasters and Beyond**. Hampshire, UK: Palgrave Macmillan, 2010, p. 171-182.

WORLD RADIO TV HANDBOOK – WRTH. Amsterdam: Billboard, 1990.